THE

PUBLICATIONS

OF THE

Lincoln Record Society

FOUNDED IN THE YEAR

1910

VOLUME 75

FOR THE YEAR ENDING 31st AUGUST 1983

STOW CHURCH RESTORED
1846–1866

Edited by
Mark Spurrell

Published for
The Lincoln Record Society
by
The Boydell Press
1984

First published 1984
for the Lincoln Record Society
by The Boydell Press
an imprint of Boydell & Brewer Ltd
PO Box 9, Woodbridge, Suffolk IP12 3DF
and 51 Washington St, Dover, New Hampshire 03820, U.S.A.

ISBN 0 901503 39 8

British Library Cataloguing in Publication Data

Stow Church restored.—(The Publications of
the Lincoln Record Society; vol. 75)
1. Stow Church 2. Churches—England—
Stow (Lincolnshire)—Conservation and
restoration
I. Spurrell, Mark II. Series
726'.5'0942535 NA5471.S82/

ISBN 0-901053-39-8

Printed in Great Britain
by Short Run Press Ltd
Exeter, Devon.

CONTENTS

LIST OF PLATES

FOREWORD

This collection of documents tells the story of the restoration of the church of Saint Mary the Virgin at Stow in Lindsey between the years 1846 and 1866. It is the story of the efforts of the perpetual curate, the Reverend George Atkinson, to achieve the work, and of the efforts of the farmers of the parish to frustrate it.

The collection touches several areas of study and interest. It shows the church administration at work, at diocesan level and in the Ecclesiastical Commission. It gives evidence for the work done in the restoration of a Saxo-Norman fabric of great archaeological importance. It gives an insight into the problems and enthusiasms of a nineteenth-century country parish priest, and depicts vividly the opposition which a village could put up. It is a local example of how the Victorian Church met and dealt with many of the problems which it faced all over the country.

The documents are arranged in chronological order so that the story is told consecutively. Extracts from the newspapers and other printed sources provide some commentary to and illustration of the events contained in the documents.

Most of the information about the opposition in the parish has been relegated to the Index, which must be used throughout in place of footnotes. The leading members of the Stow Vestry have been picked out in heavy type, and for the others the number of entries in the Index gives some idea of their relative importance.

Abbreviations in the documents have been expanded with the exception of No. 254 and the material from the Stow Vestry Book (*V*). The provenance of the material has been indicated in the headings to each document, and the code explained on p. ix of the Introduction. Numbers followed by a letter (e.g. No. 2A) indicate that the document is an enclosure. A few notes have been added to the texts, and will be found at the end of the relevant document.

I am grateful to the Lincoln Archives Office for their facilities, especially a private room to type in, and to the Church Commissioners for a full photo copy of their file No. 6498 (to which I have added this summer with a request for further repairs to be done to the Chancel).

I am glad to acknowledge the kind permission of the owners of the documents to print them in this volume: the Church Commissioners for the material from the Ecclesiastical Commissioners' files; the Diocese of Lincoln for Bishop Kaye's Correspondence; the Churchwardens and Parochial Church Council of Stow for material from the Church Book, the Vestry Book, the Vestry Committee Book, Sir Charles Anderson's correspondence and No. 225; the Incorporated Church Building Society for letters from their file on Stow; the National Society for Religious Education for No. 87; the Stow Charity Trustees for No. 220; the Lincolnshire Library Service for quotations from the *Stamford Mercury*; the *Lincoln Echo* for quotations from its predecessors, the *Lincolnshire Times* and the *Lincoln Gazette*; Mrs Duncombe for quotations from Sir Charles Anderson's journal. The illustrations are acknowledged where they are printed.

Finally I am grateful to the editor for her patience and guidance, and to my wife for her encouragement and help with the proofs and the Index.

ABBREVIATIONS AND SIGNS

AASR	Associated Architectural Societies' Reports and Papers.
Bp	Bishop
Adn	Archdeacon
CW	Churchwarden
Eccl. Com.	Ecclesiastical Commissioners for England
LAO	Lincolnshire Archives Office, The Castle, Lincoln
N	Note (used after a No.)
Quiney	Anthony Quiney, *John Loughborough Pearson*, Yale University, 1979
Sermon	Atkinson's Sermon, see p. xxxii

In No. 254 the following abbreviations may need explanation:

Carr^{e} means Carriage
E as in E Oak means English
GNR^{y}, Great Northern Railway
M.S. & Lin^{c} Railway, Manchester, Sheffield and Lincoln Railway

In the texts words in *italics* are those words underlined in the originals. Words enclosed in square brackets have been supplied either to make sense or where the text has been damaged.

In the titles to the texts the letters in brackets are explained in the Introduction, p. ix.

INTRODUCTION

I The Documents

1. *The Church Book* is a leather bound folio volume written from both ends. From it have been printed the list of church wardens (No. 1), and some Vestry minutes which were recorded in it. It also contains the church wardens' accounts and details of the church gardens which have not been printed.

2. *The Vestry Book*, a quarto exercise book, contains minutes of the Vestry meetings from 14 October 1848 until Easter Monday, 1877. It does not contain minutes of meetings which concerned the highways or the poor, but does include some meetings which were described as "Parish" or "Public". With the exception of Meetings at which no business other than the election of church wardens was done and some material concerning the charities, the book has been printed in full, and the original spelling and punctuation have been retained. (V)

3. *The Vestry Committee Book*, a small octavo note book, contains the minutes of a committee of the Vestry which met during 1848. The book has been printed in full (Nos. 43, 49–52). LAO Stow Par 10.

4. *Bishop Kaye's Correspondence* consists of a large number of bundles of letters and papers in the care of the Lincolnshire Archives Committee in the Castle. Of these two have been used here. The larger bundle, LAO Cor B 5/4/63/1, has letters from Atkinson, Archdeacon Stonehouse, and a few others written between 1846 and 1850, printed here as numbers between 7 and 127. The smaller bundle, LAO Cor B 5/4/91/7, is printed as Nos. 128 to 130. Omissions, other than topping and tailing, are indicated with dots, the material omitted concerning other parishes or matters. Where material relative to Stow has been omitted it has been noted (e.g. No. 98), and this includes all the rough drafts made by Bishop Kaye for his replies. These are largely illegible, and it is often impossible to tell which of the alternative versions was actually sent. (K) and (K2)

5. *The Ecclesiastical Commissioners' File No. 6498* concerning Stow Chancel, kept at the Church Commissioners' offices, has been transcribed with certain omissions. These are the minutes of meetings which were largely contained in the letters they ordered (Cf. Nos. 20 and 21 with No. 121 and Note); correspondence concerning damage done to the

chancel (summarised at No. 207); and correspondence concerning repairs to the chancel roof (See Nos. 221, 221A and Note). Letters to the Commissioners were addressed to the assistant secretary, J. J. Chalk Esq., and he usually signed those from the Commissioners. The file extends beyond the period; in fact it is still open. An occasional document has been quoted from File No. 6499, which concerned the Benefice. (EC)

6. *The Incorporated Church Building Society's File No. 6209* has been printed in full (with the exception of one unimportant letter), and concerns an application for a grant towards new seating in the church (Nos. 224 and 249–251). (ICBS)

7. *Sir Charles Anderson's Correspondence* which is in the possession of Stow Church has been printed in full with the exception of some of the matter referring to the Charities, and the income side of the Cash Book. The bulk of the correspondence, printed after No. 227, is from Frederick Atkinson, the brother of the Incumbent. The cash book is a copy made by Frederick Atkinson of the book used by his brother for the restoration of the nave and transepts, and is printed, out of sequence, as No. 254. (CA)

8. *Miscellaneous.* Several passages from newspapers have been printed where they fill out the narrative, or give the text of documents otherwise unobtainable. No. 220 is an excerpt from the Minute Book of the Stow Charity Trustees; and the Faculty, No. 225, is in the possession of Stow Church. No. 87 is from a file, the National Society's, School Case No. 43.

It should be noted that all letters from the Incumbent are dated from Stow Parsonage, with the single exception of No. 120 which is dated from "Malham, near Skipton".

II The Reverend George Atkinson

George Atkinson was 34 when he was appointed to the perpetual curacy of Stow. It was 1836, only four years after the Great Reform Bill, a time when, in his own words, "political dangers . . . seemed to threaten the Church as a temporal establishment" (*Sermon*, 1847, p. 13). In Stow Atkinson found the church at a low ebb. There had been no resident incumbent for the last 60 or 70 years, and the non-residents had made little impression on the parish with the result that "dissent and indifference to religion extensively prevailed". It was said that "the older inhabitants (spoke) with respect of one pastor, who certainly took an interest in their affairs which was somewhat unusual, for he joined in their sports on the Sabbath, and the football was reverently placed at the church door before the service ended every morning, that he might have the first kick" (*Lincolnshire Times*, 17 April 1855).

We have very little information about Atkinson's private life, or how the family life of the parsonage was organised. The census returns show various of his sisters living or staying with him. His brother, Frederick, who was a belligerent churchwarden in Higher Broughton, Manchester, and in conflict with his bishop, obviously idolised him, and took a keen interest in the restoration of the church. Sir Charles Anderson, the tractarian, of Lea Hall and a keen architectural student, counted him as a friend, and dined occasionally at Stow. One entry in his very brief and laconic diary reads, "dined at Stow with the Archdeacon. 12 βαρβαροι " (7 July 1841); but that may not have been at the Parsonage. In later entries we read that the day after he "heard of poor Atkinson of Stows death" he rode over "to Stow to see Miss Atkinson" (23 and 24 May 1865).

Atkinson never married, and most of his sisters were unmarried. He died intestate and it is difficult to know how well off he was. The family gave £1600 to the restoration of the church, the majority of this coming from George Atkinson himself. Yet his obituary speaks of his "slender means" and the "great self-denial" which such gifts occasioned. When applying for an augmentation of the living he never speaks of his own circumstances, but rather of what was due to the clergyman, and what was necessary for his ministry in the circumstances of the parish. After his father's death in 1850 he must have had some private means, and his sisters, no doubt, contributed to the housekeeping of the parsonage. But the parsonage had been built on a scale which his successor found quite inadequate for his needs; *he* complained of the smallness of the rooms and of the poorness of the offices and outbuildings.

Francis Atkinson, George's father, was a cotton manufacturer in Rochdale, with a mill in Cheetham Street. George was born on 29 December, 1801, and in 1820 he entered Queens' College, Cambridge, and took his B.A. in 1824. He was made deacon by the Bishop of Lincoln with the title of the curacies of Heapham and Springthorpe, villages to the north of Stow, the rectors of which each offered £50 as stipend. His letters testimonial were signed, among others, by "Old Peterloo", the Vicar of Rochdale, who, in his capacity as a magistrate, had given the order for the yeomanry to charge at the Peterloo Massacre.

Much of his character comes across in his letters. Most of the letters he wrote are contained in this volume. They are meticulously written, argumentative, confident, articulate to a fault, untiringly detailed. There is not much subtlety in them. As the Archdeacon begged leave to observe to the Bishop "it is a very fortunate thing for him that he was not brought up to a coachman—for most certainly that coach would have been upset by being driven against a post—or the side of a house—And round a corner he never could have turned" (No. 81); or in a moment of exasperation—"I have never met such a resolute obstinate person as Mr. Atkinson is" (No. 66). One catches a glimpse of him in a newspaper account of a stormy vestry meeting—"the Rev. Chairman would not allow any time whatever to be given for [discussion]; and he instantly *roared* out, 'those who are for the rate hold up your hands'; when lo! up went *one* (accompanied by groans) out of about fifty in the vestry" (*Stamford Mercury*, 29 September 1848). Yet we also catch a glimpse of him having taken the trouble to go to Lincoln to court to defend a bricklayer who lodged in the parish and had been accused of drunken and insulting behaviour. Atkinson had met him on his return from evening prayer, and he was very drunk, reeling and staggering, singing and shouting, and followed by a troop of boys who were teasing him. He said a few words to everyone he met, but was in no way insulting in his behaviour (*Lincoln Gazette*, 3 November 1860). Compassion or a sense of justice? He was buried, said his obituary, amidst "the deep regrets of the poor, whose cause he had always upheld and defended" (*AASR*, 1865, iii).

The same obituary notice mentioned his "uncompromising fidelity to the Church of England". He was tractarian in his theology. "The Church of England", he preached (*Sermon*, 1847 p. 7), "since the Reformation is the same Church of England before the Reformation . . . agreeing and uniting together in the same holy orders of the ministry derived from succession from the apostles and from Christ; one in holding the same deposit of faith contained in the three Catholic Creeds; and one in the true sacraments of the Gospel." He was strong against Erastianism—"our church is a true portion of the Church Catholic—a member of that divine society instituted by our Saviour. . . . If this be not the ground on which we take our stand, I am unable to imagine what other solid ground we have to stand upon. For surely none among us can imagine that kings, or parliaments, or the people, or any other human power can originate a true church" (*Sermon*, 1847 p. 8). This did not mean that he was favourable towards Rome—that church he said had nothing in common with the church before the Reformation other than "*its errors*"; "our true vocation appears to lie in the middle path between Papal additions and Puritan subtractions" (p. 12). His instinct and desire was to be conservative—" 'our strength is to be still'; to abide by her tried principles . . . to embody her holy doctrines and disciplines in our own teaching and conversation, that we may render our Church in practice what she is in theory", but on the same page (p. 13), he assesses the church's present situation and endorses a whole programme of reform; "The political dangers which a few years ago seemed to threaten the Church as a temporal establishment appear no longer imminent; an earnest and extensive, though as yet inadequate, effort has been making to provide for the spiritual care of the long neglected multitudes who have been suffered to grow up among us in worse than heathen ignorance and vice; the means of education by the Church are daily improving and extending. . . . While parishes, as well as dioceses, are being subdivided; while Churches and parsonage-houses are being erected and occupied by resident pastors; while the church's external means are thus augmenting; we see at the same time recognised and required among the clergy a higher standard of both attainments and duty; we see more frequent services in the Churches, those services solemnised with more decency and devotion; we see more attention paid to our sacred fabrics, especially in making them more truly 'houses of prayer'."

Atkinson's approach to the work in his own parish was typical of the nineteenth century reconstruction of the church. His first job was to establish himself as a resident pastor with an adequate house and income. After a period in rented accommodation he completed the Parsonage House, midway between Sturton and Stow, at a cost which involved an annual charge of £20 upon his stipend. The living was a perpetual curacy, a benefice impropriated by two of the prebendaries in the cathedral, Corringham cum Stow, and Stow in Lindsey. The endowments of the prebends were in the process of being made over to the Ecclesiastical Commissioners, and it was to them that Atkinson applied for an augmentation of the benefice. The income amounted to £104.4.2 plus the rent of an acre of land at £3 or £4. Against this had to be set the annual deduction of £20 to repay the money borrowed under Gilbert's Act to pay for the parsonage. Atkinson claimed that a parish of the size of Stow, about 1000 inhabitants, and the conditions prevailing there demanded a much larger stipend: "Not less than 70 [years] without a resident Clergyman until my receiving the Incumbency 7 years ago, the excessive subdivision of property, and the absence of any resident proprietor of consequence—the want of a national school, and the prevalence of dissent and indifference . . . deprive the Clergyman of the Parish of the hope of any material assistance of a pecuniary nature from his Parishioners, towards promoting Church objects, and consequently impose heavier burdens upon himself" (EC file 6499, 9 June 1843). A parish, of course, had no funds of its own for most of the work that might be done, and the clergyman's stipend was considered as the proper source for most expenses. The same background lies behind Archdeacon Stonehouse's grumble at the end of No. 45.

The Commissioners agreed to allow half an acre for a school site, and allot five acres from the prebendal glebe near the new parsonage house to the living, and to grant what was needed to raise the income to £200. In addition they promised to provide another £100 for a curate to work in Bransby, or for the provision of services there. Atkinson personally also held the vicarage of Coates in plurality. The vicarage, which had no house of residence, was valued at £60, and the population of the village was then 50 persons.

Atkinson saw the parish as consisting of three villages, Stow with about 400 persons, Sturton with a similar population about a mile from the church, and Bransby with over 100 two miles from the church. He wanted to establish a Sunday service at Bransby "where in ancient times there appears to have been a chapel", but was never successful (see Nos. 54, 58, 59). He does not seem to have envisaged a service at Sturton, as did his successors, and where in 1879 a Mission Room was eventually built to the designs of Pearson. He added an evening service "during the long days" on Sundays at Stow (No. 236) and had morning and evening services on Wednesdays, Fridays, and Saints' Days variously at 9 and 6, or at 11 and 7. Holy

Communion was celebrated on the first Sunday of the month and on the greater festivals. In later years Sunday services were at 10.30, at which Atkinson preached, and at 2.30 when he catechised (Visitation Returns, LAO, 1858, 1861, 1864).

Attendances were not good. In 1851 Atkinson claimed for the Census Sunday, 30 March, a morning congregation of 28 with 46 Sunday Scholars, and an afternoon congregation of 42 with 46 Sunday Scholars again—presumably the same 46. His average attendance was 33 in the morning and 57 in the afternoon with 40 Sunday Scholars each time. This yields an Index of Attendance figure (a relationship between attendance and the total population) of 9 which is well below the average for the district round about. Atkinson was conscious of this for he added that "the nature of the accommodation is such as to discourage attendance especially in winter". It is noticeable that the figures given by the Vestry to Bishop Jackson in 1855 (No. 212), shows a considerable variation between March and May. But given the controversy over the church rates, and the great hostility which this had aroused, and the very adequate provision by the Methodists of alternatives, a figure of 42 adults in an unheated church on a March Sunday afternoon suggests that there was something in the worship that Atkinson conducted which was not unattractive. In 1861, again in March, there was a Missionary Meeting in the National School, and Atkinson is reported to have addressed the meeting "in a very feeling and affectionate manner" (*Lincoln Gazette*, 9 March 1861).

Atkinson's successor summed up the situation within a few months of Atkinson's death. "As may be expected with the parish church one mile distant and Dissenting Chapels on the spot but a small number of Sturton and Bransby people are in the habit of attending Divine Service. Undoubtedly a considerable church feeling exists but unless some steps are speedily taken to provide one service at Sturton the larger portion of the parish will be nearly lost to the Established Church. As it is the dissenters have nearly all the Sturton children attending their schools" (EC file 6499, 30 December 1865).

Two confirmation lists survive. In March 1860 eight male candidates and 14 female were presented, of whom four males and eight females made their first communion. All those who failed to make their first communion lived in Sturton, and the only Sturton communicant lived in the house next to the Stow boundary. The Sturton candidates presumably acted together as a group. In 1863 all eight male candidates made their first communion, and three of the six females. All the candidates that can be identified came from the labouring classes, with the exception of Robert Harrison's daughter, who failed to make her first communion in 1860. In 1863 Atkinson appears to have been much more successful with his male candidates than was usual, but we have no evidence as to whether they remained communicants or not.

The "disciplines" of the Church of England to which he alluded in his

Visitation Sermon were no empty thing for Atkinson. He had doubts about permitting addresses at grave sides given by representatives of sick and burial clubs both because they were a possible "breach of the order and discipline of the Church", and also because laxity here would lead to "sectaries" making addresses in churchyards, where there had already been trouble caused by the singing of their hymns at the grave (Letter to Bishop Kaye, 31 July 1840, LAO Cor B 5/4/79). The burial registers show instances where Atkinson refused to allow the body of a young child into the church on the grounds that it had been baptised outside the parish sometimes "contumaciously", and there are twelve instances when he did this because of "heretical" or "schizmatical" baptism at the Methodist Meeting. It is probable that he exercised a similar discipline in respect of churchings (No. 212). He was anxious also to mark the churches disapproval of notoriously immoral lives at funeral services (No. 99).

Atkinson's main campaign against Dissent was, as was usual at this period, to be conducted by the building of a National School. "Another great want of the parish", he wrote in 1846, "is a National School, there being at present no Church School whatever except a small Sunday School. The Establishment of a good School would be a very popular as well as beneficial measure, as the poor have not the means at present, except at an expense beyond their power to bear, of obtaining week-day education for their children—" This was a good in itself, but also it "would enable the Clergyman to draw to the Sunday School—and to the services of the Church, nearly all, if not all, those children who are at present attending the Wesleyan and Ranter Sunday Schools established before the present Incumbent had the care of the Parish. For the want of such a school, the Incumbent regrets to state that nearly all the children in his Parish are either growing up in ignorance and neglect, or in positive alienation from the Church through attending dissenting Sunday Schools" (EC file 6499, 22 May 1846). When the school was opened in 1850 Atkinson rejoiced, "I feel no doubt of our ultimate success in getting nearly the whole education of the Parish into our hands" (Nat. Society School Case No. 43).

The school was opened first in the mistress's house and later in the converted barn, which could accommodate 83 children allowing eight square feet for each. In 1855 Atkinson reported that there was an average attendance of 20 boys and 25 girls. The average Sunday School attendance was 50 equally divided between boys and girls. In 1876 the school was transferred to the School Board, though the Incumbent retained the right to use the building for certain purposes. In 1894 the School Board gave up the premises, and it ceased to be used as a day school.

The advancement of the church in the parish entailed among other things an increase in the influence of the clergyman. This influence was partly obtained by helping parishioners in their temporal welfare, and it is probable that many of the school pence for the children from poorer families came out of

Atkinson's pocket. His rescue of the Stow Charities from abuse would have satisfied his instinct for justice, and also have extended his patronage and influence in the parish.

In his Visitation Sermon he advocated "more attention [to be] paid to our sacred fabrics", and his great work and lasting memorial was the restoration of his church. Judging from Willson's description of the church (quoted p. xxi), this was not an early priority of his ministry, and he was in no way a ritualist. Before 1846, when Atkinson reorganised the interior of the church (No. 8), the pews as they were then arranged accommodated about 250 people, of which about 50 seats only were free (EC file 6499, 1846), the remainder being allotted to the farmers of the parish. They were situated higgledy-piggledy under the tower. With the re-arrangement of the seats and their transfer to the chancel they all became free, and all faced east.

This arrangement symbolised the control that a Victorian clergyman felt that he ought to have over his church and congregation. Atkinson came to a situation where generations of non-residence had left the clergyman with very little authority or control, and making the position of the clergyman "in practice what [it] is in theory" was an innovation of some magnitude. His first clash with the parish was summed up by the *Lincolnshire Chronicle* (25 May 1838), "Everyone who is acquainted with the parish has been long aware that there are many great 'uns resident in the parish who have viewed with much suspicion the residence of a gentleman among [them], much fearing, mighty souls, that their consequence in the eyes of the parishioners might be somewhat eclipsed."

The trouble began when Atkinson, feeling himself insulted by the parish clerk, William Middleton, dismissed him, as he was legally entitled to do. He appointed in his place one, William Spurr. The great 'uns, however, instigated Middleton to force himself into the clerk's place in church, and to interrupt the service "indecently" (*Lincolnshire Chronicle*, 25 May 1838). Because of this, according to the anti-church *Stamford Mercury* (23 February 1838), on ten successive Sundays, starting 22 October 1837, Atkinson stopped the service at the absolution, and demanded that Middleton should come out from the clerk's desk. On his silent refusal, Atkinson would stop the service.

Then in February 1838, Jesse Ellis, the minister's churchwarden, according to the newspaper but not the Church Book, was charged with assault by Thomas Skill, because, on Atkinson's instructions, Ellis had attempted to stop Skill entering a certain pew. "An old man, 80 years of age, having an action brought against him for assault by a hale, healthy man of 40, is too preposterous to believe", asserted the *Lincolnshire Chronicle* (8 June 1838), which took the Church's part. Actually Jesse Ellis was only 71. As a result of this dispute Atkinson's right to appoint a churchwarden was challenged at the Easter Monday Vestry, and Edward Howard, the son of the farmer who rented Stow Hall, who was nominated by Atkinson, refused to

The Reverend George Atkinson

serve (No. 67). Thomas Skill took the chair after Atkinson had withdrawn from the meeting. The problem of the parish clerk was still unresolved; Middleton was still challenging Spurr, and occupying his desk, so that Spurr had to stand where he could, and there were always two Amens.

In the meantime there had been a dispute about the closing of a footpath across the churchyard, which had been done, and about a proposal to level the grave mounds in the churchyard. William Spurr mysteriously damaged some of the church windows while repelling the assault of a child, and had to pay 7/4d (*Stamford Mercury*, 3 May, 16 Feb. 1838). On the other hand he was assaulted by William Sergeant, "a Stow hero, and one of the friends of the editor of our contemporary, the Mercury"; Sergeant was fined 10/– and costs, and bound over (*Lincolnshire Chronicle*, 8 June 1838). But, the *Mercury* crowed, "The Perpetual Curate keeps his cure, but has been *removed* from his house by his landlord: the Rev. Gentleman has taken up his abode at some distance from the seat of his spiritual duties" (18 May 1838). Bishop Kaye, writing some years later, said of this period that "his very life was in danger" (EC file 6499, 7 July 1846).

Eventually in July a peace was patched up, which included the reinstatement of William Middleton as clerk. What concessions the parish was conceived to have made, other than perhaps giving up the claim to appoint both churchwardens, is not apparent. Bishop Kaye, in his letter of 1846 quoted above, wrote, rather optimistically, that Atkinson had "by his steady perseverance overcome all difficulties and even conciliated the good will of the Parishioners".

III The Dispute with the Vestry

As will have been seen differences between the minister and the vestry arose long before the restoration of the church was proposed. In the case of the minister's right to nominate a parish clerk or a churchwarden the rules were always slightly obscure. In general he had the right, unless there was a local custom to the contrary. William Middleton tried to promote such a custom by inscribing in the marriage register, "William Middleton, Appointed Parish Clerk and sexton by the parish of Stow may 3rd 1832", to which Atkinson rejoined, "The above entry was made by the person therein named to serve a particular purpose long after the date it bears and contains a statement contrary to fact, the Clergyman and not the Parish having the right of appointing the Parish Clerk, which right was exercised by the Clergyman the Revd C. B. Massingberd in this case—The Clergyman's right was never disputed until the year 1837, and is ascertained by an entry in the Register under the year 1752. Stow Parsonage February 23 1840."

There were parishes, notably in the City of London, where the parishioners had the right of nominating both churchwardens. Again there were parishes, such as Rochdale, where there were many more than two churchwardens, and the minister would have the right of nominating but one of them. But the presumption was that there should be two churchwardens, and if the minister and the vestry could not agree on a choice, the minister nominated one, and the parishioners the other. The churchwardens were those in whom the property of the parish, insofar as it concerned the church, was vested, and their primary duty was the care of the fabric, fittings and ornaments of the church. They were responsible for good order in and around the church at times of divine service, and had the duty to present the minister at a visitation if he were guilty of misconduct. They also had a number of secular responsibilities, which in Stow were divided between Sturton and Stow, the minister's warden looking after Stow, and the parish's being responsible for Sturton. This was entered in the Church Book in such a way that to a cursory glance it appears that Stow elected one and Sturton the other.

Church Rates were not governed by custom, but by law. Nevertheless in this area the law was even more confused and uncertain than custom. Each parish was charged by law with the maintenance of its parish church and churchyard, as well as of the roads and the poor. Rates were levied or laid by the vestry, which was an assembly of the rate payers of the parish. The incumbent of the parish had the right to be present and to take the chair. Non-payment of the poor rate disqualified a vestryman, but this disqualification did not apply in the case of non-payment of a church rate. Similarly if a parish neglected to do its duty by the roads or the poor, the civil courts could compel it to do it, but there was no civil compulsion or sanction in the case of the failure of a parish to maintain its church or churchyard.

Once a rate had been laid, then payment could be enforced. The churchwardens could sue in the ecclesiastical court, and the defaulter's goods could be distrained. This was only practicable where the churchwardens were willing to act, and where there were not too many defaulters. But if the vestry refused to lay a rate, or laid a rate which was so small as to be derisory, the secular court had no powers, and proposals in parliament to remedy this situation by putting the church rate on the same footing as the poor rate came to nothing. It was thus illegal not to maintain a church, but there was no sanction if the law was broken. In 1837 it was suggested that a minority could lay a valid rate—valid in that it could be enforced upon defaulters—even if that minority was as small as a single churchwarden. The argument went that the minority would be doing the only thing possible from a legal point of view, any other course of action being illegal and therefore out of order. This was chased through the courts between 1837 and 1853 as the Braintree Case, but the House of Lords finally decided against the validity of a minority rate.

In Stow little is heard of individual defaulters, though presumably the Spencers, as Quakers, must have refused to pay. Usually it was the vestry that refused to lay a rate. Atkinson tried to lay a minority rate in 1848 (Nos. 38, 39), but he failed in his attempt because he could get no churchwarden to sign the book. The Braintree Case at this time was being decided in favour of the validity of a minority rate.

It is not possible to make generalisations about church rate disputes in rural areas from the experience of a single parish, but it is possible to attempt to discover what the dispute was really all about in Stow. Stow was not the only parish in Lincolnshire where rates were refused. The 1856 parliamentary enquiry into cases where rates had been refused in the past 15 years lists 18 parishes where this had happened. As the returns are incomplete—St. Mary le Wigford is the only Lincoln parish—and in some cases misleading, 18 should be thought of as a minimum. Stow does not appear among the refusing parishes! The answer given to the question, Has the parish refused a church rate in the past 15 years? was, "No, not on the part of the parish." Other answers from the county suggest that the clergy were determined to present as favourable a picture as possible to encourage the retention of church rates, and many instances of actual refusal or virtual refusal—there were many parishes in which no rate had been collected for years—were hidden.

It is just possible that Atkinson gave this answer because he did not consider the refusal of the rate as other than incidental in a different dispute. It was generally assumed that it was dissenters who opposed church rates, and this is what Charles Chaplin assumed when he blamed the "dissenting portion" of the parish (No. 115). But the *Stamford Mercury* claimed (10 November 1848) that, "the controversy at Stow is out of the usual course of church-rate bickerings: it is not between churchmen and dissenters, for the staunchest churchmen are as much opposed to the movement as the most decided dissenters: it is rather between a parish of hard-struggling farmers, and a clergyman pledged to the fashionable study of archaeology—labour on the one side, the pleasure of taste on the other!" Whatever may have been the truth about other church-rate bickerings, it is true, as far as it can be seen, that the dispute at Stow was not primarily one between churchmen and dissenters. These paragraphs were written by Charles Gowen Smith, himself probably a Methodist, and the Sturton Schoolmaster, and he tended to stress not the religious question but the economic hardship which payment of rates on such a scale would entail. His language has a chartist ring about it. Atkinson is guilty of "a stretch of lawless and tyrannical power", and, when a Committee of the Vestry was proposed, "surely half a dozen respectable men—men with families and having a stake in society—must be a more tractable body for the ecclesiastical authorities to deal with, than the fierce democracy—the fiery proprietory of a hundred little freeholds!" *Stamford Mercury*, 10 Nov. 1848. See also No. 42.

The vestry claimed that "the people of Stow with the exception of a few extreme dissenters were perfectly sensible of their obligation to maintain a parish church" (No. 88), and even Thomas Spencer, if Atkinson was right (No. 65) had as his sole object the saving of his purse, even though, as a

Quaker, he was bound to bear his Christian testimony against church rates. It was the excessive demands which, it was claimed, the conservation of a Saxon Cathedral made which were resisted.

Obviously there were dissenters among the opponents of the rate—the Quaker, Thomas Spencer, is the most prominent example. Atkinson writes of a "small faction of dissenters and other opponents of the church" (No. 196), and of "a party almost wholly composed of dissenters and open oponents of the Church" (No. 74) as being the obstacle. The "almost wholly composed" gives credence to the *Mercury*'s claim that "the staunchest churchmen" were also opposed to the rate, and it is indeed possible to name some of these staunchest churchmen. But in a parish in which there were four chapels it would be almost impossible for dissenters not to be involved in the opposition. As far as one can tell, however, with the exception of Thomas Spencer, the leaders of the opposition were not the leaders of the chapels. The only list we have of Methodists is for the Bransby Ranters in the late 1840s, and none of them was prominent in the vestry. A parishioner, speaking to the *Daily News* in 1855 after Bishop Jackson's attempted mediation (No. 213), said that the Bishop's suggestion to raise £1000 on a mortgage of the rates was "objectionable" because it would infringe "on the rights of dissenters who have helped the churchmen to fight their battles" (*Lincolnshire Times*, 17 April 1855). The conflict is probably best understood as being primarily a civil and social one between the incumbent and the farmers, although, of course, one cannot exclude dissenting feelings which obviously coincided with the aims of the farmers.

"The mortgage of the rates", said the same parishioner, "would take the future power over the church rates out of the hands of the ratepayers for a long and indefinite period" (*Lincolnshire Times*, 17 April 1855). This was the crucial consideration. In 1849, John Harrison, the intruded churchwarden, had boasted openly "that the Churchwardens are now the Masters of the Clergyman and they will keep so" (No. 74), and, again, the same year Atkinson rejoiced that "the failure of this attempt to coerce the Clergyman will . . . have a salutary effect" (No. 89). In many ways the church rates issue was but the chosen field on which to fight the battle for control of the church, a favourable field because no one wants to pay more rates than he need. The vestry was prepared to raise the occasional 2½d. rate, provided they, through the wardens, had the spending of it. As soon as church rates became an issue they raised again the claim (disposed of in 1838) that they should choose both churchwardens, even though this did not affect their power to refuse a rate in the vestry.

Atkinson, however, was able to assert his right to choose one of the church wardens, and then went on to attack the administration of the charities, which provided the only income the church wardens had other than through a church rate. In Stow the Church Lands amounted to five and a half acres, and in Sturton to less than half an acre, and had been allotted for the repair of the church. They were yielding in 1837, the time of the Charity Commissioners' enquiry, £6.10s. a year, but by 1846 the income had risen to the not inconsiderable sum of £17.4.1d. The income had not been spent on the church fabric for many years, but had been used by the churchwardens to pay the ordinary expenses such as the clerk's salary and wine for the sacrament. The land was let as small gardens of a rood, or half a rood. The Edward Burgh school charity was in the hands of the possessor of Stow Hall and four freeholders, and the recipients of his money for the poor were chosen by the vestry.

By re-organising the charities with a body of trustees, the weight of whom were gentlemen from outside the parish (No. 218), Atkinson was able to gain for the clergyman of the parish the patronage which the administration of the Burgh Charities gave, and from the church lands the choice of the poor people to hold the gardens, and for the restoration fund, the income from the land.

Atkinson never obtained from the rates any real help towards the repair of the nave and transepts of the church, but he did win the battle for the control of the church. The vestry meetings from then on became merely formal gatherings, and there was no further interference in the concerns of the church. Thus far he saw "those who withstood him dispersed" (No. 226).

IV The Church Building

It is not my intention to attempt to unravel the complicated and controversial early history of the church. For the purposes of this volume it is better to suspend disbelief and accept what Atkinson and his contemporaries believed about the age and origins of Stow Church; that it was founded at the site of Saint Etheldreda's ash, that it was the ancient cathedral of Sidnacester, and that the marks of the fire on the north pier in the nave, and the lodging of the cinder in the north transept, were the result of a fire lighted by the Danes in the course of the great incursion of 870. None of this is correct, but when Atkinson laments that the "Gentlemen of the County should have taken so little interest in a work of so interesting a character as that of the restoration of the Mother Church of the Diocese" it is to this line of thought that he refers (No. 82).

Nevertheless the documents printed in this volume contain much that is of interest to the archaeologist and the architectural historian, in that they contain much evidence as to what was actually done at the restoration.

All observers agreed on the decayed, dilapidated, and neglected condition of Stow Church before its restoration. Nothing beyond a little botching had been done for years. Atkinson's description of the church in his letter to the Archdeacon (No. 94) is anticipated by E. J. Willson's account of the building which he wrote apparently about 1841 (Society of Antiquaries, Willson Collection, Vol. xiv, pp. 29–33). "The internal appearance of the church is altogether desolate and forlorn. The floors and lower parts of the walls are dirty and green owing to the accumulation of damp on the outside and the want of drainage. The mouldings and ornaments are disfigured by repeated coats of whitewash, and have been cut and broken in many parts.

"A rude gallery, or platform of timber, for the ringers to stand upon, blocks up the central space under the tower. A partition with another gallery for the singers cuts off about half the nave; and the pews and seats are of the most irregular description possible. We may however distinguish among them many curious remnants of desks and stalls of antient and rich workmanship, showing how beautifully this noble old church was once furnished."

In 1844 Atkinson was elected to the committee of the newly formed Lincolnshire Society for the Encouragement of Ecclesiastical Architecture. In January 1845 a letter was read from him "on the recent discovery of Saxon work in the church of Stow in Lindsey", and a donation of £5 was offered "to be applied to some special restoration in Stow Church, as a proof of [the committee's] interest in a sacred building originally the Cathedral Church of Sidnacester" (*AASR sub anno*).

In 1846 Atkinson began to explore around the foundations, at the same time removing the accumulated earth from against the walls. He then published a paper to the Society, *Notes, Historical and Architectural on Stow Church*, in which he stated the nature of what he had found around the foundations, and printed a picture of the church interior after he had, as the Archdeacon put it, "rooted up the whole concern as to its accommodation as a parish Church and made some temporary accommodation in the Chancel for the celebration of divine service" (No. 8). In a note at the end of the paper, Atkinson acknowledged how useful the Architectural Society's grant had been. Marks of fire indicative of date were discovered where the whitewash had been removed, and the removal of plaster in the upper parts of the chancel confirmed what the writer had always suspected, that there had been a groined stone roof. "Divine service having been celebrated in the chancel while the process of cleaning the tower arches was going on, the parishioners expressed their earnest wish that the service might be continued there. . . . Accordingly the floor of the chancel was levelled and lowered to the original depth" and the old pews from under the tower, with the superstructures of deal removed, were used for the seating (No. 94).

In 1848 the Archaeological Institute held its meeting in Lincoln, and gave further encouragement to the restoration. The newspaper reported that; "it is proposed that the church of Stow—a fabric now pronounced by the most learned archaeologists to bear more undoubted marks of Saxon origin than probably any other in the kingdom—considered also by many to be the Mother Church of the present cathedral, and whose walls have resounded with the accents of Christian prayer and praise through a series of nine hundred years—should, without delay, be rescued from its present deplorable state of decay and dilapidation, by powerful exertions in aid of parish rates and local contributions, and thus be rendered a memorial not unworthy of the nineteenth century, of our own affection towards God's service, and our veneration for the piety of our ancestors, by whom it was first erected" (*Lincolnshire Chronicle*, 11 August 1848). Well might the vestry think that "a class of men calling themselves Archaeologists have resolved to fasten upon the Church of Stowe and the Parish funds, that they may use both for the display of their skill in the Science of Antiquities" (No. 42).

The architect for the restoration was John Loughborough Pearson, whom Sir Charles Anderson introduced to Atkinson in December of 1846 (No. 10). Pearson was 29 at the time and as yet unknown. He had been brought up in Durham—a good training ground perhaps for Stow—and the son of one of the canons there had introduced him to the East Riding, where he had built several churches and where the Andersons had some property. Charles probably met him there, and employed him to restore the chancel of Lea Church (Quiney, p. 39). By 1846 Pearson had designed some half a dozen churches, but had done no major restorations: St. Augustine's, Kilburn, and Truro Cathedral were still thirty years in the future.

A distinction is made in these documents between Repair and Restoration. Repair was the effecting of "such works as might be *necessary*" (No. 23) to render the building safe and weatherproof. Again a distinction might be drawn between "decent repair" and "the least that can be done—or which an Archdeacon can compel you to do". The former might cost twice as much as the latter (No. 17). But beyond both these lay what might be called "restorations in the proper sense of the word" (No. 27)—"works which are considered by the Architect desireable, and consistent with the character of the ancient building, though not perhaps strictly falling within what might be deemed substantial repairs" (No. 26N). Ewan Christian made the same distinction, in different words (quoted No. 156), "between substantial repairs and ornamental restorations". Restoration, in the opinion of the Stow vestry, was a "luxurious and refined pleasure of the wealthy" (No. 42).

Pearson conformed to the Camden Society's definition of an eclectic restorer, in that he was prepared to destroy and substitute where he felt it desirable, and to conserve and renew, again where his judgment told him it was appropriate. In his substitutions he anticipated Violet le Duc's definition of the 1850s; "Restoring a building is not maintaining it, or repairing it, or renewing it; it is re-establishing it in a state of perfection, in which it may never have existed at any one moment in the past."

This is what Pearson did at Lea and at Stow. Where he found evidence for a feature which had been replaced, like the lancets in Lea Chancel, or the Norman windows at the east end of Stow chancel, he re-instated them, even though this might mean the destruction of a later, though still medieval, feature. He did this systematically in the chancel at Stow, but not in the nave, where he allowed thirteenth century gothic windows inserted into the romanesque transepts to remain, while he removed the west window of the nave, a perpendicular insertion.

This policy did not go without criticism. In the Ross MSS the following attack on the new east end was copied out (p. 60); "The present substitute gives a greater uniformity by harmonizing with the side windows, which are of the same character; but they have destroyed a feature that, from the claims of preservation, which its venerable age gave it, is of far greater interest to the feelings of the antiquary and the archaeologist, than any modern act for the restoration of purity can ever be made to possess." But in all probability the feelings of the antiquary would have had to have chosen between a nineteenth century version of the gothic window, rather than a medieval window, and what was actually put up.

Work began on the chancel in September 1850 (No. 125) almost exactly four years after the Bishop first mentioned the matter to the Ecclesiastical Commissioners (No. 2). The work was finished at the end of March 1852. The furniture and the floor, however, still required to be completed. The work done included all the necessary and substantial repairs, the restoration of the stone vault, the building of a parapet along the walls, and the raising of the timber and lead roof to a higher pitch. The stages of the work can be gathered from the Architect's Certificates, and what was done can be checked against the Nattes drawings in the Banks Collection in Lincoln Central Library.

Work on the nave and transepts was not begun until March 1864, (No. 254.1), and a faculty was obtained the following July (No. 225). Again the work consisted of the necessary repairs to the walls and foundations. The roof was raised to a higher pitch, re-using the old timbers where possible. The floors in the transept were re-instated at the level at which they were first put in, which were all different. The stair turret which stood in the north-east corner of the nave was removed outside, and round it was built a new vestry block. There were plans to raise the height of the tower, both to provide a lantern inside and also to compensate for the extra height of the roofs outside; this was not done and the central tower remains comparatively dwarfed by the great lead roofs. Inside a chancel screen was envisaged, and an organ. The chancel screen was never erected, and the provision of the organ lies outside the dates set for this volume.

In spite of the survival of the Cash Book (No. 254) the restoration of the nave and transepts is very much less well documented than that of the chancel, for which architect's reports and certificates have survived. We have to rely on prints, photographs, and the building itself to discover what was done. In the north transept the doorway in the east wall, near the rood screen stairs, was walled up, and the archway in the west wall was opened up to provide an entrance to the new vestries. In the south transept a hole or recess on the inside of the south wall was smoothed over. The internal ceiling of the crossing was raised a few feet. In the nave after the removal of the stair turret, the major restoration was that of the fenestration in the west wall, which involved the destruction of a large perpendicular window. The columns on the jambs of the south doorway had completely perished, and their place taken by brickwork; Pearson used the design of the columns of the west doorway, reversing the disposition. To the north of the west doorway was a small niche with an ogee shaped hoodmould; the hoodmould had presumably perished and was not renewed. Inside, the font base now appears to be a few inches higher than it was, by reason either of lowering the floor, or of inserting a thin extra course at its foot.

In the north transept was made the discovery of the Becket wall painting in the August after Atkinson's death. This is described by Frederick Atkinson in a letter to the *Stamford Mercury* (1 December 1865). Mr Trollope did identify the subject of the painting correctly.

"At the time of my brother's death the wall (behind which was the painting in question) had not been disturbed, and consequently he was ignorant that such a painting existed; but he always thought, from certain appearances in the wall, that an altar had formerly existed there, or that there had been some other arrangement connected with pre-Reformation times, and he expressed his conviction that on the removal of the wall some discovery would be made as might in all probability determine the point: his intention was to have the wall removed, but this was prevented by his unexpected death. The discovery of the painting was made by Mr Codd (Mr Pearson, the architect's head clerk) and myself early in August last: we had the walling carefully removed, and the painting then became exposed to view; but of the subject neither of us knew anything. Sir Charles Anderson, in a letter to me on the 28th September last, thought that the explanation of the painting by Mr Trollope was a very probable one."

Frederick thus shared his brother's enthusiasm for archaeology. George Atkinson's descriptions, however, of what he found in his diggings around the foundations, and of what was seen during the restoration of the chancel, are tantalizing in their lack of measurements. The following extract is typical (*AASR*, 1851, p. 320): "On the South side (of the chancel) there were strong indications of the Saxon choir having had an aisle, or possibly arches opening into a cloister. On this side the original basement course stopped short of the angle formed by the transept by some eight or ten feet, and under the foundation, or base-course, of the present Norman wall, were found three pieces of cut stonework, at nearly regular distances, which had very much the appearance of having formed the basement of piers belonging to the older structure. A similar appearance was met with in the interior, in one part where the foundation required to be laid bare."

Yet in the same paper (p. 322f) there is a vivid account of the discovery that the ancient vault had in fact been built in the chancel.

"*The Vaulting.*—The grand feature . . . is the restoration of the stone vaulting, which is now far advanced . . . [Some antiquaries] were inclined to think that the vaulting, which was evidently projected, had never been executed. Others thought that, after it had been put up, the vaulting had either fallen or had so far given way that it was found necessary to take it down. A slight outward inclination of the walls seemed to favour the latter opinion. On removing the plaster from the wall above the vaulting-piers, the doubt was set at rest. The curves of the vaulting could be distinctly traced on the wall from the tops of the piers over the upper tier of windows; and in the space included between these curves the wall had a quite different appearance from that on each side, and in places the character of rough ashlar. On taking out portions it was found that the ashlar-like stones were no other than arch stones of the old groining, with their mouldings turned inwards towards the wall. It was evident, in short, that the rents in the walls caused by the fall of the vault had been in part repaired with the materials of the ruined vaulting itself; and besides from 100 to 200 arch stones too much mutilated to be used again, we found not less than 40 so perfect that they have been placed in the restored vaulting.

"Of the smaller diagonal ribs, we found several nearly perfect specimens. The rib with the central round and the zigzag on each side we found first, and supposed that all the groins might have been of this one pattern; but after a while two other patterns were found—one with the round and plain hollow on each side; the other similar, except that in the hollow there was a knob or ball at intervals. At length, after much anxious searching, and having got traces of two other patterns which had evidently formed portions of other and more massive ribs, we found nearly perfect specimens of two larger groins, which, on being fitted to the caps of the central vaulting shafts, were found to correspond with them in size. Thus we were at length rewarded with the discovery of all the ribs for which there could be room in the groining (five in number)."

It remained to arrange them so that the most ornamental were nearest the east, which may have been a mistake archaeologically because the altar probably originally stood under the central bay.

The Restoration of Churches is the Restoration of Popery was the title of a sermon preached in November 1844, at about the time when Bishop Kaye withdrew his support for the Cambridge Camden Society. With this in mind perhaps, at the end of his paper, Atkinson drew attention to some of the later medieval alterations to the Saxon church, the rood screen cut into the piers, a beam across the eastern bay of the chancel, a holy water stoup (with a pointed arch) in the nave. These instances, he suggested quite erroneously, afforded testimony to "the simplicity of the ritual of our Church in those early times compared with what it had gradually become for some ages before the Reformation" (p. 325). He finished his paper with the words, "let these suffice to show that English churchmen, while they feel it one of their highest duties, one of their happiest privileges, to aid in preserving, and restoring where needful—and alas! through our long neglect where is it not needful?—

the sacred and venerable structures which our forefathers in the faith erected, have yet cause, in the midst of all our admiration of their wonderful beauty, to love and to be satisfied with their own pure and simple worship as it has been reformed; in which, if they are less like to the later they are all the more like the earlier Church of England, as to the pure and primitive state of the Church universal itself."

The Lincoln Archaeological Society visited Stow in 1868, and their report on the visit shows the state of affairs then existing. "But while much has been done, much still remains to be done, and although the fabric of the church is in a state of substantial repair, still nothing has yet been done in the way of internal fittings, if we except the new lectern and the seating, which have been lately placed in the church, the former as a memorial to the late Vicar. The lectern, which is of brass, was designed and executed by Hardman of Birmingham, and is a fair specimen of modern brass-work" (*AASR* 1868).

Pearson's biographer, Anthony Quiney, acclaims Pearson's restoration of the chancel as "an impressive architectural triumph, and at once a substantial archaeological success" (Quiney, p. 42). While we can agree with this, it is not perhaps unfair to suggest that some of the attractiveness of the restoration is accidental in that the loss of impetus which the restoration sustained by the death of Atkinson resulted in a failure to supply the finishing touches. What would have been the effect of the chancel screen, a reredos and altar, elaborate altar rails, and a more costly floor, and the nave and transepts crammed with pews?

Ecclesiologically the pre-restoration seating was unusual in that the pulpit and reading desk faced each other diagonally across the space under the tower, known in the eighteenth century as "the churche" at the entrance to which the singing loft had been erected in 1746 (CW accounts). The new arrangement also had its eccentricities. The Camden Society ideal of a church, which was very influential at this time, was really envisaged in a three aisled building; in the nave the pews were all to face east, the reading desk and pulpit flanked the chancel arch, with a litany desk between them, and in the chancel the choir stalls led the eye onward and upward to the single altar. Stow conformed in the chancel, but the cruciform plan, the enormous supports to the tower, and Atkinson's desire for a quite unrealistic number of seats, led him to plan for the whole church to be pewed, including the transepts. The transept pews therefore had to face inwards towards the tower, the space under the tower arches being used for children's seating. The faculty plan of 1865 (LAO) shows accommodation in the nave and transepts for a congregation of 386 adults and 72 children—but see No. 224N for a different computation. In this plan there was no provision for an organ. The pulpit was sited right in the middle of the space under the tower—a most eccentric position for a restored church—and the lectern some eight feet in front of it. The reading desk is on the south side of the chancel arch facing north. Pencil emendations cross out the reading desk, and have the word Pulpit on the north-east pier (where the pulpit had actually stood before 1846). Without these amendments, with the exception of open benches rather than the hated "pues", the arrangement was one which might have been done in the eighteenth century. There is some commentary on Atkinson's ideas in his brother's letter to Sir Charles Anderson (No. 245), which speaks of a movable lectern doing duty for a pulpit.

Haskins, Atkinson's successor, had other ideas, equally out of date. He was an evangelical—within a month of his arrival he held the first Stow harvest festival, "a most odd scene" according to Sir Charles Anderson, though "Archdeacon Giles preached a very good sermon"—and seems to have wanted to dissociate himself from the restoration. What was done curiously resembled the old state of affairs. The seating was mainly in the transepts and under the tower, and the lectern (the memorial to Atkinson) seems to have done duty for the pulpit. The organ when it was put up in 1873, filled the void left by the old stair turret in the corner of the nave, and if the singers sat opposite, they would have been under the old singing loft.

The organ, however, was moved by the next incumbent to its present position under the north tower arch, and the old pulpit re-erected on a new stone base, as a memorial to Haskins, at the south side of the chancel arch. The main seating was now in the nave, and the church conformed, as much as its architecture would allow it, to the Camden Society model.

V The Donors

The evidence for subscriptions and donations is listed in the Subject Index under Subscriptions, and includes subscription lists from the press, references in letters, and, primarily, the two items not printed in this volume: a small notebook giving a list of subscriptions, and the income side of the cash book (No. 254).

None of these sources gives a complete list of all gifts and givers, most of them partially overlap so that one donation may appear two or three times. Some donations are described by the name of the bearer or the collector, so many donors remained unrecorded, especially those who gave small gifts. Unfortunately therefore we have comparatively little evidence for the donations from the parish. The details in the list of donors of the amounts and of the identity of the donor (in square brackets) cannot be relied upon as certain.

By far the greatest givers were the Atkinson family, who gave nearly £1680 between them. Some donations look as if there was a box in the parsonage into which small gifts might be put; another appears to be a Christmas whip-round. As well as their actual gifts, Atkinson's sisters were responsible for collecting many gifts, and his brother, Frederick, was presumably responsible for all the donations from Manchester, where he had his house.

After the family the greatest gifts came from the Incorporated Church Building Society—£150—and Lord Brownlow—£125. About 30 more donors, each giving more than £15, contributed nearly £1150. Another 300 or more small donations, the sale of photographs, the collecting box in church, and other sources accounted for the remaining £700.

In the parish of Stow, William Godson and his wife gave between them £21.10s, and this was the only substantial gift. Atkinson's church wardens, Anthony Gibbs and Joseph Pycroft are represented by gifts, as was Edward Howard, probably junior, whose wife gave a donation. Her sister, rather surprisingly for she was Mrs. Knowles, the daughter of the Methodist Thomas Palmer at the Cross Keys, gave two annual subscriptions of £2.10s in 1864 and 1865. Four farm labourers we know gave money, one as much as £1, and, no doubt, the £12.6.10d collected "in small sums" in the parish came also from the poorer people. The parsonage cook and housemaid contributed generously.

The neighbouring clergy almost all contributed, as did a good number throughout the diocese. It was the country gentlemen's response which was disappointing. Atkinson attributed their "backwardness . . . to disgust at the factious spirit manifested by the majority of the Parishioners" even though the appeal had been issued under the auspices of the Lord Lieutenant and the Bishop (No. 82). The list of those who did contribute has a strong flavour of Tory magnates, magistrates and their clerks, and clergymen.

Outside the county there was a group of donations from Yorkshire, where it seems Atkinson may have had friends, for he planned a fortnight's stay there in 1850 (No. 120). Rochdale, the Atkinson home town, produced 14 donors, including Thomas Butterworth, Atkinson's brother in law. The names include Nield, Holt, Chadwick, and Livsey.

In Manchester what one guesses was Frederick Atkinson's activity drummed up 26 donors, to which may be added a further nine from other places in Lancashire, excluding Rochdale.

Miscellaneous sources of income included nearly £20 from the "Alms Box in Church", probably almost entirely contributed by visitors; nearly £17 from the sale of photographs; and £14.5s from collections taken at the Archdeacon of Stow's visitations in 1865.

VI In the End

When the dust had settled the result of all the conflict and bitterness seems to have been that Stow conformed to the pattern of what was going on elsewhere in the church and countryside. In general at this time resident clergy did become the rule; churches were restored; church rates became impracticable; the control of the clergyman over the church did generally increase; church schools were built, but Methodism was not extinguished. All this in the end was true of Stow.

Haskins was able to heal the disagreements between the staunch churchmen. The restoration was complete, or nearly so, and church rates were abolished within two years; so the task was not an impossible one. Nevertheless it is pleasant to be able to quote from the Vestry Minutes of 1876, and see old antagonists working together.

"The Parish accounts were examined and passed. Mr. Pycroft was made Minister's Churchwarden. Mr. Ellis proposed and Mr. Howard seconded Wm Godson Esq. as Parish Churchwarden

Signed Wm Godson	E. H. Haskins Rector
Joseph Pycroft	William Ellis
Edward Howard	Joseph Harrison"

Appendix 1

Church Dignitaries during the Period

Bishops of Lincoln

John Kaye (born 1783), 1827 to 19 February 1853, when he died.

John Jackson (born 1811), 5 May 1853 to 1869, when he was translated to London.

Christopher Wordsworth (born 1807), 1869 to 1885.

Archdeacons of Lincoln

Henry Kaye Bonney (born 1780), 1845 to 1862.

William Frederick John Kaye, 1863 to 1913.

Archdeacons of Stow

Henry Vincent Bayley, 1823 to 1844.

William Brocklehurst Stonehouse, 1844 to 1862.

John Douglas Giles, 1863 to 1866.

Edward Trollope, 1867 to 1880.

Prebendary of Stow in Lindsey

Peter Fraser, 1831 to 1853.

Prebendary of Corringham cum Stow

George Beckett, 1822 to 1843.

The Ecclesiastical Commission were thenceforth owners of the prebendal property and liable to the charges and duties laid upon it.

Appendix 2

Publications of the Rev. George Atkinson

Notes Historical and Architectural on Stow Church. Louth, 1846, 18 pp., two illustrations. Published thus separately, and also as part of the 1848 report of the Lincolnshire Society for the Encouragement of Ecclesiastical Architecture.

Abiding by the Church our way of duty and safety in times of agitation and danger; London, 1847, 8vo. Preached at the visitation of the Archdeacon of Stow in Lincoln Cathedral, May 1847, and published at the request of the archdeacon and the clergy.

On the Restorations in progress at Stow Church, Lincolnshire. Read at a joint meeting of the Architectural Societies of Yorkshire and Lincolnshire, held at Ripon, on Tuesday, June 17th, 1851. Published in Associated Architectural Societies Reports (AASR), 1851, p. 315. 12 pp., one illustration.

On Saxon Architecture, and the Early Churches in the Neighbourhood of Grimsby. A paper read at a meeting of the Lincoln Diocesan Architectural Society at Grimsby, May 25th, 1859. Published in AASR, 1859, p. 23. One illustration of Stow.

Proposed Restoration of St. Mary's Church at Stow, Lincolnshire. The Mother-Church of the Diocese. A leaflet of 4 pages and one illustration; no date, but 1863.

Saxon Churches: stone or wood. An article in the Gentleman's Magazine, 1863, i, pp. 755–762.

THE DOCUMENTS

1. Church Book

Easter Monday. Churchwardens Elected

1846	Christopher Page Samuel Blow (continued)
1847	Christopher Page Samuel Blow (continued)
1848	John Spinks Robert Foster
1849	William Taylor John Harrison
1850	John Harrison George Burton
1851	John Harrison Robert Gilbert
1852	John Harrison Henry Walker
1853	John Harrison parishioners Anthony Gibbs minister
1854	Anthony Gibbs minister John Harrison parishioners
1855	Magnus Hugh Duncan minister John Harrison parishioners
1856	Joseph Smith minister John Harrison parishioners
1857	Joseph Smith minister John Harrison parishioners
1858	Jonathan Elwis minister John Harrison parishioners
1859	Jonathan Elwis James S. Gelder
1860	Jonathan Elwis James S. Gelder

1861 { Jonathan Elwis
James S. Gelder }

1862 { Jonathan Elwis
James S. Gelder }

1863 { Jonathan Elwis
James S. Gelder }

1864 { Jonathan Elwis
James S. Gelder }

1865 { Joseph Pycroft
James S. Gelder }

1866 { Joseph Pycroft
James S. Gelder }

Note: The Court of Queen's Bench declared that the Wardens for 1852 were W. Hutchinson and John H. Locke. See No. 198.

2. To Eccl. Com. from Bp Kaye, Riseholm (Copy), 1 Aug. 1846 (EC)

My dear Sir,

I beg leave to acknowledge the receipt of your letter of yesterday enclosing a copy of one addressed to the Perpetual Curate of Stow on the subject of the Augmentation of his Benefice, I enclose one from him relating to certain repairs which are required in the Chancel of the Church at Stow

2A. From the Revd. George Atkinson to the Bishop of Lincoln

Stow, Gainsborough
July 28th 1846

My Lord,

I beg leave to recall your Lordship's attention to the defect which I have already mentioned in the foundation of a part of the North Wall of the Chancel of Stow Church.

In consequence of the heavy fall of water from the eaves, and the earth lying against the walls to a considerable height above the proper ground line—the foundation along the whole length of the North side is in a decayed state

The repairs which have been done for a long time past, where any have been done at all, have been executed in a very penurious and imperfect manner, and the whole of the foundation of the Chancel—especially on this the North side will ere long require a thorough examination and repair.

In the mean time there is a portion of the footing of the North wall which is in so very decayed a state—the stones of the basement course being quite loose—the wall above them for at least a foot inward from the exterior surface being in consequence left without support—that I think it would be wise to have some temporary reparation made until the whole can be done satisfactorily.

I do not at the same time think from the vast solidity of the wall that there is immediate danger to its stability—The reparation of the Chancel as your Lordship is aware belongs to that portion of the Tithes lately held by Sir John Beckett and now in the possession of the Ecclesiastical Commissioners

Should your Lordship think proper to communicate with the Board on this subject, I beg further to say that I shall be glad if authorized by them to superintend whatever work they may think proper to have done, and to see that it is done properly at a reasonable cost indeed the expense of what would be necessary at present would be trifling

I should be glad also if I might be allowed to order 3 wire screens to be put up before the openings of the windows by which we air the Chancel—In consequence of there being nothing to prevent the birds getting in when the windows are open, they build in the Church and both disturb the Service by their noise, and make the Church very dirty

These matters I beg respectfully to lay before your Lordship And remain &c

(Signed)
George Atkinson

3. To Bp Kaye from Eccl. Com. (Copy), 3 Aug. 1846 (EC)

My Lord,

I have the honor to acknowledge your Lordships communication respecting the Chancel of the Church at Stow which I will lay before the Board on Wednesday next.

4. To Atkinson from Eccl. Com. (Copy), 28 Aug. 1846 (EC)

Sir,

Stow Chancel

Your letter of the 28th ulto to the Bishop of Lincoln having been forwarded to this Office by his Lordship has been laid before the Ecclesiastical Commissioners for England and I am directed in answer to it to state that upon referring to the documents relating to the Prebend of Corringham, which have come to the possession of the Commissioners it appears that the Prebendary of Corringham as holder of a portion of the Tithes of Stow was liable only to repairs on the south side of the Chancel of Stow—and I am therefore with regard to the repairs of the North side to refer you to the Prebendary of Stow the Revd Peter Fraser in whom the remainder of the Tithes is still vested.

5. To Bp Kaye from Eccl. Com. (Copy), 28 Aug. 1846 (EC)

My Lord,

I have the honor to inclose a copy of a letter respecting the repairs of the Chancel of Stow Church which by direction of the Commissioners I have this day addressed to Mr Atkinson.

6. To Eccl. Com. from Bp Kaye, n.d., Copy of Extract (EC)

The Lessee of the Stow Prebendal property, who is bound to repair one side of the Chancel, will shortly communicate with you on the subject; the Commissioners are bound to repair the other side and the East end.

7. To Bp Kaye from Adn Stonehouse, n.d. (K)

My very good Lord

Mr Peel & Mr Atkinson are very anxious that I should issue a monition to the Church Wardens at Stow to repair their Church—I believe with regard to those Churches which have been peculiars—my authority extends no farther than to visit—If I am correct your Lordship will perhaps take order therein. Mr Peel says the Stow People will not take any steps to borrow the money, until they find the Ordinary is resolved to compel the reparation of the Church— . . . .

8. To Bp Kaye from Adn Stonehouse, Owston, 2 Nov. [1846] (K)

My very good Lord—

On my return from Riseholme—I called at my Cathedral Church of Stow to see what was going on as in duty bound so to do—I found Mr Atkinson in the Church and that he had rooted up the whole concern as to its accommodation as a parish Church and made some temporary accommodation in the Chancel for the celebration of divine service—Mr Atkinson said that he had your Lordship's sanction for his proceedings, which being granted when you were on Visitation, and during inhibition was very "singular good"—

But "my duty and service duly remembered" I do opine that your licence to Master Atkinson may peradventure place him in somewhat similar circumstances to the late Archdeacon of Stow when he had demolished in a very considerable degree Broughton & Bottisford Churches without knowing, or having duly provided the means for building up—and when Our departed Friend was hard pressed for the ready by those whom he had set to work—He exclaimed—"Take my watch" which I suppose meant that he would be answerable even to part with that personal chattel

I think that the best thing to be done with Stow Church—is this—First to get the Chancel put into a substantial state of repair—by those parties who are legally liable to these repairs which are the Ecclesiastical Commissioners as to the east end and north side & the Revd Mr Samuel Hall as to the south side—Your Lordship will manage the Ecclesiastical Commissioners much better than I can—and as I have some influence with the Revd Mr Samuel Hall who is a right minded man I will try to manage him

This Chancel which is by far the most beautiful and interesting part of the Church, would accommodate 200 persons—and as the repairs can be easily accomplished it would be the best thing we could do to carry this into effect I suggested this to Mr Atkinson but he replied—I have a population of a 1000 What is accommodation for 200 to do for me? Let us subject this assertion that he has a population of a 1000 to the most disagreeable of all operations a dry analysis—That population of a thousand being analysed—will be found to consist of the following ingredients—

Imprimis

	250	Infants—
In secundo	250	people to nurse them
In Tertio	150	In statu Pupillari
	100	Dissenters
In Quarto	100	People who go to no place of worship with the aged & infirm who cannot go—
	8500	[*Sic*]

This calculation leaves him with a congregation of 150—to which we may add 70 children if he gets a good School—for which a loft might be built at the west end of the Chancel—

I have made this calculation from an accurate analysis of the population of Owston given me by the Registrar of Births—Secondly will the congregation average 100 grown up people—

You will find Atkinson a Man who will have nothing but his own way—which I think is a very great hindrance to the effecting good works—

I shall feel much obliged if your Lordship will present my very best respects to Mrs Kay—and tell her that I have not been negligent to seek out for an ass—but though I have seen several—they have not good characters for docility &c—But if Mrs Kay has not got suited I feel certain that I can get an old Grey Poney about the size of an ass—broad on the back—short and thick in the legs—very sure footed—This poney was for several years the property of Mr Pooley who gave him to Mr Hill a parishioner of mine under condition that Mr Hill should not part with him he rode the poney for several years—and now does not do so because he says he can walk as fast—so I suppose we may say literally of this old poney—what I said figuratively of the late Dean of Lincoln you cannot lash him into a trot. I asked Mr Hill what he would take for him—and he said I'll neither give him to you nor sell him to you—but if you want him for Mrs Stonehouse to ride upon you may have him as long as you please—I told him I wanted him for another Lady—Very well said he you shall have him, and your friend may send him back when she is tired of him—In fact Hill is tired of keeping the poney now he has no use for him, but wont forfeit his word—If Mrs Kaye has not got suited with an ass—I think she would do well to have old Pooley on trial.

P.S.

The only way in which the nave and transepts of Stow Church can be repaired is by a subscription—If a considerable sum was raised in that way—perhaps the Parishioners might be induced to borrow money from the Board of Works—I am convinced by experience that the best way to go to work is to get the subscription first & then go to the Parish and say—I have got so much money—a free gift—on condition you will borrow so much—The fear of losing the gift, as the Americans say works elegantly—

I *should* esteem it a great favour if your Lordship would inform me if you can give Mr Middleton the Chimney Doctor as good a Character as I have given the old poney—as I think he exercises his art in your place, and also if you would give me his direction with many thanks for your kind hospitality I remain . . .

9. To Adn Stonehouse from Hall, Wolfreton House, 18 Nov. 1846 (K)

Dear Mr Archdeacon,

It grieved me to learn from you that the Chancel of Stow Church is in so dilapidated a state. Though not ignorant that it belonged to me to keep in repair a portion of the structure, I was not previously aware of the extent of my liability which you correctly describe. Being, I confess, a little afraid of London Architects, as not having like the Commissioners a building fund to draw upon, I have taken steps to obtain through a competent person nearer home, an estimate of the expence of the necessary repairs of the south side of the chancel. Possibly the Ecclesiastical Commissioners might not be unwilling on receiving from me a sum of money in fair proportion to restore my part along with their own. I should be glad to come to such an arrangement, & if you can assist me in making it, shall feel much obliged, & be most desirous of meeting in a liberal spirit any offer from them.

Should anything bring you to Hull, I am but five miles distant from it & should be happy to see you.

[P.S.] I hope you received through the Gainsborough Bookseller the volume of sermons by Mr Codd.

10. To Adn Stonehouse from Atkinson, Stow, 31 Dec. 1846 (K)

Dear Mr Archdeacon

On my return to Stow I found that Mr Hall's Agent—Mr Gourlay from Fenton—had been over to survey the Chancel in my absence. I was informed however by Mr Hall's Tenant at Stow Park Mr Burnham, that as Mr Gourlay wished to look over the chancel in company with me—he would come to Stow again for the purpose. He accordingly came on Monday December 14th and I pointed out to him those parts of the North wall (the repair of which devolves upon Mr Hall) which appeared to be most in need of repair.

It so happened that Sir Charles Anderson had staying with him at Lea about that time a Mr Pearson a very able Architect from London for the purpose of surveying Lea Church—and furnishing a design for its restoration. This Gentleman I met at Lea on the Friday previous and he was so kind as to examine the Church at Stow in order to give us his opinion as to its condition and what was necessary to be done in the way of repair and restoration. The first thing he stated to be the *roofs*, all of which he says are from their very low pitch, and from the very faulty way in which they are constructed exerting a very injurious effect upon the walls, and tending to endanger their stability.—The weight of the roof being thrown upon the middle of the Tie-beams instead of the ends, has caused those beams to bend or "sag" in the middle in this way

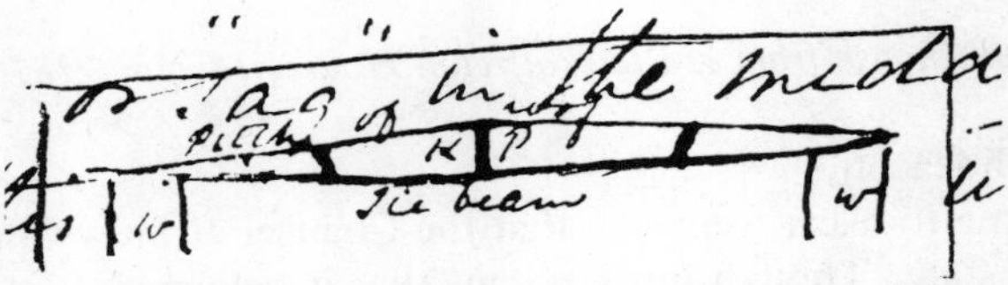

And so the Tie beams instead of bracing the walls together, are acting upon the inner edge of the walls, which are thus a fulcrum on which the Tie-beam as a Lever exerts a pressure which must of necessity tend to press the walls outward, and as the walls are already out of the perpendicular (inclining outwards) the removal of these roofs and the replacing of them by others of higher pitch and better construction is in Mr Pearson's opinion of the first importance to the preservation of the structure. I requested Mr Gourlay to make a note of this—and he promised to do so with regard to the Chancel roof. Should Mr Hall refer to you in this matter before he concludes as to the Amount to be expended on his part, you will perhaps, if this point should not have been sufficiently brought to Mr Hall's notice, have the goodness to explain it to him. Mr Pearson I casually learnt is known to Mr Hall—and Sir Charles Anderson states that he bears a very high character as an Architect, his statement therefore *which he made very emphatically* as to the injurious and indeed dangerous effects of the present roofs on the stability of the walls must be considered worthy of very serious attention.

Our temporary alterations are now nearly concluded—they have given great satisfaction to the Parishioners, and promise to lead to much improvement both in the attendance and devotion of the congregation.

11. To Pearson from Hall, Wolfreton House (Copy), 4 Jan. 1847 (K)

Dear Sir,

I have a letter this morning from Archdeacon Stonehouse, inclosing one addressed to him by the Revd. G. Atkinson, Incumbent of Stow near Gainsborough—from which I learn that you have lately had an opportunity of seeing his church, to the repairs of the *south* side of the chancel of which I am liable. I am glad of this, as I was only waiting for your coming again into this neighbourhood (& I understood from Kirby that you were expected in a short time) to avail myself of your opinion on the subject.

I shall hope to see you here on your next visit to Ferriby & perhaps you could give me a day or two notice that I may be in the way, when you call.

There is, I believe, some intention of completely restoring Stow Church—the ancient cathedral of the Diocese of Lindsey & for several centuries the residence of the Saxon Bishops—cannot you furnish a design! I am sure your friends in this part would use all their influence in your favour.

Note: See No. 26 for a correct statement of the position.

12. To Adn Stonehouse from Atkinson, Stow, 7 Jan. 1847 (K)

Dear Mr Archdeacon

In thanking you as I now beg leave to do for your kind Note of the 2nd Inst. I beg leave also, as an evidence of the very satisfactory effect your correspondence with Mr Hall is producing with regard to the Chancel of our Church, to enclose a copy of a Note from Mr Hall to Mr Pearson, the Architect whom I mentioned as having looked over the Church here lately. This Note has been sent to me by Mr Pearson for my perusal—and I cannot but think that so far all is proceeding under the happiest auspices. Mr Pearson from what I have seen of him, as well as from what I have heard from Sir Charles Anderson respecting his professional abilities appears just the person we need in a work such as we hope in due time to accomplish. Mr Hall's testimony is to the same effect—Mr Pearson is a Gentleman—and a person upon whom we may most thoroughly depend. The fact of his being a friend of Mr Hall's, and the influence which that Gentleman is prepared to use in his favour, would be the most likely thing in the world to induce my Parishioners to put confidence in Mr Pearson too, in as much as two of the principal Farmers in this Parish Mr Robert Burnham, and Mr John Skill—the latter in part—the former wholly—*Tenants of Mr Hall's*. I trust if the other parties to the restoration should agree to choose Mr Pearson as their Architect—the Ecclesiastical Commissioners will do so likewise—as it is very important that the whole of the work should be under one management.

For the kind terms in which you are pleased to signify your appointment of myself as the Preacher in the Cathedral at your Spring Visitation—I beg to return my sincere acknowledgements. The having had the happiness to gain and secure the friendship of our most excellent Brother, the Rector of Willingham—a friendship which has ever been most generous, active and unvarying on his part,—I have always looked upon as one of the great events of my life.

Note: This sermon was published (see pp xii and xxxii), and is quoted in the Introduction. The Rector of Willingham was the Rev. Frederick Peel, also Rural Dean.

13. To Adn Stonehouse from Hall, Wolfreton House, 8 Jan. 1847 (K)

Dear Mr Archdeacon,

I feel obliged by your transmission to me of Mr Atkinson's letter, which in compliance with your request I now return. The faulty construction of the chancel roof is a serious matter & worthy of attention. Not considering Mr

Gourlay's statement quite satisfactory, I had determined on consulting Mr Pearson with respect to the repairs of the chancel, & was waiting for his arrival in this neighbourhood, having understood that he was expected at Ferriby, where a new church is being built after a design by him. As the time of his coming now appears to be uncertain, I shall write to him on the subject.

Mr Atkinson mistakes the side of the chancel to the repairs of which I am liable: you correctly stated it to be the south side.

I hope in the course of another fortnight to get over to Stow & see the church. *The proposed arrangement with the Commissioners is certainly desireable for me, but I feel a difficulty in proposing terms, & should be glad of an offer from them, if they were at liberty to make it.*

Note: The final sentence was underlined by the Archdeacon. See No. 14.

14. To Bp Kaye from Adn Stonehouse, Owston, Jan. 16 [1847] (K)

My very good Lord,

I herewith send you the letters anent Stow chancel which in my humble opinion are satisfactory—I have underlined a sentence in Mr Hall's letter to which I beg leave to call your Lordship's attention as to what answer I should return to it—Would this do—Archdeacon would advise Mr Hall to inform the Ecclesiastical Commissioners through the Lord Bishop of the diocese that if they will complete the repairs of the whole chancel—he will pay his share, but this offer is not to extend to any works of an ornamental nature—

or thus

If the Ecclesiastical Commissioners will send Mr Hall a statement of the expense of the necessary repairs of the whole Chancel—he will endeavour to agree with them on equitable terms to do his part—

As I have taken copies of all these letters your Lordship had better keep them—

15. To Adn Stonehouse from Hall, Wolfreton House, 26 Jan. 1847 (K)

Dear Mr Archdeacon,

On the same day on which I addressed you last, I wrote to Mr Pearson & requested him to send me an estimate of my proportion of the necessary repairs of the Chancel of Stow Church, which after the view taken by him he seemed to think himself competent to give. I have not as yet received his answer, but I conclude that when obtained his estimate will have its due weight with the Commissioners & under this impression I do not hesitate to accede to the arrangement recommended in your favour of the 22nd Inst. If you are likely to be in communication with the Bishop, & will kindly inform him of my readiness to bear my share of the expence of completing the necessary repairs of the Chancel & in case of dispute (which I hope will not arise) to abide by the decision of a person appointed by himself or his ordinary, I shall feel much obliged.

Should any more formal agreement be deemed necessary, I shall of course be ready to execute it.

16. To Adn Stonehouse from Hall, Wolfreton House, 4 Feb. 1847 (K)

Dear Mr Archdeacon,

I have received a letter from Mr Pearson, in which he gives the estimated cost of the several works that are necessary & those also that it would be desireable to have done at the chancel of Stow church. The inclosed extract from it is an exact copy, so far as it relates to the immediate object of this correspondence, with the exception that I have supplied three underlined words inadvertantly omitted, as it is evident Mr Pearson is writing not of the church but of the chancel.

Mr Pearson informs me that his plans for the restoration of the church are now nearly complete & will soon be forwarded to Stow. If they should be eventually carried out by him, I hope he may also be employed by the Commissioners for the Chancel, as it is desireable to have only one Architect engaged.

16A. *(Copy)*

London 31. Keppel Street
January 29. 1847

Dear Sir,

"I find after measuring the plans that the restoration of" (*the chancel of*) "Stow church will cost about 110£s; the necessary repairs alone will require from 50 to 60£s. The roof of the present structure is extremely bad & must be replaced, in which case it becomes necessary to give it much greater height with proper gutters &c according to the style. The floor is also in a very wretched state & the place is much dilapidated. To effect an entire restoration including the stone groining that has been thrown down, (parts of which remain) the cost would be about 1300£s; without the groining & with only a roof intended to have groining under it (which would thus be concealed) & therefore of common construction & in deal and leaving out tiles for floor and substituting stone instead, the cost would be reduced to 780£s, (in both cases the roof to be covered with lead as it is now.) The cost of the new roof alone with the lead covering will be about 300£s."

17. To Bp Kaye from Adn Stonehouse, Owston, 11 Feb. 1847 (K)

My very good Lord

I was aware of the obscurity of Mr Pearson's valuation of the repairs of Stow Chancel; but I was afraid to make any observations—lest I should make the matter worse. explanations often have that effect—

The impression which Mr Pearson's statement leaves on my mind is this—by "The restoration of the chancel of Stow Church" Mr Pearson means—The decent repair of the chancel will cost 110£. The least that can be done—or which an Archdeacon can compel you to do—will cost from 50 to 60—

Then comes the obscurity does this 110 or 60 include any repairs to the roof? I opine it does as far as botching goes—

What he says about complete restoration is clear enough—but I am sure that a slate roof is preferable—

How far will the Ecclesiastical Commissioners feel themselves justified in going beyond necessary repairs?

I am of the opinion that as Mr Hall has stated that he is willing to let the Ecclesiastical Commissioners effect the whole of the repairs of the Chancel—and to pay his share of the expenses, subject to an appeal to the Bishop or his ordinary—That proposition had better be communicated to Mr Murray—The Commissioners will then send down *their own Architect* who will make a report—furnish plans—&c &c &c—When we have ascertained what they are willing to do—we can get Mr Hall to consent to pay his share—And then Mr Atkinson will be able to see what sum he must raise—to have the Chancel made & restored as he wishes—

Whatever statements as to repair we may send to the Ecclesiastical Commissioners I am convinced they will not stir a peg until they have obtained a complete account of the state of things at Stow from their own Architect. . . .

18. To Eccl. Com. from Bp Kaye, Riseholm (Copy), 12 Feb. 1847 (EC)

My dear Sir,

I have more than once brought under your notice the repairs of the Chancel of Stow Church, part of the expense is to be born by the Commissioners, part by the Lessee of the Prebendary of Stow. The Lessee is prepared to pay his portion of the expense to the Commissioners, on the understanding that they shall get the repairs done. What course will you pursue? will you send down an Architect to survey the Chancel and make an estimate? I understand that a new Roof is necessary: which if covered with lead would cost £300. I prefer a slate covering to lead

19. To Bp Kaye from Adn Stonehouse, Owston, 22 Feb. [1847] (K)

My very good Lord

I think the estimate for the complete restoration of Stow Chancel was 800 *l* I will desire Mr Atkinson to let your Lordship know the exact sum

20. Eccl. Com. Minutes (Copy), 4 Mar. 1847 (EC)

Read

A letter from the Bishop of Lincoln respecting the necessity for repair of the Chancel of Stow Church Lincolnshire for a portion of which the Commissioners are liable as the holders of certain property lately belonging to the Prebend of Corringham cum Stow.

It having been also intimated by the Bishop to the Assistant Secretary that the Church of Stow being one of considerable antiquarian interest in the county a local subscription for its restoration might possibly be set on foot in case such repairs should be undertaken by the Board.

Resolved,

That application be made to the Bishop for his opinion as to the steps which the Commissioners should take with a view to effecting the repairs to which they are liable having reference to the prospect of a subscription.

Confirmed. 11th March 1847.

21. To Bp Kaye from Eccl. Com., 8 Mar. 1847 (K)

My Lord,

I have submitted to the Board your Lordship's letter respecting the repairs of the Chancel of Stow Church, and I also mentioned the verbal communication which you made to me as to the possibility of a local subscription being made towards restoring the edifice, and I am directed to inquire of your Lordship what steps you would think it expedient for the Commissioners to take with a view to effecting such repairs as they are liable to, having reference to the prospect of the subscription alluded to.

22. To Eccl. Com. from Bp Kaye, Riseholm (Copy), 8 Mar. 1847 (EC)

My dear Sir,

It appears to me that the first step to be taken by the Commissioners is to obtain an estimate of the expenditure which will be required to effect the *necessary* repairs of the Chancel at Stow, and then to enter into some arrangement with the Lessee of the Prebend of Stow respecting the portion to be borne by each party. I conclude that the Commissioners will not feel themselves at liberty to expend money in what is called restoration, the local subscription therefore to which I allude will be applied to that purpose

23. Eccl. Com. Minutes (Copy), 11 Mar. 1847 (EC)

Read,

A letter (No. 817/47) from the Bishop of Lincoln, stating his opinion with reference to the repair of the Chancel of Stow Church, that, the Commissioners should procure an estimate of the expenditure which will be required to effect such works as may be *necessary* and then enter into an arrangement with the Lessee as to the proportion to be borne by each party; and that the subscription to which his Lordship had alluded on a former occasion would be applicable only to such work as is usually called "restoration"

Resolved,

That inquiry be made of the Incumbent of Stow, as to whether with reference to the contemplated subscription any local Architect has been consulted, or any, and what steps taken towards effecting a general restoration of the Church, and also whether he has any suggestions to offer on the subject.

Confirmed. 18th March 1847

24. To Atkinson from Eccl. Com. (Copy), 15 Mar. 1847 (EC)

Sir,

A representation has been made to the Ecclesiastical Commissioners for England that certain repairs are required to the Chancel of the Church at Stow and that the Lessee of the Prebendary of Stow (who with the Commissioners is chargeable therewith) is prepared to pay his portion of the expense if the Commissioners will get the work done but before any steps are taken in the matter the Commissioners have directed me to ask you with reference to an intimation which they have received to the effect that, if they undertake such repairs there is a probability that a local subscription may be raised for the general restoration of the Church whether any local Architect has been consulted or any arrangement made towards effecting such restoration and if not whether you have any suggestion or observation to offer to the Commissioners with reference to any part of the subject.

25. To Eccl. Com. from Atkinson, Stow, 23 Mar. 1847 (EC)

Sir

I beg to acknowledge the receipt of your Letter of the 13th Inst. respecting the repairs of the Chancel of Stow Church—and the prospect there may be of effecting a general restoration of the Church. I shall be most happy now and at any future time to answer any communication with which the Ecclesiastical Commissioners may be pleased to favour me on this subject, and to afford every information in my power; and I beg gratefully to express my sense of their courtesy in making the Communication to which I now proceed to reply.

1. Stow Church being a structure of extraordinary antiquity and of singular interest, especially as "the Mother Church" of the Diocese in the earlier Saxon Times, is generally regarded as having a peculiar and very strong claim on the County of Lincoln—and there is every reason to believe that a call for subscriptions towards its restoration would be liberally answered.

2. It has always appeared to myself, and to those friends with whom I have conversed on the subject, that an appeal to the public for aid, could not with full effect, nor indeed with fairness, be made until we should be enabled to inform the public that those upon whom the charge of repairs legally devolved were prepared to do their part. This can now be done so far as the Chancel is concerned, when the Ecclesiastical Commissioners shall have determined upon the Amount they will expend towards its restoration.

3. The next step, after we shall be enabled to name the sum proposed to be advanced by the Tithe-Owners for the Chancel, would be, I conceive, to call upon the Parishioners to raise a fair sum towards the repair of the rest of the Church—not by a single heavy Church rate, but by borrowing on the credit of the rates a sum to be repaid, say, in twenty years.

4. This Amount being likewise ascertained, we should then be in a condition to issue our appeal to the County and to the friends of the Church at large, stating what the whole cost of the proposed restoration would be—what the Tithe-Owners, and the Parishioners respectively would contribute, and then the Amount to be raised by subscription would at once be seen. I would therefore respectfully suggest that the repair of the Chancel be postponed until the effect of this plan for raising funds for a general restoration shall have been ascertained.

5. A design for the restoration of the Church has been furnished at my request by Mr Pearson an Architect Employed by Sir Charles Anderson to prepare plans for the restoration of his Church at Lea in this neighbourhood. Sir C. Anderson has long been, himself, a warm advocate for the restoration of Stow Church, and will I am sure use his utmost influence to promote it. Mr Pearson is likewise well known to Mr Hall the Lessee of the Prebend of Stow, and would be likely, I think, through Mr Hall's influence, to be acceptable to my Parishioners, inasmuch as two of the principal farmers in this Parish are Tenants of Mr Hall's who is a considerable Landowner here as well as Lessee of the Stow prebendal Tithes. I [have good] reason to believe that Mr Pearson is fully competent to superintend the work of restoration—and it would be very satisfactory to myself, should it be so to the other parties concerned, to have the restoration placed under him as Architect.

6. Though it appears obviously to be very desirable that the whole of the works should be effected under one and the same management—still the funds for the restoration of the Chancel might be kept distinct from those for the restoration of the Nave and Transepts—it being understood that the chancel, as well as the other part of the Church is to have a share of the funds which may be raised by subscription, in order to the rendering the restoration of the whole more complete. To effect this restoration in a satisfactory manner, with the best materials and workmanship, according to Mr Pearson's estimate a sum of not less than £4000 would be requisite.

7. Though a structure of great magnitude, this Church from the peculiarity of its plan would not afford more than sufficient accommodation for a proper proportion of the Parishioners. The Nave and Transepts if filled with open seats Mr Pearson estimates to contain somewhat under 600 sittings for a population of 1100. At present Divine Service is celebrated in the Chancel, temporarily fitted up, which will not hold 200. This temporary provision it would be expedient to retain until the other portion of the Church should be so far proceeded with as to be in a fit state for Divine Service.

All this I beg humbly to submit for the consideration of the Ecclesiastical Commissioners for England, and I venture also to transmit herewith a copy of a paper on Stow Church lately printed by the Lincolnshire Architectural Society. The illustrations may serve to convey some slight [impression] of some of the very peculiar features of this Church.

26. To Wm Railton from Eccl. Com. (Copy), 17 Apr. 1847 (EC)

Dear Sir,

Stow Chancel

I am directed by the Ecclesiastical Commissioners for England, to request that you will survey the above Chancel, and report as to the works necessary to putting it into *ordinary* repair, and the cost at which such works may be estimated.

For your guidance in this matter, I should explain to you, that the Commissioners as holders of a portion of the tithes, are said to be liable to repair the south side, and east end, and the Prebendary of Stow, as holder of the rest of the tithe is liable to the repair of the other part of the Chancel. The Lessee of the Prebendary is I am informed willing that the whole repair should be done under the direction of the Commissioners and will pay his share of the cost, but as I have reason to think that the north side may be in worse condition than the south—I have mentioned the above division of liability, in order that if it should hereafter be arranged that the cost should be borne by the Commissioners, and Prebendary, in any other proportion than that of equal moieties, you may be prepared to apportion the cost between them fairly.

I send you a copy of a letter from the Incumbent, which will shew you what has been and is proposed to be done, and I think it not improbable that the Commissioners may in their future proceedings adopt the principle suggested.

The Incumbent is the Revd George Atkinson, Stow near Gainsborough, whom it is desirable that you should see; he takes great interest in the Church, and has written a pamphlet on it, which has been published with engravings by the Lincolnshire Architectural Society.

Note: Letter written in accordance with a Minute of a meeting held on Thursday 15 April 1847; see Introduction, p. ix.

27. To Adn Stonehouse from Atkinson, Stow, 5 May 1847 (K)

Dear Mr Archdeacon

Having learnt from Mr Peel that his Co-rural Mr Carr had made an official report to you, I inferred that the report which you requested might be sent in by me for Mr Peel would not be considered necessary—If however it should be your wish to have any further information relating to Stow Church I will hold myself in readiness to obey your wishes after the Visitation. Since my last communication to you I have had a letter from the Secretary to the Ecclesiastical Commissioners asking for information as to our plans and intended proceedings in respect of the proposed restoration—and wishing me to make any suggestions I might think proper with reference to any part of the subject. I accordingly stated my views to them. Last week I received a letter from Mr Railton Architect to the Commissioners informing me that he was directed by the Commissioners to survey the chancel and asking me to give him the meeting and go over that part of the fabric with him. He came last Thursday, and carefully examined all parts of the Chancel. He considers it necessary to have a new roof of higher pitch—and to have the lead relaid in a much improved manner—a parapet instead of dropping eves—a new floor laid on concrete—a thorough repair of all the stonework inside and out—including the underpinning of the foundations, and the renewal of the basement courses—and I understood him that the Commissioners would be willing to contribute the sum which a thorough repair of the Chancel would cost towards its restoration, though they do not undertake any restorations in the proper sense of the term. This was in fact what I ventured to suggest that they should do in my reply to their Communication to me.

Mr Hall has also been staying at Lea and Mr Pearson with him, they came over to see the Church together and Mr Hall seems to enter into our plans with much interest and liberality. Mr Railton and Mr Pearson appear to have agreed very much in their respective reports.

Note: Similar reports from the Rural Dean can be found in *A Stow Visitation. Ven. W. B. Stonehouse 1845*; ed. Canon N. S. Harding, 1940, pp. 89, 93, 97, for the years 1850, 1851, 1852 respectively.

28. To Eccl. Com. from Wm Railton, 12 Regent St., 12 May 1847 (EC)

Dear Sir,

Stow Chancel

In accordance with your instructions I have carefully inspected this Chancel which is large and of great antiquity having massive and lofty walls with the remains of considerable architectural embellishment

The side walls have a considerable inclination from the perpendicular, the buttresses have in some instances become detached and fractures and decay exist to a large and general extent

The masonry of the East window is in a very dilapidated state and the glazing both in this and the other windows very defective

The absence of drains and the consequent dampness of the soil has had an injurious effect on the foundations which require reparation and the introduction of proper means for conveying away the water from the roof appears necessary

The roof and floor are in a very defective state

I conceive the cost of putting the fabric into a due state of ordinary repair would be about five hundred pounds and that this sum should be contributed in the following proportions—viz—

By the Ecclesiastical Commissioners for England three hundred pounds and by the Prebendary's Lessee two hundred pounds

29. To Atkinson from Eccl. Com. (Copy), 21 May 1847 (EC)

Dear Sir,

I am directed by the Ecclesiastical Commissioners for England to forward to you a copy of Mr Railton's Report on the Chancel of Stow Church, and to inform you that they are ready to contribute their share of the expense accordingly.

I have written to the Lessee of the Prebend of Stow, but as I do not know his address I have enclosed it in this packet and shall feel obliged by your forwarding it.

Note: Minute, 20 May 1847, refers.

30. To Bp Kaye from Eccl. Com. (Copy), 21 May 1847 (EC)

My Lord,

I am directed by the Ecclesiastical Commissioners for England, to transmit to Your Lordship a copy of Mr Railton's report on the Chancel of Stow Church, and to inform you that the Commissioners are ready to contribute their share of the expenses accordingly.

31. To Hall from Eccl. Com. (Copy), 21 May 1847 (EC)

Sir,

It having been intimated to the Ecclesiastical Commissioners for England, that you were willing to cooperate with them in some arrangement for the repair of the Chancel of Stow Church, I am directed to send you a copy of the Report of their Architect on the subject, and to inform you that they are prepared to contribute their share of the expense as therein estimated.

It is I believe the intention of the Incumbent of Stow to raise a subscription for the general restoration of the Church, in which event a portion would I apprehend be expended on the Chancel over and above Mr Railton's estimate.

I shall be happy to receive any communication from you, or to give you any further information in my power.

32. To Eccl. Com. from Atkinson (Copy), 24 May 1847 (EC)

Dear Sir,

I beg to acknowledge the receipt of your letter accompanying the report of Mr Railton relative to the repairs of Stow Chancel, and to express my grateful thanks to the Ecclesiastical Commissioners for England for this communication—The next step will be to call upon the Parishioners to contribute to the substantial reparation of the other portion of the Church, and on this point I hope to consult the Bishop of the Diocese.

I have sent the communication enclosed for Mr Hall to that Gentleman's address which is the Revd S. W. Hall, Wolfreton House Hull.

33. To Eccl. Com. from Hall, Wolfreton House (Copy), 4 June 1847 (EC)

Sir,

I beg to acknowledge the receipt of a communication on the part of the Ecclesiastical Commissioners for England, and will thank you to inform them that I accede to the arrangement therein proposed, and am prepared to contribute my share of the expence of repairing the Chancel of Stow Church, as estimated by Mr Railton—

34. To Atkinson from Eccl. Com. (Copy), 11 June 1847 (EC)

Dear Sir,

Stow Chancel

I am directed by the Ecclesiastical Commissioners for England to inform you that Mr Hall, the Lessee of the Prebendary of Stow, has consented to contribute his share of the expense of repairing as estimated by Mr Railton in the Report, of which I sent you a copy on the 21st Ultimo

35. To Bp Kaye from Eccl. Com. (Copy), 11 June 1847 (EC)

My Lord,

I am directed by the Commissioners to inform Your Lordship that Mr Hall the Lessee of the Prebendary of Stow has consented to contribute his share of the expenses of repairing the Chancel of Stow Church, as estimated by Mr Railton in the Report, of which I had the honor to inclose you a copy on the 21st Ulto.

36. To Eccl. Com. from Atkinson (Copy), 14 June 1847 (EC)

Dear Sir,

I beg to acknowledge the receipt of your letter of the 11th Inst. informing me that Mr Hall has consented to pay the sum towards the repair of Stow Chancel which was specified in Mr Railton's report.

I passed a few days with Mr Hall since the report was forwarded to him and he stated to me that he should acquiesce in Mr Railton's Estimate.

I have also by desire of the Bishop of Lincoln just obtained an Estimate from Mr Pearson of the Expense of putting the nave and transepts into a proper state of ordinary repair in order that it may be laid before the Parishioners at a Vestry meeting which will shortly take place at the request of the Archdeacon of Stow. When anything shall have been effectually settled I shall do myself the honor of communicating it to you.

Note: There are no more letters on Ecclesiastical Commissioners' Stow Chancel file until 30 April, 1850, No. 95.

37. To Bp Kaye from Adn Stonehouse, Owston, 4 Sept. [1848] (K)

My very good Lord—

On my return home from Leamington I had an interview with the Revd Mr Atkinson about Stow Church. He said that the principal parishioners were ashamed of such nonsense being put forth as that resolution in the Newspaper and requested that a Vestry should be legally called, and a proposition submitted to borrow the Money from the board of works—and that the Church Wardens wished to have an interview with me—

The Church wardens came this Morning—with Mr Atkinson and three other parishioners—After some desultry conversation about peculiars being done away with—and the best means of effecting such reparations—I gave them to understand that I was determined to enforce the repairs without delay—and finally it was agreed upon that notice should be given next Sunday for a Vestry meeting to lay a rate for the due reparation of the Church—

This is the present state of affairs at Stow. It is my opinion that the parishioners of Stow having neglected to keep the Church in repair during the time when it was a peculiar—are very unwilling to take to it now—and the more so because the burden is become so very heavy—that they will not be influenced by any offer of subscriptions—and that they will not consent to borrow the Money until a rate has been made & the payment enforced on some refractory individuals.

I will let your Lordship know how we progress

Note: This meeting was described in the *Stamford Mercury*, 29 September 1848. "On Monday the 4th. the Incumbent, the churchwardens, and Messrs Sergeant, Gelder, and Watson, had an interview with the Archdeacon, who stated to them that an architect's estimate for the nave of the church alone, exclusive of the chancel (which belongs to Mr Hall and the Ecclesiastical Commissioners) was £2500; but, as a matter of course, the parish might have an architect of their own, for the Venerable Gentleman told them, in a *very clever oration*, they were not obliged to take the estimate of any particular architect. He also proposed that the Churchwardens should give notice for a Vestry meeting to be held at the first opportunity to consider about and lay *a rate*."

38. Church Book

A vestry meeting was held in the Parish Church of Stow, on Thursday the 14th day of September 1848 pursuant to Notice duly given in obendience to a monition directed to the Churchwardens of the said Parish by the Ven. W. B. Stonehouse Archdeacon of Stow requiring them to take immediate steps to repair the Parish Church, the same being in great need of repairs. The said

Vestry was called for the special purpose of making a Church rate for and towards the repair of the said Parish Church: Present the Minister of the Parish The Revd George Atkinson in the Chair—the Churchwardens—Messrs John Skill, Robt Burnham. The Revd G. T. Hutton, Thos Spencer, Wm Taylor, George Burton, Robt Harrison, James Gelder, George Credland, Wm Sergeant, Wm Ellis, Joseph Jarvill, John Abraham, John Harrison, Joseph Harrison, Christopher Page, and other Parishioners of the said Parish. Mr John Spink proposed and Mr Robert Foster seconded, they being the Churchwardens of the said parish, that a rate of six-pence in the pound be now made for and towards the repairs of the said Church—upon the said proposition being submitted to the meeting and a show of hands being taken, a large majority appeared against the rate—and the Churchwardens and others there present there and then proceeded no legal amendment being moved to the said rate—to make the rate in manner and form following—

We the Churchwardens and other Parishioners of the Parish of Stow in the County of Lincoln, and Diocese of Lincoln whose names are hereunto subscribed, do hereby this fourteenth day of September in the year 1848 at our Vestry Meeting, in pursuance of due Notice, for that purpose assembled rate and tax all and every the inhabitants of the Parish aforesaid, hereunder mentioned, for and towards the repair of the Church of the said Parish and for such other expenses as are by Law chargeable on the Church rate the several sums following, being at the rate of six-pence in the pound.

Signed

Note: This attempt to levy a minority rate was boldly recorded across two pages of the Church Book by Atkinson, but no signature was added. See Introduction p. xviii. For a description of the meeting see the *Stamford Mercury*, 29 September 1848 (quoted here p. xi) and 6 October 1848.

39. To Bp Kaye from Adn Stonehouse, n.d. [Sept. 1848] (K)

My very good Lord

According to my promise I send Mr Atkinsons statement of the proceedings of the Vestry at Stow concerning the rate for the reparation of that fabric—

In these proceedings Mr Atkinson as Chairman has committed two mistakes 1st When the rate was proposed and seconded He called for a shew of hands which left him in the minority This he ought not to have done—He ought to have thrown the onus of objecting to the rate on his adversaries by proposing an amendment—if they had proposed an illegal amendment, which would most probably have been the case, he should have refused to submit such a motion to the Vestry—If after such refusal no legal amendment was proposed—the rate would have been carried in the eye of the Law nemine contradicenti—This Method of proceeding would have relieved Mr Atkinson from the necessity of having recourse to the extreme measure of making a rate by aid of the Minority.

His second mistake was dissolving the Vestry because the Church warden refused to sign the rate which he himself had made & proposed because if the Minority could make a rate they could make it without him. See the first vol of Dr Phillimore & 9o edition of Burns Ecclesiastical Law Article Proceedings against Church Wardens—

I have seen Mr Atkinson and have endeavoured to explain the matter to him and have advised him to call a second Vestry with as little delay as possible; & if the Church Wardens refuse to do so I will issue a fresh admonition

I fear the spirit of these people is very hostile to doing anything—and that I shall have to dodge them thought every possible evasion of the Law—If a rate is obtained it will have to be enforced on some of the most refractory parishioners either by summary proceedings before the justices. . . .

Note: The rest of this letter is missing.

40. Vestry Book

Stow Saturday Octr 14.1848

A vestry meeting was held in the Parish Church, according to Notice duly given by the Churchwardens, on the 14th Day of Octr 1848 at 4 o'Clock in the afternoon, present the Churchwardens, John Spink & Robert Foster, Thos Spencer, George Burton, James Gelder, George Credland, Wm Ellis, Joseph Fox, Jonathan Rose, The Revd G. P. Hutton and other Parishioners—The Revd George Atkinson Minister of the Parish in the Chair.

A proposition having been made and seconded that a Committee should be appointed to view the body of the Church and to report to the Parishioners, the Chairman being of the opinion that the Vestry had no power to invest such a Committee with any legal functions—the motion was by consent withdrawn and the Vestry adjourned to Monday week the 23d Instant at the hour of four oClock in the afternoon to give time for the Chairman to obtain proper legal advice respecting the appointment of such Committee when the proposition is again to be brought forward.

George Atkinson M.A.
Chairman.

41. Extract from a communication to the Stamford Mercury *from Atkinson, dated 12 October and published 20 October 1848.*

1. The idea of calling upon the parishioners to raise 4000*l.* or 5000*l.* "to restore a Saxon Cathedral" never entered the minds either of the Ecclesiastical authorities, or of any other person taking an interest in the matter: much less has any such idea been expressed. On the contrary, it has been on every occasion most distinctly stated that all that was or could be expected from the parishioners was that they should contribute, just so far as every other parish is liable to contribute, to the ordinary substantial repairs of their parish church, and to the fitting it for divine service.

2. The sum of 4000*l.*, or from that to 5000*l.*, has never been named except as the amount which might be necessary for the complete restoration of the whole fabric, including the chancel. To the repairs of the chancel, as is known to all, the parishioners have to contribute *nothing*: to what is meant by "restoration" over and above the necessary repairs, they contribute *nothing*: nor, in the case of Stow Church, have the ratepayers been asked to raise the whole sum which the necessary repairs would cost. Mr Pearson's estimate of the necessary repairs (not including the chancel) was about 2500*l.*; but even this sum it was never proposed to the parish to raise. It was intimated to them that the Ecclesiastical Authorities and other influential persons would be disposed to assist the parish by taking a considerable part of the cost of the *necessary* repairs upon themselves, and so relieving the parish to that extent from a legal burthen. They did this, trusting that the feelings of interest and veneration which are known to prevail throughout this county and elsewhere towards the ancient "mother church" of the diocese, would enable them to raise the funds which might be necessary to complete the repairs; and accordingly a subscription was commenced, headed by the Bishop and the Lord Lieutenant, the further progress of which is only suspended until the parishioners should have agreed to raise a fair and reasonable sum *towards* the necessary repairs, for the whole of which they are legally liable.

3. As to the alleged "impoverished condition" of the parishioners, their inability to maintain so large a fabric, and the amount of Tithe paid, it may be remarked that the parish of Stow contains in the whole about 4700 acres of land, certainly not inferior in average quality to its neighbours, nor is it subject to any peculiar burthens, or causes of "impoverishment" beyond other populous rural parishes. The church, though apparently large, will not really afford accommodation to more than a fair proportion of the inhabitants, the population being at present over 1000; while the church, it is found, will not conveniently seat more than half that number. As to the expense of repairing the fabric past and to come, not one penny has been expended upon it by the parish for the last 12 or 15 years, and nothing more than a mere trifle for very many years previously. The nature of the repairs or restoration now proposed, instead of involving considerable additional outlay

in keeping up the church, would reduce the expense to almost nothing for generations after. In regard to tithe, that has been commuted by voluntary agreement between the land-owners and tithe-owners, on such terms that the amount now paid in money has been acknowledged not to be more than one-half of what it was when paid in kind.

4. It ought to be known, moreover, that when the churchwardens and some others of the parishioners waited on the Archdeacon, he advised them to call in an architect on their own behalf, if Mr. Pearson's estimate was not thought satisfactory. At a subsequent meeting in the parish, it was agreed to adopt this course: but this resolution has not been carried into effect, though the Archdeacon has suspended proceedings for some weeks in order to afford time for such estimate to be prepared.

5. In conclusion, if those wishes on the part of the parishioners are really sincere, as expressed in the article to which these remarks refer, "to put their parish church into such a proper state of repair as will render it fit for devotional services, and to that end are willing to tax themselves to full extent which . . . their condition will enable them to bear"—if this be so, a very easy mode of effecting this most desirable object *has* been suggested, viz., that as the Board of Works is in the practice of advancing some money to parishes whose churches require any considerable outlay (such sums with interest at 4 per cent. to be repaid in 20 years), the parish of Stow should avail themselves, as other parishes are constantly doing, of this provision of the legislature, by borrowing not 4000*l*. or 5000*l*., nor yet 2500*l*., but the sum of 1500*l*., which there is reason to believe would be accepted, and the parish guaranteed from any further expense. A rate of sixpence in the pound annually on the average of the 20 years would pay off this sum principal and interest. This mode of raising the funds required is the only just and proper method, because thus all who occupy lands in the parish during any part of the 20 years will have their share to pay; and this is the way approved and advocated by some of the principal occupiers of land in the parish who really wish to see the church repaired; while those who complain most loudly of the hardship and oppression which the repairing of the church will inflict on the ratepayers, would make the whole weight of the burden fall upon those individuals who may happen to occupy farms during the one or two years in which the church is undergoing repairs, inasmuch as these are the very parties who oppose the proposition to borrow the necessary amount from the Board of Works to be paid off in 20 years.

42. Vestry Book

Stow Monday Octr 23. 1848

A vestry meeting was held in the Parish Church on Monday Octr 23d at 4 oClock in the afternoon by adjournment from Saturday the 14th Inst to take into consideration the proposition then made, and to be brought forward on this occasion—present The Minister in the Chair, the Churchwardens, Messrs John Skill, Thos Spencer, George Sikes, Wm Watson, Jas. Gelder, Robert Harrison, George Burton, John Homer, Joseph Jarvill, Wm Sergeant, George Harrison, John Harrison, Samuel Blow, George Credland and others.

Mr Thos Spencer proposed that William Watson, William Taylor, Wm Ellis, George B. Sikes, William Sergeant, William Wilkinson and James S. Gelder be a Committee to view the body of the Church with the Wardens and to report to a future Vestry.

This was seconded by Mr James S. Gelder.

The Chairman having consulted the Archdeacon & having also had other legal advice as to the power of the Vestry to appoint such committee, or to give or delegate to it any power or responsibility in respect to the inspection or repairs of the Parish Church—and being confirmed in his opinion expressed at the former meeting that the Churchwardens alone are the Officers to whom the duty of seeing to the repairs of the Parish Church is by Law committed, and that the Parishioners in Vestry assembled are the only legal body of the nature of a Committee so far as the repairs of the Parish Church are concerned—declined as Chairman of the Vestry to submit the motion proposed, to the Vestry.

The Chairman having enquired whether any other business was intended to be brought forward, and it being stated that no other business would be proposed so long as the Minister continued in the Chair, The Chairman accordingly declared the Vestry dissolved and having recorded the proceedings of the Vestry quitted the Chair.

George Atkinson. M.A. Minister
Chairman

The Chairman having declined to insert the propositions, Mr Spencer was proposed as Chairman by Mr Sergeant and seconded by Mr Watson, the proposition was carried unanimously. The meeting being duly opened it was proposed that C. G. Smith should be vestry Clerk *pro tem* and was unanimously chosen by a show of hands. The following resolutions were unanimously carried *viz*

1 Resolved.—That William Watson, William Taylor, William Ellis, George Booth Sikes, William Sergeant, William Wilkinson, and James S. Gelder be a Committee to view the body of the Church with the Wardens, and report to a future Vestry.

2nd Resolved.—That it is the opinion of this vestry that the "Mother Church of this Diocese" has been sadly spoiled of her inheritance. There is an ancient tradition in the Parish that she had revenues sufficient for her support, and that these have been wrongfully diverted. But notwithstanding, the people of Stowe are willing to do as much for their Church as has been done by any

Generation for the last 300 years—as much as the Law requires. Only they claim the right to "deliberate and determine how and in what manner this may be best and most effectually and withal most conveniently and fairly between themselves performed and carried into effect".

3rd Resolved.—That the requirement of the Archdeacon that £2,500. be expended on the body of the Church would involve a most improvident outlay. One half of the sum would give the parish of Stowe, with its abundance of material, a new Church, fully equal to the Churches of the surrounding villages, and afford Church accommodation very far beyond the average of all England.

The present Church is a huge structure, *never* a quarter part filled; reported to have been erected in other times, when Stowe was the seat and see of a Bishop, and had a large and wealthy population. If it could be restored, which is the object aimed at, it would be sorely out of Place in the midst of a people, already impoverished by the withering drain of nearly £1000. a year in Tithes. And moreover it would entail a burden upon the Parish which the Law of the land never contemplated.

The conservation of a Saxon Cathedral, and the maintenance of a Parish Church are very different affairs.

4th Resolved.—That it is evident from the Incumbent's letter to the Stamford Mercury, that a class of men calling themselves Archaeologists have resolved to fasten upon the Church of Stowe and the Parish funds, that they may use *both* for the display of their skill in the Science of Antiquities. And this meeting is astonished that Ecclesiastical Authorities should stoop to countenance such a proceeding; for while it is the duty of all good subjects to obey the Law, it is also incumbent upon all superiors and persons in authority not to demand more than the Law requires. To use the Law of the land—to spend the money of hard working men in pursuit of the luxurious and refined pleasures of the wealthy would be a crime against the peace of Society and the more so at the time, when the oldest Institutions of Europe are crumbling to dust before our own eyes.

5th Resolved.—That this Vestry hold in the highest estimation the manly conduct of the Churchwardens in refusing to sign a rate when the Chairman attempted to *choke* the liberty of speech, and to drag money out of the Pockets of the Parishioners without their consent—and it will idemnify and bear them harmless while they keep to the Law and the rights of Englishmen. On the other hand it will hold them accountable for any misapplication of Parish funds—the hard earnings of a struggling people.

6th Resolved.—That the present highhanded attempt to drive the People of Stowe into ruinous and illegal expences can only end in renewing those scenes of tumult—that animosity between Priest and People—which a few years ago so lamentably disturbed the peace of the Parish, and so sadly retarded the spiritual welfare of its people.

Here the meeting closed.

Signed in the vestry by

Thomas Spencer. Chairman
Charles Gowen Smith. Clerk
Geo: Booth Sikes
William Wilkinson
James S. Gelder
Wm Sergeant
William Taylor
William Watson
William Ellis
William Buttery
John Harrison
Robert Harrison
Joseph Jarvill
Henry Walker
William Marshall
George Burton
George Knowles
Samuel Foottit
Charles Brocklesby

Thomas Ingham
Joseph Harrison
William Pearce
Robert Credland
Henry Clayton
William Baxter
Jonathan Rose
George Credland
John Jollands
George Harrison

Note: The Vestry confused Atkinson's letter, No. 41, with the report of the Archaeological Institute in the Lincolnshire Chronicle quoted in the Introduction, p. xxii.

43. Vestry Committee Book

We, the undersigned, being a Committee legally chosen, to view the body of the Church with the Wardens, and report what we have resolved upon. We accordingly examined the Church on Saturday afternoon the 28th of October, and our report to this Vestry is as follows.

1st We found some of the foundations in a dilapidated state and in need of repairs.

2nd. We found some of the walls, pillars, windows, and leads which are wanting repairs.

3rd We agree that the Churchwardens shall lay a rate of 2½d in the Pound; towards defraying the expenses of the same, and other incidentals.

(Signed) John Spink
Robert Foster } Churchwardens

Geo: B: Sikes
James. S. Gelder
William Watson
William Ellis

William Sergeant
William Wilkinson
William Taylor

44. Vestry Book

Stow Thursday Novr 2. 1848

A Vestry meeting was held this day in the Parish Church according to Notice duly given for the purpose of making a rate or assessment for the repairs of the Parish Church, and for such other expenses as are by law chargeable upon the Church-rate. Present The Revd George Atkinson the Incumbent in the Chair, the Churchwardens Messrs John Spink and Robert Foster, George Credland, William Watson, James Shankster Gelder, George Booth Sikes, Henry Walker, William Ellis, John Milnes, John Homer, William Buttery, Joseph Jarvill, William Sergeant, William Taylor, John Jollands, James Stothard, William Marshall, William Wilkinson, Thomas Spencer, Joseph Fox, Robert Cottam, John Harrison, Richard Lawrence and others.

Mr John Spink one of the Churchwardens proposed that a rate of 5d in the pound be granted for the purposes above stated, and Mr Robert Foster the other Churchwarden seconded this proposition.

The Chairman read the report and Estimate of Mr Pearson Architect in order to shew that the rate proposed by the Churchwardens was far short of the Amount required—whereupon Mr William Ellis proposed as an amendment on the proposition of the Churchwardens that a rate of d2½ (two pence half-penny) in the pound be granted, and Mr James Shankster Gelder seconded this Amendment, but no estimate or statement from any architect was offered on their part.

The Amendment having been submitted by the Chairman to the Vestry a shew of hands was taken upon it, when the Amendment was declared to be carried.

The original proposition was then put and negatived by a majority *viz* Messers Wm Ellis, James Shankster Gelder, Robert Harrison, Joseph Jarvill, William Marshall, William Wilkinson, Thomas Spencer, John Harrison, Robert Cottam, Henry Walker, John Milnes, John Jollands, Charles Brocklesby, Thomas Holmes, William Watson, William Sargeant, George Credland, William Hunt, Joseph Fox, William Taylor, John Butler, Robert Gilbert, William Buttery, Thomas Lanes, George Spurr, William Spurr, Samuel Footitt, John Gibson, John Homer, William Gee, Christopher Page, Robinson Spencer, John Stothard, George Booth Sikes, Thomas Revill, John Credland, Richard Lawrence, Thomas Ingham, James Stothard, Thomas Smith.

Signed
George Atkinson M.A. Chairman
George Hutton
John Spink } Churchwardens
Robert Foster }

Note: The *Stamford Mercury* (10 November 1848) reported the meeting '. . . The Rev Geo. Atkinson was in the chair; and after he had opened the meeting, he was asked several questions by a ratepayer, and as often waived them. The ratepayer then said,

"I have understood, Mr. Chairman, that you told a man present at this vestry that you intended a fivepenny rate, and the church done as you liked." The reverend gentleman would still give no answer. . . . [After the rate was passed] It was then proposed and seconded that Messrs Wm Sergeant, J. S. Gelder, W. Ellis, W. Watson, W. Wilkinson, W. Taylor, and G. B. Sikes be a committee for watching the expending of the parish funds, and advising with the Wardens: this motion the Rev. Geo. Atkinson declined to put, but it was eventually carried by a majority of this vestry.'

45. *To Bp Kaye from Adn Stonehouse, Owston, 5 Nov. [1848] (K)*

My very good Lord—

I mentioned in my last note that I hoped soon to [be] able to give your Lordship a further account of the proceedings of the Sinners at Stow anent the repairs of their parish Church—which I now will endeavour to do.

At the first Vestry meeting held on the seventh of September although the proceedings were not according to Law—the result was that the rate proposed by the Church Wardens was not granted on the plea that the parishioners objected to Mr Pearsons valuation and wished to employ another architect. Soon after they engaged the services of An Architect from Sleaford—Then they determined not to employ any architect—and called a Vestry Meeting to appoint a committee to assist the Church wardens in effecting the repairs, or in truth to hinder them by every means in their power from doing their duty—This meeting was adjourned at the suggestion of the Chairman the Revd G Atkinson to enable the Church Wardens to ascertain from the Archdeacon at his Michaelmas Visitation held at Lincoln on the 19th of October if such a proceeding was legal—On that day by and with the advice of Mr Swan, I told the Church wardens—that such a proceeding was of no use—The Committee could do [no] legal act—I then admonished them to call another vestry meeting as soon as possible and to propose a rate to provide for the expense of some part of these repairs—this admonition they obeyed as I shall presently set forth—In the mean time the adjourned Vestry meeting for the purpose of appointing this committee was held on Saturday the 21st of October—When the Chairman informed them that such a committee was altogether null and void in Law—and would be of no use whatever—Nevertheless in defiance of the Law the supporters of this measure proceeded to a distant part of the Church elected another Chairman—and appointed a Committee of seven persons—with instructions to survey the state of the Church—and to make a report thereof—

When the Vestry was held (in obedience to my admonition at my Visitation) on Thursday the second day of November—A rate was proposed by the Church wardens and duly seconded of fivepence in the pound to enable the

Church wardens to commence the repairs—The Committee then handed up to the Chairman their report—He very properly refused to recognise those proceedings in any way—Then they proposed by way of an Amendment a rate of two pence halfpenny in the pound, which was carried. Now concerning things of which we have written this is the sum—

I wish for your Lordships advice on these points—

First The amount of the repairs as estimated by a Skilful Architect is 2500£—Is this amendment of a rate of 2½ in the pound which = 50£ collusive or a fraudulent attempt to defeat the effectual repairs altogether?

If it is I fear the rate proposed by the Church Wardens is in the same predicament—

Would you advise me under these circumstances to proceed against the supporters of this Amendment—by citation in the Court of Arches—for I have no confidence in Crassus as a Judge?

Secondly would it not be as well to give these persons notice that I intend to do so? This is a safe measure—

If you think they cannot safely be proceeded against on this ground of a collusive rate—Ought the Church Wardens to proceed to collect the rate granted, and proceed to repair the worst part which is the South Transept, and when that is expended—call for another rate—and so on until the whole of the repairs have been effected? This method of proceeding though somewhat tedious would in the long run bring them to their senses by passing a resolution to borrow the Money?

If the Churchwardens proceed to effect any repairs; and the committee interfere how are they to be dealt with?—Will the Court of Queen's Bench grant a Mandamus—to restrain them?

It is my humble opinion that it would be as well to try the safe measure of giving notice to every one of those who supported the amendment of what I intend to do—if this produces no good effect We can only apply to the Ecclesiastical Court at last—

Verily if these snobs knew what & what Atkinson is in a very unhandsome fix—and places me also in somewhat of the same situation—I think they might have cited him in the Ecclesiastical Court for tearing up all the seats without a faculty for so doing—taking all the plaster of the walls—And injuring the foundations by injudiciously removing the earth.

I beg your Lordships kind indulgence for observing that I did not undertake the duties of the Archdeacon of Stow subject to these peculiars—I might have refused to have anything to do with them—But I thought it best to act as I have done—Now I have undertaken them without one sixpence of remuneration I might refuse to incur any expence—But I dont mind that—All I wish for is to obtain the best advice I can to prevent me from expending money foolishly—and there is no advice "in this universal airth" in my opinion equal to yours—which must be my apology for troubling your Lordship with long Epistle

Nattes' drawing of Stow Chancel looking west in 1793, from the Bankes Collection

Exterior of Stow Church from the north-east, taken soon after the completion of the restoration of the Chancel in the spring of 1852

46. To Bp Kaye from Haggard, Doctors' Commons, 8 Nov. 1848 (K)

My dear Lord

The view that you have taken upon the Church-rate question at Stow is, in my opinion, quite correct. In Greenwood & Spedding v Greaves & others (on appeal from York to the Delegates in 1832) the marginal note, in 4 Vol p 77 of my Ecclesiastical Reports, is thus:—"Estimates for the repairs of a Church, and the lawful and necessary expences of the Church Wardens, amounting to £111, laid before a Vestry, & a rate to that amount proposed; but a rate of £50. 17– only granted, whereupon two church Wardens exhibited Articles against two other Church Wardens and ten Parishioners for refusing to make a sufficient rate. A decree, rejecting the Articles, affirmed with Costs. *Semble*, that the Ecclesiastical C[ourt] cannot decide on the quantum of a rate; and therefore, that Parishioners, who do not contumaciously refuse to make a rate, but grant one not manifestly collusive, are not liable to be articled for a refusing a sufficient rate."

The Churchwardens, then, of Stow, must, I think, proceed to collect the 2½ rate, expend it, & then apply for another. They alone are responsible for the expenditure of the sum collected; & it does not occur to me how a Committee—constituted by a section only of the rate-payers can get at the funds so as to interfere with the Wardens in the payments they propose to make out of the rate. The opposition throws an additional responsibility upon the Church Wardens, & they should be careful not to lay out the rate upon repairs not sanctioned by the Vestry, & such as are [not] strictly warranted by law. The interference of a Committee cannot be recognized; but until I am informed in what manner they do interfere with the Church Wardens in the discharge of their office, I am not in a condition to advise as to the mode of dealing with them.

The *pleadings* in Gorham's Case are, I understand, progressing: it will scarcely, I think, make its appearance before Xmas.

47. To Bp Kaye from Adn Stonehouse, Owston, 10 Nov [1848] (K)

My very good Lord

. . . Accept my best thanks for your excellent advice about the Sinners of Stow and their Church rate—I will follow that advise [*sic*] to the letter—and have this day Admonished the Church wardens of Stow to collect the rate and when they have got the money to commence the repairs of the worst part which is the south transept (this rate will hardly pay for the erection of the scaffold) and I also admonished them—that the law would require them to employ a skilful and experienced person to effect these repairs—and if any damage took place as to the fabric owing to the ignorance and incapacity of the workmen implied [*sic*] by them, the Law would hold them responsible for the same—

I have sent Mr Atkinson a copy of your Lordship's note He wants a forward movement and says—"I cannot help having the impression, that notwithstanding their blustering they are loosing [*sic*] confidence and that a well directed attack upon the committee men, and two or three others would produce a panic"

We must watch our opportunity to take advantage of any foolish & illegal acts which these sinners may commit—In the meantime rest assured that I will obey the commanding Officer by following that sound advice which your Lordship has been so kind as to give me for which I know not how to be sufficiently thankful

48. Vestry Book

Stow Saturday Decr 2d—1848

A Vestry meeting was held this day in the Parish Church according to Notice duly given to ascertain the most equitable mode of collecting the Church rate of the Parish of Stow, there being an alleged inequality in the respective assessments of the two districts of the Parish to the poor. viz—that Sturton and Bransby are assessed higher to their own poor than the rest of the Parish, i.e. Stow, Normanby and Stow-Park are assessed to their poor (Sturton & Bransby having separate poor from Stow, Normanby & Stow Park) so that the respective assessments to the Poor would not afford a fair and equal Assessment for collecting the Church rate by throughout the whole Parish—with a view to the adjustment of this inequality Mr Thomas Spencer proposed and Mr William Ellis seconded the following motion that a Committee be appointed consisting of rate-payers from the respective parts of the Parish to consider and determine upon the best mode of equalizing the Assessment to the Church-rate—the said Committee to be composed of six persons besides the Churchwardens Viz—Mr Wm Ellis, Mr Wm Sargeant, and Mr Wm Wilkinson from Stow &c. & Mr Wm Watson, Mr Wm Taylor and Mr Jas S. Gelder from Sturton and Bransby—and that after investigating the matter the Committee report to a Vestry meeting to be holden for the purpose.

George Atkinson. Chairman
John Spink }
Robert Foster } Churchwardens
William Ellis
Wm Sergeant
Wm Taylor

49. Vestry Committee, 13 Dec. 1848

The Committee having met on Wednesday the 13th inst. Mr Wilkinson moved that Mr Gelder be Chairman Mr Taylor seconded the motion and it was carried unanimously.

Mr Wilkinson proposed that this meeting be adjourned till 3 oclock Saturday the 16th day of December to the Red Lion Sturton—Mr Ellis seconded the motion, it being put, it was carried without a dissentient—the meeting then dissolved

Signed { James. S. Gelder
Chairman

50. Vestry Committee, 16 Dec. 1848

We the undersigned, being a Committee legally chosen, in vestry assembled; (to ascertain the most equitable mode of equalizing the present 2½d rate only granted by the parishioners in vestry assembled on 2d of Novr upon the Townships of Sturton and Bransby with Stowe, Stowe Park, and Normanby) met on Saturday the 16 inst. by adjournment from Wednesday the 13 inst.—our report to this vestry is as follows.—

We, the Committee with the Churchwardens, have, according to the best of our abilities made the aforesaid rate, of the former and latter places, before mentioned, equal, or as near so as it will admit of—and further, we do request the Churchwardens to convene a vestry, to be held in the Church on Thursday the 28 inst, ensuing at 5 oclock in the Afternoon, on purpose to give all that are interested in this report, a chance of hearing the same.—

J. S. Gelder. Chairman
William Sergeant
William Taylor
(Signed.) William Wilkinson
William Watson
William Ellis
John Spink } Churchwardens
Robert Foster

51. Vestry Committee Book, 16 Dec. 1848

Acres		£ s d		£ s d
2711	Stowe Gross Rental	3115 – –	per acre	1. 2. 11¾
2034	Sturton Gross Rental	2590 – –	per acre	1. 5. 5½
			Difference per acre	£– 2 5¾

Stowe Poor Rate	10d in the pound	£116.16.4½	at 2½d p.p.	£29.4.1.
Sturton Poor Rate	10d in the pound	97. 1.10	at 2½	24.5.5½

There appears to be a difference one tenth per acre in the assessment— } deducted 2 – 8 – 6½

Which amounts to	
which leaves for Sturton	21. 16. 11½
Stowe.	29. 4. 1
Amount altogether including tithe	51. 1. 0½
Deduct 10 per Cent	5. 2. 0
Deduct for tithe of Sturton	2. 0
Deduct for Stowe	2. 6
	£45. 14. 6½

52. *Vestry Committee Book, 16 Dec. 1848*

A notice is hereby given that a vestry meeting will be held at the Church in Stowe on Thursday the 21st day of December at 2 OClock in the afternoon to receive the Report of the Committee appointed to Equalize the Rate.

Dated at Stowe the 16. day December 1848.

53. *Vestry Book*

Stow December 28. 1848

A Vestry meeting was held in the Parish Church according to Notice duly given to receive the report of the Committee appointed by the Vestry held on Thursday the 2d Inst "to consider and determine upon the best mode of equalizing the Assessment to the Church-rate" throughout the Parish—present The Revd George Atkinson the Incumbent in the Chair, The Churchwardens Mr Thomas Spencer, Mr Wm Ellis, Messrs Taylor, Watson, Gelder, Wm Buttery, Robt Credland, George Credland, Thos Smith, Henry Walker, Wm Sargeant and others.

The report of the Committee was read by the Chairman in which it was stated that the Committee met on Saturday the 16th Inst, by adjournment from Wednesday the 13th Inst. and that the said Committee with the Churchwardens had according to the best of their abilities made the rate of the former and latter places—(i.e. Stow, Normanby and Stow Park, and Sturton and Bransby) equal, or as nearly so as it will admit of—and that the Rate-books now produced by the Churchwardens are in accordance with the result at which the Committee arrived after they had made due investigation—the whole rateable value for Stow, Normanby and Stow Park being set down at £2520..12..6 and that for Sturton and Bransby being set down at £1857..18..11.

Mr Henry Walker moved a resolution that the report of the Committee be accepted by the Vestry which was seconded by Mr Thomas Spencer—This resolution was carried unanimously, as was the following proposed and seconded by the same gentlemen—that the labours of the Committee having been arduous, and they having rendered valuable services to the Parish in this business are justly entitled to the thanks of this Vestry which are hereby tendered to them.

Resolved that the Churchwardens and Parishioners of Stow are not sensible of any gross neglect in respect to the collection of the two pence half-penny rate, and they are surprised that the Archdeacon should make such a charge. This resolution was proposed by Mr Thos Spencer seconded by Mr Wm Sergeant and carried.

George Atkinson M.A. Chairman
John Spink, Robert Foster } Churchwardens
William Ellis
James S. Gelder
William Watson
Wm Sergeant

54. To Bp Kaye from Atkinson, 29 Jan. 1849 (K)

My Lord

It did not occur to me at the time when I made the return to your Lordship's annual queries, that I ought to have accompanied it by some statement of the reasons which had prevented the intended weekly service at Bransby from being established. I now proceed, in reply to your Lordship's Letter, to supply the omission.

I have never lost sight of this object, and the sole reason which has hitherto prevented its attainment, has arisen from my inability to obtain the use of a room in which the service might be held.

There is a building in the hamlet which is used at a meeting-House by the Ranters—this sometime since was sold with some other property, and now belongs to Mr Spencer. The Ranters have for some years past been rather declining, and I have entertained hopes that they might become so weak as to be unable to pay the rent of the building in which case I would have taken it, if practicable—they however contrive to maintain a precarious existence, and it may be prolonged for an indefinite period.

The only alternative, then, for the present is a room in some house. There are five farms at Bransby, besides a few very small holdings. Of these, the whole except two farms belong to Mr Spencer. Mr Spencer, though a Quaker, has until lately professed good feeling towards the Church, and a disposition to throw his influence rather into the Church's scale, than into that of the forms of dissent which are found in this Parish, viz, Wesleyanism, and Ranterism. I mentioned (at the time this benefice was augmented) the intention that provision should be made for a weekly Service at Bransby, to Mr Spencer, in the hope that he might recommend the object to his tenants—He has not done so, and I have now too much reason to believe that Mr Spencer's professions of friendly feelings towards the Church, & to myself as a clergyman, were insincere. He has now taken the lead in opposition to the repair of the Church—and he is the only person of any considerable weight in the Parish on that side—and so nothing can be expected from him, if he interferes at all, but that he will endeavour to prevent the service at Bransby altogether. There is some probability, I have reason to believe, that he may leave Bransby altogether, and go back to reside in America.

The only remaining farms are the property of a Mr Mason, a Notts Gentleman. The matter has been already proposed to the Tenant of one of them, but without effect so far as inducing him to grant the use of a room is concerned. The tenant of the other farm does not reside in the Parish, and has a labourer occupying part of the house. This labourer is a dissenter—his Master is, I believe, a Churchman but as he seldom comes to Bransby I have never yet met with him, though I have had it long in my thoughts.

This appears to be the only feasible plan at present—viz—to try to obtain a room in this house. I believe Mr Peel is acquainted with some members of Mr Mason's family, if not with Mr Mason himself. I will, therefore, consult him as to the best mode of getting at Mr Mason—and if we can obtain the Landlord's sanction first, I hope there will be no serious difficulty with his Tenant. The result I will communicate to your Lordship without loss of time.

55. To Bp Kaye from Adn Stonehouse, Owston, 15 Feb. [1849] (K)

My very good Lord,

Having been informed that the Church Wardens of Stow had collected the rate of 2½d. in the pound granted some time since I appointed a day to meet them in the Church and to give directions as to the commencement of the repairs—

Accordingly I went and found a considerable portion of the parishioners waiting to meet me—as they intimated it was their intention to do—

After I had surveyed the Church—I directed the Church Wardens to expend the money in their hands—in repairs to the foundations of the North Transept and the West end of the Nave—I stated that the Church Wardens were the only persons whom I could deal with officially—nor would any of the parishioners be justified in interfering with their operations—

Mr Spencer then beg leave to ask me what I really intended to do—I answered to put the Church into a complete state of repair—He inquired if I intended to enforce the expenditure of 2500£ according to Pearson's valuation? I answered if the Parishioners were dissatisfied with that valuation—they ought to have procured another, as the people at Kirton have just now done." Then he delivered a sort of rigmerole speech about bad times—a year of famine & the impossibility of raising the money—&c &c—I answered that I had not come there to ask for money or to make a rate—but only to direct the Church Wardens how to expend the small sum which had been raised. Then several of the parishioners began to abuse Atkinson on diverse counts; which he rendered innocuous by answering not a word—And I kept out of that scrape by saying Mr Atkinson's operations in the Church were completed before the Archdeacon had any jurisdiction over peculiars—If Mr Atkinson had done any wrong, he must answer it before the proper tribunal.

I then left the Church—and Spencer came to me and said I hope you will be as favourable with us as you can—a speech which I think deonotes—that they were firmly convinced—that I was resolved to proceed—And therefore I trust that my visit had some good effect—

It is my humble opinion that Mr Atkinson's operations were premature—to say the least, and could only have been justified by his having agreed to undertake and complete the repairs—for a certain sum under the sanction of a faculty—I think also that his "diggings" under the foundations have been very injudicious and injurious—If the parishioners were to proceed against him in the spiritual court for tearing up all the pews—&c &c—how could he justify his proceedings? How can I compel the parishioners under these circumstances to new pew the Church?

I have great doubts as to any power in our hands to enforce anything about the roof beyond reparation—it does not appear to me in bad repair—and as to what Pearson says about it being badly constructed—that I fear will not enable us to compel the parishioners to make a new one—

Under present circumstances we are at a dead Lock—it will be several years at least before the walls are repaired—I think it would be wise to get the chancel repaired at any rate—as the seats could easily be removed into the body of the Church—if necessary—. . . .

56. To Bp Kaye from Adn Stonehouse, Owston, 19 Feb. [1849] (K)

My very good Lord

Accept my best thanks for your last kind & obliging note anent the affairs Ecclesiastical of Stow and Kirton—

As your Lordship thinks with me that it would be judicious to proceed immediately with the restoration of the chancel of Stow Church, I shall feel extremely obliged if you will graciously condescend to communicate your wishes to the Ecclesiastical Commissioners or their agent on this behalf—

I will inform Mr Atkinson of our sentiments on this matter—

I still hope that if I follow the doctrine taught in the parable of the poor widow and the unjust judge, or in familiar phrase "keep on dinging at em"—the Stowegians will yet avail themselves of the permission granted by the Legislature to borrow money on security of the rates—

I do opine that every word which your Lordship has written about the Ecclesiastical Architecture association is the truth—the whole truth, and nothing but the truth"—I have had several blanditious Missives as *Baaley* used to say, to join the aforesaid Association—But I foresaw that many inconveniences might arise to me as Archdeacon from doing so—That restless little jail bird Master Ousby said that he should not wish any restoration of the roof of Kirton Church without the approval of the aforesaid Society—I scorched with a look—and I hope caused him to reflect seriously on the vanity of Human wishes. . . .

57. To Bp Kaye from Atkinson, 23 Feb. 1849 (K)

My Lord

I am requested by Archdeacon Stonehouse to answer your Lordship's enquiry respecting the Amount of the Estimate for the restoration of the Chancel of Stow Church. Your Lordship's impression is quite correct that the Estimate for the necessary repairs was £500 of which the Ecclesiastical Commissioners are to pay £300 and Mr Hall £200. Mr Pearson's Estimate of the Cost of a thorough restoration given some time ago was about £1300 i.e. £800 in addition to the £500.

Mr Pearson happening however to be here the early part of this week on his way from Lea where he is superintending the restoration of the Church, I had a conversation with him respecting the restoration of the Chancel here, and his Estimate for it, and particularly whether it could be done for somewhat smaller cost.

He said that if no unforeseen defects should disclose themselves during the progress of the work—which he states is often the Case—and the timber of the present roof should prove to be sound enough to go into the new roof to a considerable extent—it might be done pretty well for £1000 or £1100.

His estimate therefore for a perfect restoration including all risks is £1300 for a less perfect restoration but still well done, subject to casualties, £1000 or £1100.

58. To Bp Kaye from Atkinson, 27 Feb. 1849 (K)

My Lord

I was prevented from consulting Mr Peel respecting the best mode of applying to Mr Mason for a room at Bransby longer than I expected, but I had an opportunity of doing so last week and wrote to Mr Mason the next day. I received an answer from him yesterday which is just of such a nature as I expected.

Mr Mason as I have long known by the report of those who are acquainted with him, is a person of a serious and religious turn of mind, but so extremely lax in his views, as to be much more of a Dissenter than a Churchman though I believe professedly a Churchman.

In his Letter he says, he will not *oppose* my having the room, if his Tenant wishes it, but before he can *recommend* my design to Mr Holmes he must know whether my views are in accordance with those of the party commonly called "Tractarian, or High Church".

I have written to him this morning a Letter which I shall be glad to shew your Lordship, stating that my views are those of the Church as expressed in their simple and obvious sense in the Articles and Liturgy, and not in accordance with either of the Extreme parties into which the Church is unhappily divided—and I have asked Mr Mason's leave to refer him to your Lordship for further satisfaction in respect to the soundness of my doctrine if he should still think it necessary.

As I wish to consult your Lordship on one or two other matters, I should be glad to come over to Riseholme some morning in the early part of next week—Monday I think would be most convenient to myself—if your Lordship will be at home.

59. To Bp Kaye from Atkinson, 7 March 1849 (K)

My Lord,

I beg to inform your Lordship that on my return from Riseholme I found an answer from Mr Mason respecting the room at Bransby. It is unfavourable, as we were led by the tenor of his former letter to anticipate would be the case.

Your Lordship will see from the Copy which I subjoin that Mr Mason would afford no assistance to any Clergyman who does not belong to the party to which he avows his adherence.

(Copy)

Hakes's Hotel
March 3. 1849

Sir

I take blame to myself for not having distinctly stated in my former letter that my own sentiments are what are called evangelical or low Church: from which you may conclude that I must feel some scruple about taking any step towards *actively* promoting the Ministry of any Clergyman who at all *leans* to the views of the opposite party. If the "doctrines" of our "Articles and Liturgy" were so "obvious" as you appear to consider them, two parties in the Church would not exist—I can therefore come to no conclusion from your avowed declaration of adherence to them. I am ignorant of the side which the Bp. of Lincoln may espouse: but the majority of the Bishops evidently are favourable to the Tractarians: and it is natural to expect them to view with complacency a system which gives to the clergy so much power over the laity, and to themselves over the clergy—

I remain
Sir
Your faithful Servant
W. Mason

I have written to Mr Pearson requesting him to call upon your Lordship some morning next week between the hours of 10 & 11.

I enclose with this a statement of circumstances connected with the old Tithe Yard.

59A. To Bp Kaye from Atkinson, 7 March 1849 (EC file 6499)

My Lord,

I avail myself of your Lordship's kind permission to make the following statement of circumstances connected with the piece of Glebe land in the village of Stow which formerly was the "Tithe Yard" belonging to the prebend of Corringham, and on which I hope hereafter to see a National School erected.

On this piece of ground which is in extent about half an acre—exactly 2r. 7p.—when it came into possession of the Ecclesiastical Commissioners were an old Tithe Barn, and a house, both constructed of timber and mud, and both in ruins—there were also two ponds in it—and from a large portion of the remaining surface, the soil had been wholly carried away in removing the manure from time to time—the fencing was quite gone to decay round the whole circuit.

I have removed the remains of the old buildings—filled up the ponds—led soil upon it from a distance, drained and fenced it, at an expense to myself of £40—a sum equal, at the least, to the value of the fee-simple of the land in its former state. For the present I occupy it as a potato-garden.

When the Ecclesiastical Commissioners signified their approval of my proposal that this ground should be appropriated as the site of a school—my meaning and impression was that it would be conveyed to the living together with the other glebe which they, at my request, were so good as to assign to the Incumbent. It was not, however mentioned with the other glebe in the Gazette containing the Augmentation.

The favour which I have now to request your Lordship is, that you will lay before the Ecclesiastical Commissioners my humble petition, that they will be pleased, in consideration of the expense I have been at in improving this piece of ground, and of the favourable position it will place me, as the Incumbent of the Parish, to appear as the Donor of the site, with respect to the obtaining subscriptions and other means of forwarding the erection and maintenance of the proposed school, to assign this land to the living of Stow—in order that the Incumbent may hereafter, grant it, either wholly or such part as may be sufficient, for the site of a school.

60. To Bp Kaye from Atkinson, 15 March 1849 (K)

My Lord

I thought your Lordship might like to have the draught of the proposed appeal in behalf of Stow Church, during your stay in London, as this might afford an opportunity of submitting it to Lord Brownlow if he is in town.

It is longer than I wished it to be, but it will I think be printed upon a sheet which will not exceed 1d. postage. The details it contains will serve to shew those who take an interest in such matters that this Church has a very peculiar claim—while such persons as will not be at the trouble to read so long a paper, will perhaps take the fact of the Lord Lieutenant and the Bishop feeling a strong interest in its behalf as a sufficient guarantee, that the Case is one deserving of assistance.

Any alterations which your Lordship or Lord Brownlow may suggest, I shall be happy to receive, and they may be noted on the blank pages which have been left for this purpose.

After the consent of the Bankers and others has been obtained to receive subscriptions a notice to that effect may be added at the End—and also, perhaps, the names of subscribers received previously to its being printed.

I have had a letter from Mr Pearson stating that he was obliged to go down into Devonshire on Monday morning last, but he hopes to find your Lordship still in Town on his return towards the End of the week.

61. To Bp Kaye from Adn Stonehouse, 28 March [1849] (K)

Minutes of the correspondence of the Archdeacon of Stow with the Revd Mr Atkinson and the Church Wardens of Stow anent the reparation of the foundations of Stow Church—

Feb 22. 1849—Being informed by Mr Atkinson that the Church Wardens of Stow intend to effect the repairs which I ordered on my parochial Visitation to that place in a very [d]efficient manner and that Mr Pearson the Architect had informed him that such repairs would only be Money thrown away—I wrote to the Church Wardens to caution them on this behalf—and told them that if they persevered in this method of proceeding I should have their work surveyed by an Architect, and if he pronounced it badly done, I should compel them to do it better—

Feb 27—Received a note from the Church Wardens of Stow stating that "they had with the advice of certain Parishioners purchased a quantity of tooled yorkshire flag-stones to repair the foundations—

Answered by return of post—

That the Archdeacon was informed by Mr Pearson that such a Method of repair would be only money thrown away—The Archdeacon also stated that he had reason to believe that he should be able to obtain directions from Mr Pearson without any expense to the parish as to an effectual repair of these foundations, and advised them to suspend operations until they heard from him on this behalf—

March 24th

Received a Communication from Mr Atkinson in which he informs the Archdeacon that the Church Wardens of Stow notwithstanding his advice to the contrary had proceeded to execute the repairs to the foundations of the worst possible manner—that is to say by setting up flag Stones on their edge—which as Mr Pearson says is only concealing the mischief instead of repairing it—

All these letters are in the possession of the Archdeacon—

This Bishops opinion is requested as to what proceedings the Archdeacon ought to adopt under these circumstances—

62. To Bp Kaye from Atkinson, 4 April 1849 (K)

My Lord,

Before the account of the Church is printed I wish to ask your Lordship's opinion on a point which has been suggested by a friend to whom the Manuscript had been shewn. He thinks it is deficient in containing no estimate of the probable Cost of the restoration—and the Sum which will require to be raised by subscription—and that this want of precise information will probably injure the Subscription as people in apportioning the Amount they may be disposed to give will be likely to be guided in some measure by the amount required.

I was not unaware of this but felt the difficulty of making a precise statement—in the present position of the Case with respect to the legal repairs by the Parishioners.

Mr Pearson's estimate for a complete restoration of the whole fabric was over £4000. The amount required to be raised by subscription would not be less than £2000 even if the Parishioners had been disposed to come forward properly.

There appears to be a danger on both sides—if we state the full sum it may appear so large as to be impracticable to raise it—if we state no sum at all—the want of information may have an unfavourable effect on the other hand as if little were required.

Perhaps it might be the best course to state the amount of the Estimate for a general restoration—intimating that the works would be proceeded with gradually as funds might be supplied.

But on this point I should feel much obliged by the favour of your Lordship's opinion.

I had a very obliging Note from Sir John Thorold on Monday last offering a donation of £50 for which I have written to thank him.

63. Church Book

Stow Easter Monday April 9, 1849

At a Vestry meeting held according to Notice duly given, in the Parish Church on Easter Monday 1849 for the purpose of electing the Churchwardens for the parish of Stow for the year ensuing—the Minister appointed Mr Edward Howard of Stow—& Mr William Taylor of Bransby was chosen by the Parishioners—and they were accordingly declared to be the Churchwardens for the year ensuing.

George Atkinson M.A. Minister
Chairman—

After the election of the Churchwardens as above recorded had taken place and had been recorded and signed by the Chairman—Mr John Harrison of Stow was proposed by Mr James Gelder and seconded by Mr William Wilkinson, as a Churchwarden of the Parish, and (a majority of votes *del*) the Chairman while protesting against the assumption of any such right on the part of the Parishioners, agreed to record the fact that such assumption had been put forward, and this at the request of the parties to this proceeding, in order to enable them to use the record of this claim for such purpose as they may think proper—the ground of such assumption or claim being the allegation that the Parishioners have the right to choose both Churchwardens.

George Atkinson M.A. Chairman

We the Churchwardens whose names are here undersigned, were present (with other parishioners) when the above record of the proceedings was made by the Chairman as witness our hands the day and year above written.

John Spink }
Robert Foster }

Note: Vestry Minutes henceforth were always recorded in a separate "Vestry Book".

64. To Bp Kaye from Stow Parishioners, n.d. (K)

We the undersigned, being parishioners of Stow, do protest against Mr. Atkinson's having any legal authority to choose a Churchwarden. It being the custom, as it appears by the records of the parish, for the parishioners to choose both churchwardens—such custom being from A.D 1693 to A.D 1839.

And we the parishioners, in vestry assembled, on Easter Monday, 1849, did propose, second, and declare duly elected as Churchwardens Messrs. Wm Taylor and John Harrison.

And we further protest against Mr. Ed Howard being allowed to make the declaration as churchwarden, he not being duly elected.

W Sergeant
Wm Watson
Wm Wilkinson
James. S. Gelder
Wm Ellis
Edward Howard Junior
Joseph Harrison
Joseph Fox
Thomas Spencer
George Burton

65. To Bp Kaye from Atkinson, 1 May 1849 (K)

My Lord

The Circulars of which I send your Lordship a copy were printed last week. I requested Messrs Brooke to send some to Riseholme but in case they should have omitted to do so your Lordship may procure any number from the printers. They stated that the expense of printing 500 would be about a guinea and a half—so that the cost is moderate, and they will keep the type standing and any requisite number may be printed at a reasonable rate. Messrs Brooke undertook to supply the Bankers and booksellers who receive subscriptions with so many as they might require. I suggested them to send some to Lord Brownlow if they could ascertain that he is at Belton. If your Lordship should happen to have any communication with Lord Brownlow shortly perhaps you would inform him that the circulars are to be had of Messrs Brooke, if he has not received a supply.

In your last letter to me your Lordship mentioned Archdeacon Stonehouse's opinion that when we should be in a condition to say to the Parishioners "we have so much money subscribed towards your Church, if you will meet it with an equal sum we will take the repairs off your hands"—the parties now opposed to us would come in to these terms. I am sorry that I cannot share the Archdeacon's expectation, at least until these persons have been made to feel that they can and will be compelled to repair the Church themselves without help if they continue obstinate. In that case I feel sure they would soon come to reasonable terms—at least to make the best bargain they could. At present their hope and intention is to slip through without any real repair at all by merely hiding with plaster &c. the decays of the building—and they are even doing positive mischief by their present operations. If legal proceedings should be taken to enforce a real repair—the cost of resisting the law would fall upon two or three at most of the leaders, and I think it would fall upon Mr Spencer alone—as the rest neither could nor would make themselves responsible for legal expenses—and as Mr Spencer's sole object in opposing the repair is to save his money, he would be likely to desist on finding that continued resistance would only involve him in additional expense. The Archdeacon has directed me to ask Mr Pearson to survey what has been done by the Churchwardens, and to report to him thereon. I have written to Mr Pearson on the subject, and I believe he will be at Lea in a short time.

In the meantime our proceeding with the Chancel can hardly fail to have a good effect. At least it will shew them how the work ought to be done.

P.S. The following Subscriptions have been communicated to me directly by the parties themselves since the paper was printed.

Revd J. H. Pooley, Scotter	£5: 0: 0
Revd J. H. Shepherd Clayworth	5: 0: 0
Revd D. C. Legard Lea	5: 0: 0
Revd S. W. Hall, Wolfreton House Hull	20: 0: 0
James Barker Esqre Severn Stoke	10: 0: 0
Revd J. K. Miller, Walkeringham	5: 0: 0
Mrs Miller	5: 0: 0
Miss & Miss M. Miller	5: 0: 0
Revd Dr Parkinson, Ravendale	5: 0: 0
Mrs Parkinson	5: 0: 0

66. To Bp Kaye from Adn Stonehouse, Owston, 12 May [1849] (K)

My very good Lord—

. . . .

With regard to Stow Atkinson has contrived concerning the election of Church Wardens a confusion equal to that of King Agramant's Camp—

He asserted his right to appoint one Church Warden. This was opposed by the parishioners on the ground of Custom (but which Custom would stand no legal investigation)

But which is worse—After he had appointed one Church Warden, and the parish another Mr Atkinson acted so foolishly as to enter a minute, after the book was signed—to this effect that the parishioners had appointed a second Church Warden against which he protested—To this it was replied that Mr Atkinson signed the book in spite of the persons present—and as Chairman had not adjourned the Vestry—Then what made matters worse—The Church Warden whom Mr Atkinson had appointed refused to take the declaration.

Under these circumstances I thought it my duty to receive the declarations of those persons present who were willing to make it. And Dr Bonney says that I acted judiciously—I told Mr Atkinson that he must apply to the Court of Queens Bench for a Mandamus to compel the person whom he appointed to undertake the duties of the office—which he said he would do—under the peculiar circumstances of the case a most injudicious proceeding. I never met with such a resolute obstinate person as Mr Atkinson is.

. . . . . .

Note: King Agramant's Camp is a reference to Ariosto's *Orlando Furioso*.

67. To Bp Kaye from Atkinson, 18 May 1849 (K)

My Lord,

I beg leave to draw your Lordship's attention to the proceedings which took place at the Archdeacon's Visitation held last week at Lincoln with respect to the Churchwardens of the Parish of Stow, and to the position we appear to be placed in, by those proceedings in reference to any further steps towards the repair of the Church.

I must premise that on Easter Monday at the Vestry meeting held for the purpose of choosing the Churchwardens for the ensuing year, after I had named Mr Edward Howard as Minister's Churchwarden, and the Parishioners had named Mr William Taylor, and I as Chairman had declared them duly elected, some of the persons who were present said that they proposed to elect another on the part of the Parish, and after the names of two persons had been severally proposed, both of whom refused to stand, a Mr John Harrison, a Miller was named. I had, in the mean time recorded the election and signed the Vestry Book stating that the election was complete, and that they had no ground of right or law to elect another. They however persisted in nominating "a third man" as they called him. I refused to put it to the Vestry, but at their request made a subsequent entry in the Vestry Book that such a proposition had been made on their part, and that they alleged a right by Custom to elect both the Churchwardens. In reply to this allegation I shewed them the records in several successive years in the Vestry Book signed by those of the parishioners who were present at each Vestry meeting, as well as by myself, of the Minister having elected one Churchwarden and the Parishioners the other. After the Vestry I wrote to Archdeacon Stonehouse a full account of these proceedings and that I would attend his Visitation in order to give any Evidence or explanation which might be required.

I accordingly attended on Thursday the 10th Inst. at the hour named to me by the Archdeacon, when I found that he had decided in my absence upon admitting Harrison to the office of Churchwarden, Howard (whom I had elected) refusing, no doubt by an understanding with the other parties, to make the declaration. I objected, when the Stow Churchwardens were called, to Harrison's being admitted on the ground that *he was not elected*, and that it is distinctly laid down in Burn's Ecclesiastical Law as a thing settled by the Temporal Courts that if a Mandamus be applied for directing the Archdeacon to swear in a certain person the return by the Archdeacon *that the person* in question was not elected is a good return. I also stated in the Court (what I had communicated to the Archdeacon previously) that some of the other parties to the present proceeding had done precisely the same thing once before, by presenting two persons on behalf of the Parish before the late Archdeacon Bayley at his Visitation held at Gainsborough in 1838 to be admitted as Churchwardens, I having elected another person which happened to be the same Mr Howard. Archdeacon Bayley after hearing what my opponents had to say stated that on their own showing they had no case, and that he should admit the person chosen by the Minister and the first of the two names presented by them. My opponents then withdrew their last name, and Mr Howard and the other were admitted and served the office. Every year since I have elected one of the Churchwardens and the Vestry the other without any question or dispute whatsoever, until this present year.

Archdeacon Stonehouse while stating that he considered himself bound to admit Harrison, if he required it, to make the declaration, said that all those persons whom he had had an opportunity of consulting on the Case, agreed with him that the alleged right or custom was a mere pretence without any foundation either in law or fact, and that if they would lay the Case correctly before any respectable Lawyer he would tell them so at once.

But however frivolous and vexatious this proceeding might be, since the Archdeacon has thought proper to admit this person whose right to act as Churchwarden is open to question, I conceive that until the point is settled the Archdeacon can take no further steps in regard to the repair of the Church and that even if the Vestry were willing to grant a rate, no valid rate could be made. Moreover, the object of this proceeding being obviously and indeed avowedly to thwart the Authorities and to prevent the repair of the Church, it is certain to be renewed every year with the same purpose, if no effectual steps are taken to prevent it.

68. To Bp Kaye from Atkinson, 26 May 1849 (K)

My Lord

I have been prevented by an attack of acute rheumatism in the wrist and hand from sooner acknowledging the receipt of your Lordship's letter of the 22d Inst. respecting the late election and admission of the Stow Churchwardens.

I do not see how any other view can be taken than that which your Lordship expresses that "the matter is now placed upon such a footing that either the question must be tried or a precedent for the appointment of both Churchwardens by the Parish will be established"—and this it is obvious would inflect a permanent injury on the interests of the Church in the Parish.

The Archdeacon was under a mistake in supposing that it was my intention to apply for a mandamus to compel Howard to make the declaration. Willing as I am to make any sacrifice in my power to protect the Church from injury, I could not venture to take up this case on my own responsibility—nor do I think that the Archdeacon could, on reflection, expect me to do so, especially as this difficulty has arisen out of the proceedings which the Archdeacon himself has had to adopt in the course of his official duty.

Neither would an application for a mandamus, in this case as I conceive, be the proper mode of proceeding. Burn states that if any person elected Churchwarden refuses to take the oath, he may be compelled thereto by excommunication, and that, I presume, upon the motion of the Archdeacon. This was the Course indicated by Dr Stonehouse himself in the Case of Spink, one of the late Churchwardens of Stow, who refusing to make the declaration last year, Dr Stonehouse wrote to him stating that if he did not do it before a certain day, he should proceed to compel him.

The proper proceeding, I imagine, would be to apply to the Queen's Bench for a writ of Quo Warranto against Harrison calling upon him to shew upon what ground he claims to hold or exercise the office of Churchwarden. This would lay the burden of expence upon the right parties. Harrison, the Miller, is in no circumstances to maintain a suit, and if the party who are his instigators would not guarantee the costs he would be anxious to get out of the matter—if they should make themselves responsible those who are most guilty would suffer.

Howard though blamable acts more through fear than any bad feeling, and Harrison's party would not in the least degree be touched by any penalty which might fall upon Howard.

69. To Bp Kaye from Adn Stonehouse, Owston, 30 May 1849

My very good Lord—

The words which Mr Atkinson made use of when Howard refused to take the declaration as Ch Warden were these "I will assert my right." argal in order to do that he must apply for the quo warranto.

As to the last paragraph in your Lordship's note "Still if no steps are taken—a precedent for the appointment of two Church Wardens by the parish will be established." I beg leave to observe that the Stowegians shewed at the Visitation from their vestry book that the Parish had appointed two Church Wardens ever since the year 1693—until the year 1836—when they suffered Mr Atkinson to appoint one—and the exercise of this right for 14 years was the ground on which Mr Atkinson claimed to appoint—That is the question which he will have to try with his "quo warranto—"

This question therefore of a precedent is not raised now—but if he allows things to remain as they are of course His adversaries will be more resolute next year—

I think we might make out a strong case against peculiars in this Archdeaconry of Stow—The Churches in ruins—all ecclesiastical affairs in utter confusion.

70. To Bp Kaye from Adn Stonehouse, Owston, 1 June 1849 (K)

My very good Lord,

I get on better at Kirton with Church repairs than I do at Stow. Since I last wrote to your Lordship I have had an interview with several of the parishioners who have promised me that there shall be no more factious opposition to a rate for the complete restoration of the roof of Kirton Church— . . . .

The Stow people have been wrangling about the equilization [*sic*] of the Church rate—and now another question arises—which may perhaps affect the validity of the rate granted, on its being inforced upon a recusant—which is this. At Stow there is no vestry room—in the Church or adjoining to it—but they always held their vestries in the nave. And did so when the present rate was granted—But by a late act of William the fourth—it is enacted that where there is no vestry such meeting shall be held elsewhere—but *not in the Church*. May I request the favour of Dr Haggard's opinion. . . .

71. Adn Stonehouse to Haggard and back, undated (K)

In the 29 Sec of the 1 & 2 of Wm IV Chap 80[(a)] it is enacted

"That in any case in which the Vestry Room of any parish shall not be sufficiently commodious for any vestry meeting such meetings shall be held elsewhere within the said parish or place, but *not in the Church or Chapel thereof*.

At Stow there is no vestry room in the Church—The parishioners have always used the Nave for that purpose—and did so when a rate was granted which the Ch Ws are now about to collect—Is a rate granted in *a Vestry held in the Church valid*?

[*Dr Haggard's writing*] Not invalid on that ground

JH.

(a) Has the Stat: been adopted at Stow? JH.

72. Vestry Book

According to public notice duly given, a Vestry meeting was held in the Church on Thursday evening, June 28th, 1849, for the purpose of "ascertaining the minds of the Parishioners wether a rate should be laid and the repairs of the Church proceeded with as commenced by the late churchwardens (Messrs Spink and Foster) and if such be the mind of the parishioners, to pass such Rate, or otherwise; and for any other business that may come before the said Vestry".

Present,—The Churchwardens; Mr Ellis in the Chair; and Messrs Gelder, Sergeant, Rose, Credland, Palmer, Spencer, Josh. Harrison, G Credland, Walker, Smith, Buttery, &c, &c.

The minutes of the meeting are as follow:—

Mr H. Walker proposed that C. G. Smith be vestry Clerk. This motion was seconded by Mr. J. Harrison, and carried unanimously.

Mr Harrison proposed that the sense of the vestry be obtained wether a rate be proposed for continuing the repairs of the church as commenced by Messrs. Spink and Foster the late Churchwardens: This motion was seconded by Mr. Taylor and carried unanimously.

Mr Taylor proposed that a rate of 2½d. in the pound be granted for the repairs of the Church. Mr Harrison seconded this motion. And as an amendment upon this proposition Mr. H. Walker proposed the following:

Resolved,—That the parish of Stowe in common with the agricultural community is suffering from an unfair competition with foreigners;—and further that the destructive floods and long continued rains of last year reduced the annual produce of the parish to half the usual average, so that Rents, rates, tithes and taxes have been mainly paid out of the farmers' capital;—and that under these sufferings it is most expedient to postpone the consideration of a rate untill the results of the approaching Harvest be better known.

Upon a show of hands being obtained the following is the result:—

For the amendment	9
Against the amendment	3
Majority for the amendment	6

William Ellis	Chairman
Charles. G. Smith	V. Clerk
Wm Taylor John Harrison	Churchwardens
James. S. Gelder	William Watson
Henry Walker	Thomas Spencer
William Buttery	William Marshall

73. To Bp Kaye from Atkinson, 3 October 1849 (K)

My Lord

In the last communication which I had the honour to receive from your Lordship respecting the attempt made by the Vestry Meeting of this Parish last Easter to deprive the Incumbent of the right of electing one of the Churchwardens by electing both themselves, you stated that you would consult the Archdeacon as to the steps necessary to be taken in order to prevent their establishing a precedent for doing this in future.

As the commencement of the Michaelmas Term is approaching, as well as the time when the Archdeacon's Autumn Visitation is usually held, I feel anxious to know what has been the result of your Lordship's correspondence with Archdeacon Stonehouse on the subject.

I forbear at present from troubling your Lordship with any particulars of the intruding Churchwarden's conduct since your Lordship's visitation (when as your Lordship will remember the presentment from this Parish conveyed an insinuation against my moral character) further than to say that subsequent experience has fully realized what I had reason to expect it would be from my knowledge of the motives of those persons whose instrument he is.

Note: The bishop's draft reply discouraged Atkinson from any legal proceedings. Nothing is known about the 'insinuation'.

74. To Bp Kaye from Atkinson, 15 Oct. 1849 (K)

My Lord,

The copy, which your Lordship's letter of the 5th Instant contains of the Archdeacon's Statement respecting the election of Churchwardens for this Parish has greatly surprised me. He says "that the people of Stow shewed at the Visitation from their Vestry Book that the Parish had appointed two Churchwardens ever since the year 1693 until the year 1836, when they suffered Mr Atkinson to appoint one." I can only account for this statement by supposing it to arise, on the part of the Archdeacon from an imperfect recollection of what took place, or that the Vestry Book had been altered and interpolated by the opposing party on purpose to afford countenance to such a statement. Since my coming into this Parish I have thoroughly examined all the Vestry Books, as well as the Registers and I can speak most positively to the fact that they contain no evidence whatever of the Parish having elected two Churchwardens *in any instance*, much less from 1693 to 1836. What they do contain on this point, is simply the *names of the Churchwardens* of the Parish, and their accounts for each year; but as to the mode of their election, nothing whatever appears. In fact until after the former attempt to claim for the Parish the election of both Churchwardens, there is not a single entry in the Vestry Books of any election of Churchwardens at all. The first of such records was made by myself, in accordance with the advice of Archdeacon Bayley and Mr Swan, in order to prevent future disputes, and ever since Vestries have been duly held, and the proceedings recorded by myself in the Vestry Book, by which it will appear that the Minister elected one, and the Parishioners the other. This record was on each occasion attested by the signatures of several of the Parishioners present.

As to their statement that in 1836 "they *suffered* Mr Atkinson to appoint one"—this is equally unfounded. When I first came to Stow no question was made about the Clergyman's right to appoint one Churchwarden. In that year I appointed for the Stow part of the Parish as I was informed the custom had been aforetime. In 1838 after the disputes about the Clerk had arisen, the claim for the Parish to elect both was first heard of—but no evidence in support of it was ever attempted to be adduced—and upon enquiry I was informed by two respectable farmers, who had resided many years in the Parish, that it had always been understood and acknowledged in the Parish that the election of one of the Churchwardens belonged of right and custom to the Clergyman. For a long time before my incumbency no clergyman had resided in the Parish—and from this circumstance the Minister may have often left it to the Parish-meeting to name both, yet without relinquishing his right. One instance was adduced, and is well known in the Parish, in which my immediate predecessor Mr Massingberd directly exercised his right by appointing one John Harrison of Stow (uncle to the present intruding Churchwarden) who is now living, and who acknowledged to Mr White (now of Barnetby) that he was appointed by Mr Massingberd.

When the party opposed to the Clergyman in the disputes about the Clerk presented their two nominees to Archdeacon Bayley, he asked them what evidence they had to shew of their right or custom. They acknowledged they had none, and withdrew one of their men—My nominee was admitted, and ever since I have exercised the right without dispute, and, if the Parishioners had not been called upon by the Archdeacon to repair the Church, this claim, would never more have been heard of. It is on that account that this move has been made by the opponents of the Church-repair, not so much with a view of depriving me of my right, as of thwarting the Archdeacon's authority, and I cannot but feel that I have a just claim to be assisted in vindicating the one as well as the other. Such a claim I possess too on this additional ground—Sometime previous to the Visitation I wrote to the Archdeacon informing him of the intention of our opponents to present two persons for admission, and requesting to be informed of the precise day and hour of his Visitation at Lincoln, stating that I would attend to give any explanation which he might require, and that I could be there, if necessary, by a railway Train as early as 9 o'Clock in the morning. In his answer he said that the hour of Visitation was 12 o'Clock at noon—And that there was a Train from Gainsborough which would bring me into Lincoln at that hour, by which I should be quite in time. On my arrival by that Train I did not lose a moment in going up-hill, when I found that the Archdeacon had heard and decided the Case in my absence. I called afterwards on Mr Swan, and made a statement of the Case to him. He said that if I had been present when the Case was under discussion to make that Statement, he should have advised the Archdeacon *not to admit* Harrison, as not having been elected at all, and that he was satisfied that there did not exist any legal ground for the claim to elect both. The Archdeacon himself also, in the Consistory Court, when admitting Harrison, declared that same opinion, which he added was confirmed by that of all whom he had had an opportunity of consulting upon the point. He named the Archdeacon of Lincoln, Mr Swan, and Mr Bromehead as being of this opinion and told the Churchwardens that if they would consult any respectable Lawyer he would tell them the same thing.

With regard to the effect upon the interests of the Church in this Parish which this proceeding of theirs, if suffered to remain unquestioned, must of necessity produce, I need not be at any pains to prove to your Lordship that it cannot but be of very evil consequence. It is the proceeding of a party almost wholly composed of dissenters and open opponents of the Church—and was avowedly adopted, primarily indeed to thwart the Ecclesiastical Authorities in regard to the repair of the Church, but also to depress and hamper the Clergyman in his influence and labours in the Parish—and your Lordship had an opportunity of judging at your late Visitation whether these Churchwardens and their instigators are likely to spare any means which may tend to lower his Character and credit. I cannot therefore contemplate the consequences of such a precedent being established without the greatest pain and alarm for the welfare and advancement of the Church in this Parish—for it must be quite clear that the point once gained the same proceeding will be repeated every year.

Of the probable result in respect to the personal comfort and peace of the Clergyman in the Parish I have had some experience already. Harrison the intruding Churchwarden has openly boasted that the Churchwardens are now the Masters of the Clergyman and they will keep so: he has threatened to insult me publicly when he can find a fitting opporunity—and some weeks ago, meeting with one of my sisters at the Parsonage Gate, he insulted and reviled her in the grossest manner without the slightest provocation.

Under the circumstances I feel constrained most respectfully but most earnestly to appeal to your Lordship as my Bishop for support and protection.

This hostile movement against myself as the Clergyman is entirely in consequence of the Archdeacon's interference about the repair of the Church—an interference, as your Lordship and all the world knows, not without the most urgent necessity. When I informed the Archdeacon from time to time of the factious disposition manifested by the opponents, he encouraged me by letter after letter to persevere, assuring me that he would spare neither trouble nor expense to subdue their opposition, and to enforce the repair of the Church.

The factious party who have given all this trouble, are really weak in every respect, except their ability to command a numerical majority at a Vestry meeting. With the exception of Mr Spencer, the Quaker, the largest and most respectable farmers stand quite aloof from their proceedings, though they will not come forward as they ought to do, to oppose them. In reference to any further proceedings to enforce the repair of the body of the Church, I am of opinion that it would be wise to wait until we have at least *begun* the restoration of the Chancel, and see what effect that may have. This matter of the Election of Churchwardens would obviously be prejudiced by delay. I would therefore suggest that good legal advice should be had on a Case properly drawn up. The expense of this preliminary step would not be great, and I am willing to bear my proportion of it. Should we be advised that the claim set up for the election of both Churchwardens by the Parishioners cannot be maintained—and the other party should be made aware that legal proceedings would be adopted if necessary to try the right, I believe they would never contest it. Harrison I am sure is in no circumstances to do so, and, even were he disposed to litigate the matter, I think he would find few or none to support him with pecuniary assistance.

I beg respectfully to submit these matters to your Lordship's consideration and through your Lordship to that of the Archdeacon—

75. To Bp Kaye from Adn Stonehouse, Owston, 19 Oct. [1849] (K)

N O 1

My very good Lord

After an attentive perusal of Mr Atkinson's memorial, I think it right to send you the documents presented to me at the visitation in May last—I do not see how Dr Haggard can give a safe opinion without an attested copy of the vestry book—

Mr Atkinson has omitted to state one thing, which is this—That the Archdeacon directed all the three candidates for the office of Church Warden to take the declaration—That the person chosen by Mr Atkinson refused—That the Archdeacon told Mr Atkinson the Court of Queens Bench would compel him to do so—. . .

76. To Bp Kaye from Atkinson, 25 Oct. 1849 (K)

A true copy of the record in the Vestry book of the Parish of Stow of the proceedings of a vestry meeting in the Parish Church on Easter Monday 1849. . . .

Note: See No. 63 for the text.

77. *To Bp Kaye from Haggard, Doctors Commons, 29 Oct. 1849 (K)*

My dear Lord

I have the honour to acknowledge your note of the 27th inst, & the four documents, relating to the Election of Churchwardens at Stow, which accompanied it. My impression, upon a perusal of those documents, is, that the claim, on the part of the Parishioners, to nominate two Churchwardens, in exclusion of the Perpetual Curate, cannot be sustained. Mr Atkinson has not, I think, by the minute as to the appointment of Harrison, prejudiced his own claim to a nomination: the minute is entered under protest, & the whole is to be taken together. But it is, I think, rather unfortunate that prompt measures were not adopted to put this conflict of claims in a course for judicial decision; & whether, at the Visitation, Howard (the nominee of the Minister) refused to attend, or, attending, refused to be admitted into office, a monition might forthwith have been served upon him. I am not competent to say whether until Howard has signed the declaration of Office, the question of custom in Stow, as to the appointment of Churchwardens can be raised; but as custom governs these appointments, it seems to me desirable to get Howard admitted; & under the circumstances of his contumacy in respect of the Archdeacon's Visitation, & upon the statement of Mr Atkinson as to what passed before & at that Visitation in reference to the Stow Churchwardens, I presume to suggest that the Archdeacon should serve Howard with notice to appear before him (or his Surrogate) in the Vestry room at Stow, at a certain hour, to make & sign the declaration as Church Warden. I thus suggest, assuming that the Archdeacon has received (& had at his Visitation received) a formal notice of the Minister having appointed Howard. To act formally the Archdeacon should be provided with a presentment on formal notice, & he should be attended by his Registrar, or a Notary Public. As the Annual Visitations are now over, it seems to me, in the absence of Howard having been served hitherto with a monition, that an objection may be obviated by not attempting to cite him to Lincoln; but on this point, the objection would not avail, if at the Visitation he was presented as Church Warden, & a fortiori, if in that character (as named) he was present, & refused to be admitted. I return the documents:

P.S. In regard to Stow, unless Howard is willing to be admitted I incline to think, so far as the papers your Lordship furnished me, that it may be as well to let the matter rest until next Easter, & that then Mr Atkinson should be prepared with a Nominee & put the claim in order for a legal inquiry. Were *he* to call upon Howard now to take office, & Howard to resist, it might compel Mr Atkinson to show his *right* to enforce upon *Howard* the acceptance of the office (& thus have an hostile person to deal with) there being already two Church Wardens admitted, & perhaps no *regular* announcement at the Visitation of a nominee on the part of the Minister. I do not recollect that this matter was noticed at your Lordship's Visitation. . . .

78. To Bp Kaye from Atkinson, 29 Oct. 1849 (K)

My Lord

Having procured the Vestry Books in order to furnish your Lordship with the Copy, which I sent, of the proceedings of the Vestry meeting on Easter Monday last, I have since examined them very carefully, and I beg now to submit the result of this investigation.

1. It enables me to confirm the statement, I have already made, that these Books, which extend from 1693 to the present time, afford no evidence or trace of the existence of any custom in this Parish, for the Parishioners to elect both Churchwardens—nor of their having done so in any instance.
2. They shew that down to the year 1812, the election of Churchwardens had always taken place on *Easter Monday*, but there is no record of the proceedings, in any instance, of these Vestry meetings. The Books contain nothing more than the names of the Churchwardens, and their accounts for each year.
3. It appears from these accounts that it was the practice to have a dinner at the Village Inn every Easter Monday when the Churchwardens were elected, of which generally about 6 persons appear to have partaken. Besides the old and new Churchwardens, who would probably be present, this number appears to have included the Clergyman and the Schoolmaster, the latter of whom appears to have acted as a sort of Vestry Clerk in entering the accounts of the Churchwardens in the Book. The accounts of the two Churchwardens were for a long time kept separately and each generally puts down half the Expenses.
4. This item of expenses on these occasions is found throughout the whole series of accounts till the year 1812, and is generally thus expressed, from the commencement of the year 1756 "Spent on Easter Monday—so much . . . From 1785 downwards it is generally thus "paid for (so many) dinners—" generally 6 sometimes 4 or 5—. After 1812 the item ceases altogether, and the election of Churchwardens—as I learnt had been the Case for sometime when I first came into the Parish—appears to have taken place irregularly as to time.
5. In the year 1756 in the account of what was spent on Easter Monday this item occurs—"Pd Mr Broughton and the Schoolmaster's dinner" 1s 4d. Mr Broughton was the Incumbent. During the latter period of Mr Broughton's incumbency, Mr Basset was his Curate, and in the years 1778 and 1779 both were present. Till 1785—i.e. from 1756 the Clergyman is mentioned by name, afterwards the number of dinners only without the names. Thus for about 30 years in succession there is positive evidence of the Clergyman having regularly attended the Vestry meetings, at the canonical time, for the election of Churchwardens.
6. I have here set down several of the entries which are expressed more fully—thus in

1768	Spent on Easter Monday *when the new officers were nominated*	*s* 5	*d* 0
	Paid for Mr Broughton's dinner		6
1771	Spent on Easter Monday *when we chose the new officers*	10	0
	Paid the Clergyman's dinner		6
1781	Spent on Easter Monday *when we chose new officers*	10	0
	Paid that day for Mr Bassett's dinner		8
1782	Spent on Easter Monday *when we chused new Officers*	10	0
	Paid for Mr Bassett's and Wm Swift's (the Schoolmaster's) dinners	1	4
1783	Spent on Easter Monday *when we chose new officers*	5	0
	Paid for 3 dinners	2	0
1784	Spent on Easter Monday *when we chose new Officers*	5	0
	Paid for Wm Swift's and Mr Bassett's dinners	1	4

I apprehend that—in the absence of any indication to the contrary—the fact of the elections having always taken place on Easter Monday, would be of itself presumptive evidence that they were conducted in conformity with the Canon, and the regular attendance of the Clergyman at these elections seems to negative the supposition of any custom, which excluded him from taking part in them—and, in short, in the absence of any positive evidence either one way or the other—must be taken as affording sufficient proof that the Clergyman of this Parish exercised the same right in the election of Churchwardens as in the vast majority of other Parishes.

79. To Bp Kaye from Atkinson, 3 Nov. 1849 (K)

My Lord

Since my last letter to your Lordship was sent, in which I gave the result of a fresh examination of the Churchwarden's Accounts in the Vestry Books, from which it appeared that the Clergyman regularly attended at the Vestry meetings on Easter Monday when the Churchwardens were elected, another circumstance has come under my notice which I will now beg permission to lay before your Lordship.

I had previously observed that the Name of John Brown of Normanby occurred as Churchwarden for a long series of years in succession—and it is the only instance of the kind, the same person being very seldom found to have served the office more than one year at once.

Upon observing that the person in question, who was one of the principal farmers, had been Churchwardens so long, I made enquiry, and ascertained, that (as I had some faint recollection of having formerly heard) he was connected with Mr Broughton, the Incumbent of the Parish at that time. I was told that Mr Broughton married Mr Brown's daughter. Upon referring to the Register I found this to be correct. The Marriage took place in 1759 and that same year Mr Brown's name appears as Churchwarden—and during the next *thirty* years—he was Churchwarden *27* times.

The explanation of this circumstance appears sufficiently obvious—viz—that Mr Brown was so repeatedly elected because of his connection with the Clergyman, and that the Clergyman had, consequently, the choosing of one Churchwarden. This fact connected with the evidence contained in my last letter, appears to bring the matter as near a demonstration as anything short of positive testimony can do.

80. To Bp Kaye from Atkinson, 13 Nov. 1849 (K)

My Lord

I received your Lordship's letter containing the opinion of Dr Haggard with regard to the Case of the Stow Churchwardens, for which I beg to express my thanks, and to state that if it were in my power to act upon the suggestion he makes, viz, that I should be provided with a nominee next Easter, who would willingly come forward to be admitted, I would acquiesce in the course he intimates to let the matter rest till that time.

I regret, however, to say that there is not a single eligible person in the parish upon whom I could rely to come forward to take the declaration in opposition to the party who nominated Harrison, and who will, no doubt, again nominate a second person next Easter, if no proceedings are previously taken.

There are several farmers in the Stow part of the Parish, (from which the Clergyman has always chosen his Churchwarden) who have taken no part with the opponents, and are on the whole favourably disposed, but there is not one of them who will come forward to oppose the party hostile to the Church—they wish to keep out of the dispute altogether, to save themselves from being involved in trouble.

Howard is himself one of this class—he is not hostile to me or to the Church, and if I had to choose again I could not name any person in the parish less likely to offer resistance. I know too that his landlord has desired him not to make any opposition to the proceedings of the Authorities in repect to the repair of the Church. It so happened, in fact, that Howard was my nominee in 1838, when, on occasion of the disputes about the Clerk, the same parties who have put Harrison forward, presented two persons to be admitted. On that occasion Howard tried to escape just as he has done now—but Archdeacon Bayley and Mr Swan telling him that he could be compelled, he took the declaration, and served the office, the other party withdrawing their second nominee.

Such being the Case, it appears evident that we should be in a worse position another year than we are at present. Harrison the intruder would have served a whole year without having been called to account. Howard the Clergyman's nominee, by simply refusing to make the declaration, would have escaped serving—and this could hardly fail to have the effect of encouraging the opponents of the Church again to present two for admission—while the person who might be nominated by the Clergyman would again hold back in the hope of escaping as Howard had done.

I beg to add in reference to Dr Haggard's surmise that "perhaps there was no *regular* announcement at the Visitation of a Nominee on the part of the Minister", that such announcement was made, and that Howard was cited, and attended the Visitation, and was present when the other Churchwardens made the declaration.

Most respectfully submitting these Statements to your Lordship's further consideration I remain. . . .

P.S. I find on further enquiry and examination that the "John Brown" who was Churchwarden so long, was *brother* to Mrs Broughton (not her father who was also John Brown). It is remarkable that he was first appointed at Easter 1759, the Incumbent marrying his Sister in May of that year, & that in 30 years from that time he served the office 27 times, as I informed your Lordship in my last letter. I have since found that Mr Broughton was buried March 10th 1789, that his brother in law Mr Brown who had served so long as Churchwarden, and for the 10 years previous in succession, went out of office at Easter following, and did not serve again, tho' he lived till 1798, so that Mr Brown's first year of office was that in which the clergyman married his sister, and his last the year of the Clergyman's death.

81. To Bp Kaye from Adn Stonehouse, Owston, 19 Nov. [1849] (K)

My very good Lord—

. . . .

As to Mr Atkinson I beg leave to observe that it is a very fortunate thing for him that he was not brought up to be a coachman—for most certainly that coach would have been upset by being driven against a post—or the side of a house—and round a corner he never could have turned.

Most assuredly will I act on Dr Haggard's suggestion—and I will take care before my next visitation to get the case well up—I will obey the commanding officer—but no body else

82. To Bp Kaye from Atkinson, 8 Jan. 1850 (K)

My Lord

I will write a circular in the terms suggested by your Lordship to those persons who have promised subscriptions towards the restoration of Stow Church, requesting them to pay the amount into the Bank, and I thought I might name the 1st of February as the day previous to which they should be paid.

I beg to thank your Lordship for your kind offer that the whole of your subscription of £50 may go towards the restoration of the Chancel, and gratefully accept it on the understanding mentioned by your Lordship, viz "that you shall not hereafter be expected to contribute towards the restoration of the Church." The whole of my Father's subscription as well as my own which were intended to go towards the general restoration will, in like manner be applied to the Chancel.

The Amount of Mr Pearson's Estimate for the restoration of the Chancel is £1300 but he stated as I believe I informed your Lordship at the time, that it might be done in a fair way, though of course, not so perfectly for £1100. The subscriptions which have come to my knowledge are not much short, I think of £550 this with the £500 from the Ecclesiastical Commissioners and Mr Hall, does not leave us very far short of the lower Estimate, and I have had intimations from a few other friends of an intention to contribute something when they see the work actually begun. I should propose that the work be done by contract in order that the outlay may not exceed the funds in hand—and that the necessary and substantial repairs and restorations should be first let and proceeded with. The floor and the glazing, and some few other portions of the work, might form the subjects of a subsequent contact, if it were found that our funds would not in the first instance cover the whole. This, however, would be ascertained more nearly after Mr Pearson has made a complete plan and specification of the works to be executed, for which purpose it will be necessary that he should examine and measure the Chancel more minutely than he has hitherto done.

It is much to be lamented that the Gentlemen of the County should have taken so little interest in a work of so interesting a character as that of the restoration of the Mother Church of the Diocese, especially when recommended to them under such auspices—from what I have heard expressed by the Gentlemen of this immediate neighbourhood, their backwardness may be attributed to disgust at the factious spirit manifested by a majority of the Parishioners in refusing a reasonable contribution towards the necessary and legal repairs.

83. To Bp Kaye from Atkinson, 22 Jan. 1850 (K)

My Lord

I beg to state that after receiving your Lordship's last letter in reference to the payment of the subscriptions to the Stow Church restoration fund, it occurred to me that it would be proper to communicate with Lord Brownlow on the subject before I should write to the other subscribers. I did so last week mentioning that I had been in correspondence with your Lordship about the matter. I received Lord Brownlow's answer yesterday in which he expresses an opinion "that it is now time to begin the restoration of Stow Church in good earnest." His Lordship suggests that a list of subscribers should be published and he authorises me to put his name down for £100 instead of the £70 as it stood before. I have this day sent to Messrs Brooke two copies of the subscription list, with a short notice that as it is intended to begin the works in the ensuing spring, they are requested to pay their subscriptions before the 8th of February—and have requested Messrs Brooke to procure their insertion in the next numbers of the Lincolnshire Chronicle, and Stamford Mercury.

Mr Fraser promised a subscription some time ago, but I thought it would be better not to put his name down in the published list until I have heard from him again upon the subject.

84. Vestry Book

Stowe, Feby. 23rd, 1850

A vestry meeting was held in the church this day by adjournment from June 28th 1849 "to reconsider the postponed 2½d rate; that is, a rate of 2½d. in the pound, for continuing the repairs of the church". Present—Mr. Skill (in the chair) Messrs Spencer & Gelder; The Churchwardens, &c.

Mr. Taylor proposed that a rate of 2½d. in the pound be granted for the continuing of the repairs of the Church. This was seconded by Mr. John Harrison and carried unanimously.

John Skill Chair Man
Wm Taylor } Church Wardens
John Harrison }
Wm Wilkinson
William Watson
Robert Foster
Thomas Palmer
George Burton
Joseph Harrison
Henry Walker

Interior of Stow Church looking east after the installation of the organ in 1873

The nave of Stow Church, fitted up temporarily for divine service, after 1850

85. To Bp Kaye from Atkinson, 4 March 1850 (K)

My Lord

Before the repairs of the Chancel of Stow Church can be commenced, it will be necessary to have another part of the Church temporarily fitted up for divine Service. As the Transepts are at present quite unfit for the purpose, and access to the Chancel for the workmen and materials during the repairs can only be had through the Transepts, the Nave is the only, as it is in all respects far the most suitable portion of the Fabric for divine Service. The present seats which are in the Chancel being all removable together with the pulpit and Communion Table, can be readily placed in the Nave. In order to separate the Nave from the rest of the Church, the Western Arch of the Tower would require to be bricked up, and it would be desirable to brick up also the North, and West Doorways for the sake of warmth, and this with some levelling of the floor which is at present so uneven that the benches would not stand, would be the whole of the alterations required to fit the Nave for a temporary Church, and the Expense would be inconsiderable. The plan was mentioned by me to the Archdeacon when he was in the Church sometime since, and was approved by him. The Churchwardens are now collecting a rate of 2½d. in the pound which was granted the week before last—it will produce about £40 which I conceive will be more than sufficient to effect the necessary alterations as specified above.

As it is desirable that the Nave should be prepared as soon as practicable both on account of commencing the Chancel repairs, and while the Churchwardens have funds in hand, I beg to submit the matter to your Lordship, in order that such steps may be taken as the Case may require.

I shall be ready to write to the Archdeacon if your Lordship thinks proper, to request him to give such directions to the Churchwardens as he may think necessary, unless your Lordship should prefer communicating directly with Dr Stonehouse on the subject.

Note: There are photographs in the Lincoln Central Library showing these arrangements as carried out.

86. To Bp Kaye from Atkinson, 7 [March] 1850 (K)

My Lord

I have written a letter to the Archdeacon of Stow in accordance with your Lordship's suggestion requesting that he will give directions to the Churchwardens to prepare the Nave for divine service.

I did not attend the Vestry meeting of the 23rd of February at which the Church rate of 2½d in the pound was granted, but I am informed that there was only one person dissenting, and he proposed 1¼d instead, but no one seconding or supporting his proposition, it fell to the ground, and the rate was carried without further opposition.

I attribute this unanimity to a conviction that they are compellable to repair the Church, and to a fear on the part of the Churchwardens that they should be called to account at the Archdeacon's Visitation which is approaching, if they had not taken some steps towards those repairs. I am still of the same mind I have always been, that if they were dealt vigorously with, they would come to terms, such as perhaps it would be expedient to accept, though I think in the present depressed state of farming, and until we have made some progress with the Chancel restoration in order to shew them that we are in earnest, and also to set before them a pattern how Church work ought to be done, it would be better not to urge them.

If your Lordship should attend the meeting of the Diocesan Board of Education, which I am informed is to be held during the assize week, you will find that I am an applicant for a Grant towards the expense of fitting up some premises belonging to the prebend of Stow for a school. The obtaining these premises is a source of great satisfaction to me, and I trust the plan will meet with your Lordship's approval.

Note: This letter was mistakenly dated 7 February.

87. *To National Society from Atkinson, 18 March 1850 (Misc)*

Application to the National Society for the Education of the children of the Poor in the principles of the Established Church, for a Grant towards a proposed School in the Parish of Stow in the County and Diocese of Lincoln, by the Revd George Atkinson—Perpetual Curate.

Statement.

1. The population of the Parish exceeds 1000 and there is no Church-Day School whatever—nor any efficient School for merely secular Education even. There is a Church Sunday School, which numbers from 20 to 30 children only, and as this is taught in a room to which they are admitted only on sufferance they are liable to be excluded from it at any time. There is no girls' school in the Parish above the degree of a Dame-school, except one small school the mistress of which finds herself unable to obtain more than 10 or 12 scholars on the average owing to the charge being higher than the people in general are able to pay.
2. As there appeared to be no reasonable prospect of raising any funds in the Parish towards the erection of a school-house, the Incumbent has agreed with the Lessee of the Prebendary of Stow, to rent from him certain premises comprised in his Lease, for the purpose of providing school-accommodation.

3. These premises are situated near the Church, and consist of a barn, house and garden. The barn which it is proposed to adapt for a school-room is a substantial brick and tile building, comparatively new and in good repair. Its interior dimensions are 36 feet by 18 feet, which allowing 6 square feet for each child, would accommodate 108 children. There is ground, adjoining the Barn, suitable of being levelled for a play-ground. The house which is a very good and roomy Cottage would be for the residence of a Master and Mistress.
4. An experienced Mistress has been already engaged by the Incumbent, and she will commence teaching in the Cottage, as soon as possession is obtained of the premises which will be at Lady Day next, until the alterations necessary to fit the barn for a school room can be effected. The Incumbent will pay the Mistress a fixed salary himself receiving the Children's pence towards it, and as soon as the number of scholars may require, a Master also will be procured.
5. The rent of the premises which (with that of a separate paddock of about half an acre) will be £10 per annum the Incumbent will pay. The Lessee has agreed that the Incumbent shall have undisturbed possession of them during the continuance of his Lease—and as they are Church property these premises may be considered as permanently secured for the purposes of a school, so long as the rent is paid. The Incumbent will pledge himself to pay the rent during his Incumbency,
6. The Incumbent has felt so deeply the deplorable want of a sound religious education in the Parish combined with proper instruction in secular knowledge, that he has been induced to make this effort to supply it at his own pecuniary risk. He does not expect to meet with any assistance towards the Expense, from the owners and occupiers of land in the Parish. The Diocesan Board of Education have made him a Grant of £25 towards the first Cost, and he now respectfully and earnestly requests the assistance of the National Society towards the same object. No Estimate has yet been procured of the probable Cost of the alterations, but including the necessary fencing, and the levelling and draining of what is now a farm yard, for the play ground, they will not fall short in all probability of £100. As the Incumbent will be responsible for the Teachers' salaries as well as for the rent of the premises and has no prospect of aid towards the first Cost of fitting the premises for their intended purpose, besides the Grant already received from the Lincoln Diocesan Board, and what he may obtain from the National Society, he respectfully submits this statement to the favourable consideration of the Committee of the National Society in the hope that they will render such assistance in this Case, as it may appear to them to deserve.

N.B. The School will be open to children from the adjoining small Parish of Coates, of which also the undersigned is Incumbent, on the same terms as to those of the Parish of Stow.

Note: See Introduction, p. xv for the outcome.

88. Vestry Book

Stowe April 1, 1850

This day was held, according to notice duly given by the churchwardens, a meeting for the following purposes:—viz., "To elect churchwardens for the year ensuing; and to take into consideration copies of a monition recently received from Archdeacon Stonehouse ordering us the undersigned churchwardens, to immediately remove the seats out of the chancel into the nave of the church—to level the floor of the said nave,—to brick up the western and northern doorways of the said nave,—to brick up the western arch of central tower,—to remove the pulpit reading desks communion table and rails into the aforesaid nave, so that divine service may be celebrated therein in lieu of the chancel which can no longer be used for that purpose on account of the repairs which it is about to undergo;—and for consulting how the funds are to be raised to enable us to carry out the aforesaid commands."

Present: Messrs Spencer, Gelder, Rose, Ellis, Walker, Skill, Knowles, Smith, Robt. Harrison, Howard, Jollands, T. Palmer, Watson, Foster, Lawrence, Josh Harrison, Burton, F. Spencer, (*sic*) Strafford &c; Messrs Harrison & Taylor churchwardens; The Rev. G. Atkinson Chairman.

Proposed by Mr. Robt. Harrison & seconded by Mr. Jollands that C. G. Smith be vestry clerk *pro temp*.

Moved by Jonathan Rose and seconded by Robt. Harrison, that—whereas the Clergyman vacated his seat to perform a funeral service and has not returned to occupy it according to agreement—William Ellis take the chair. Carried. It was a second time proposed by Robt. Harrison and seconded by John Jollands that C G Smith be vestry clerk pro temp. This being put to the meeting the Chairman declared it carried unanimously.

Moved by Mr Watson and seconded by Henry Walker that Mr John Harrison and Mr. George Burton be elected churchwardens for the ensuing year. A show of hands being obtained on this motion the Chairman declared it carried unanimously.

The Churchwardens then laid the Monition from Archdeacon Stonehouse before the vestry and applied for funds to carry out his commands; and in answer thereto Thomas Strafford proposed and Mr. Josh. Harrison seconded the following resolutions: which were carried unanimously:—That the parishioners of Stow are too poor at this time, to vote more money for building purposes, having just granted a rate to carry on the repairs of the church, and having a half-yearly tithe-call for nearly £500 immediately at hand which must to a great extent come out of the Farmer's capital, and not out of his profits; for it is doubtful whether he has any.

That whereas the Incumbent of the Parish apparently for the gratification of his own architectural taste, and in hot pursuit of antiquarian discoveries literally gutted the church; tore down the galleries; scraped away 12000 square feet of plaster; removed the family pews of the parishioners; placed the present seats improperly in the Chancel; and all without the consent of the parishioners legally assembled; This vestry would therefore respectfully suggest to the Archdeacon that the Incumbent is the proper person to take the seats away again and not the parishioners, whose feelings were outraged by their removal;—and who have never ceased to mourn for their lost homesteads in the Church.

That whereas certain persons, strangers to the parish of Stow, are about to expend large sums of money on its church, not in the substantial and necessary repairs to which the parishioners are bound by law but on works of taste and antiquity;—it is the opinion of this vestry that such persons should form their own workshops, and make their own preparations, and not impose onerous burdens on a parish of poor Farmers. The parishioners of Stow are for the most part hardworking men—small farmers with large families perpetually engaged in a struggle for existence and utterly destitute of means or opportunity to indulge in the pleasureable perceptions of architectural beauty, and the delightful emotions which a cultivated taste for antiquities are so well calculated to produce;—and they do not think that they should be taxed to maintain such enjoyments for the gratification of their more wealthy neighbours.

That the people of Stowe with the exception of a few extreme dissenters are perfectly sensible of their obligation to maintain a parish church and to provide all things decent and comfortable for the performance of Divine service as by *law* established; and they are willing to incur as large expence as has been incurred by any generation of parishioners since the days of the Reformation: but they cannot afford to be made the conservators of a dowager minster. And they look with jealousy upon the progress of a scheme for restoring a Cathedral character to their parish church because it will burden their already groaning lands with a large annual expenditure. To build up the magnificence of a Minster; to fill it with architectural embellishments; to crowd it with antiquarian reminiscences; to give a cathedral character to Stow church and then to impose the keeping up of such an expensive establishment so far beyond the requirements of the law upon a body of poor husbandmen would be ruinous to them—destructive to the true interests of the church—and a sad stumbling-block in the way of the people.

Signed in and on behalf of this meeting.

William Ellis — Chairman
Wm Taylor, John Harrison — Churchwardens

Edward Howard, William Wilkinson, Joseph Harrison, Henry Walker, William Buttery, George Harrison, Wm Millns, Thomas Spencer, James. S. Gelder, Thomas Strafford, Robert Harrison — Parishioners

89. To Bp Kaye from Atkinson, 4 April 1850 (K)

My Lord

I beg to inform your Lordship that at our Vestry meeting on Monday last, I nominated Howard as Churchwarden. The usual opponents, in order apparently to be first, proposed Harrison the present intruding Churchwarden, and another, the moment I had read the notice calling the meeting. This gave me an opportunity of making my nomination in the exact mode directed by the Canon—I stated that as I could not agree to the proposed choice, I would nominate one, which I then did, and called upon them to elect another. They answered that they should choose two as before. I then said that it was my wish to be candid, and if they presented two on their part to the Archdeacon, the third person should understand fully the responsibility which he would incur—I then stated the substance of the evidence which a careful examination of the Old Vestry books, since last Easter, had disclosed, with respect to the Clergyman taking part in the election of Churchwardens. Mr Spencer and others of the more intelligent evidently feel anything but sure of their ground. Harrison the present Churchwarden having possession of the Vestry Book refused to let me have it to make the usual record as I have always heretofore done—and they appointed one of their own party who would write what they pleased. Having again demanded the Vestry Book in order to record the proceedings, and this being again refused, I made a record upon a sheet of paper which I had with me.

The proceedings of the Vestry meeting were adjourned on account of a funeral, and after the funeral I did not return to the Church so that I cannot state what or whether any subsequent proceedings took place in the Vestry meeting.

I wish to make a statement to your Lordship respecting this funeral, especially as it will probably reach your ears in an incorrect form.

On Thursday night last, a small farmer of this Parish, William Sargeant, after attending a sale at Thorney where he became intoxicated, stopped, on his return at a beer-shop at Saxilby—where at length he was got to bed. After being in bed some two hours, as is reported, he got out, and when the Landlord who was in the same bed attempted to get him in again, Sargeant struck at him more than once, and began to swear. He then attempted to go down stairs, but missing his footing, fell headlong down, and broke his neck. He died instantly. The last word he spoke was an oath.

This unhappy man had been a confirmed drunkard, and for the last four or five years it is said, he had never gone to bed sober in a single instance. He never came to Church—nor attended any other form of worship—and was altogether a man of most reprobate character—at one of the last Vestry meetings I attended, he was drunk in the Church, and very violent and abusive.

I had little thought when I conversed with your Lordship lately at

Riseholm, on the subject of burying such characters with the service of the Church, that I should so soon have to meet so painful a Case. However after mature reflection, it appeared to me, that if any Case ought to be marked by a Clergyman this was such a Case. I accordingly wrote a note to the family to inform them that when the corpse was brought to the Churchyard-Gate I should proceed straight to the grave to bury the body, and after the service at the grave was over, I should be prepared to proceed into the church to read the rest of the service. In a short time one of the deceased's Sons with another person came to the parsonage to try to prevail upon me to take the body into the Church—I reasoned with them, and concluded by saying that I must adhere to what I had said in my note. After going away one of them came again, and not prevailing with me to alter my mind, he proceeded to threats. Shortly after they sent me word that the funeral would not be at half past three, the hour they had fixed, but at 5. Their object evidently was to have more time to concert their plans, and to be sure of the Church being open. I have reason to believe that in the meantime, they employed themselves in mustering as many of my usual opponents as possible to take part with them. About 5 oClock they came, and their party in the Vestry proposed at once that the Vestry meeting should be adjourned till after the funeral. I made no opposition to this, and met the corpse at the Church Gate, proceeding thence towards the grave reading the opening sentences—but instead of following me, they carried the corpse into the Church—Harrison the Churchwarden taking up the stools on which the coffin had been placed, and leading the way into the Church. The Clerk I am glad to say, who always carries them, refused to do so in this instance.

After waiting a few moments at the grave—Taylor the other Churchwarden and Mr Spencer, in a proper and respectful manner came to me, and entreated me to read the Service in the way the friends of the deceased wished, for the sake of peace. On my saying that it was a matter of conscience and principle with me not to do so in this very dreadful Case, they said they could not urge me further. I then went into the Church—the funeral people had taken their seats in the Chancel, and there was a considerable number of persons standing about in the open part of the Church. I desired that the Sons of the deceased might be called. Upon their coming to me under the Tower, I enquired if they were willing to have the corpse carried back to the Gate, and to follow me with it to the grave—Harrison the Churchwarden and others urged them not to consent and they declined accordingly. I then said—"When you are willing to do so"—and I again pointed out to them the rubric, as I had done several times previously, which gives the Clergyman the option of going from the Gate, either into the Church, or towards the grave—"I shall be prepared to perform the funeral service, due notice being given me." I then took off my surplice, left the Church and came home—no interruption of any kind was offered—nor any word spoken in my hearing. After I had been a short time at home, the Churchwardens with two or three others came to prevail upon me to go back, and bury the body. I stated that I would do so at once, if they would comply with my note—Harrison and the two more violent persons said they would not have the body buried in that way and Harrison said he would have the Coffin left in the Church unburied for a fortnight before it should be buried in my way.

Taylor however the other Churchwarden said it must be buried—and it appears that as soon as they got back the party finding they could not carry their point the body was carried to the grave and buried without further disturbance.

I had told the relatives of the deceased at the first interview that my wish was that no service whatever should be read—and if they would consent to that I should feel greatly relieved—This wish of mine was in fact eventually gained without my incurring the responsibility of a direct refusal to read the service—

I cannot but believe that the failure of this attempt to coerce the Clergyman, will, after the feeling of the moment has died away, have a salutary effect for the future. In this Case the Church can lose nothing from the offence taken by the relatives of the deceased—they being all irreligious persons who never came to Church, with the exception of the widow, who I believe is a Methodist.

90. Vestry Book

Stowe, April 11th, 1850

A vestry meeting was held in the Church at Stow, pursuant to notice duly given by the churchwardens, on Thursday the 11 day of April, 1850, (in accordance with a requisition which they last week received from the Inhabitants of the Parish); viz, '"for the express purpose of taking into consideration the conduct of the Minister of the parish, in refusing to read the Christian burial service in the usual manner over a parishioner."' Present;—Messrs. Taylor & Harrison, churchwardens; and Messrs Sikes, Watson, Knowles, Josh. Harrison, Lawrance, Credland, J. Palmer, Thos. Palmer, Ellis, Wilkinson, Burton, Walker, Rose, Page, Burnham, &c.

Mr. W. Ellis proposed and R. Lawrance seconded that Mr. G. B. Sikes take the chair. This motion was agreed to.

Henry Walker proposed and Mr. Joseph Harrison seconded that C. G. Smith be Vestry Clerk *pro tem*.

Mr. Watson proposed and Mr Page seconded—That a petition be presented to the Lord Bishop of the Diocese praying him to take into consideration the conduct of the Incumbent of the Parish (The Rev. Geo. Atkinson) in refusing to read the Christian burial service in the usual manner as set forth in the Book of Common Prayer, over a parishioner who died according to the *verdict* of the Coroner's Jury an "*accidental death*". This motion was then put and carried unanimously.

Proposed by Mr. Ellis and seconded by Mr Joseph Harrison—That the Vestry clerk be requested to draw up a petition for the above purpose, and to present it to the Inhabitants for signature. The motion being put to the vestry it was carried unanimously.

Signed in and on behalf of the vestry by

Geo B. Sikes, Chairman
Chas. G. Smith, Vestry Clerk
Wm Taylor
John Harrison } Churchwardens

William Ellis
Joseph Harrison
Henry Walker
John Sergeant
William Webster
William Hill
John Butler } Parishioners

91. To Bp Kaye from Adn Stonehouse, 20 April [1850] (K)

My very good Lord,

In order that the repairs of the chancel of Stow Church may be proceeded with, I have at Mr Atkinson's request, twice admonished the Church Wardens to prepare the nave for the celebration of divine service, by placing the seats Pulpit &c which are now in the chancel there. These monitions I am informed they intend to resist to the utmost—

The case is not a common one—and I should be very much obliged if you will get me Dr Haggard's opinion. It is this. About the time that Stow ceased to be a peculiar Mr Atkinson, without any *legal* authority—pulled up all the seats Pews Pulpit reading desk &c which were situated partly in the nave & partly under the centre Tower and placed them in the chancel. Very extensive repairs are about to be effected in the chancel now—during which divine service cannot be performed in that part of the Church. The Archdeacon has admonished the Church Wardens—to place the seats in the nave—so that the performance of divine service may go on during these repairs—The Church Wardens refuse to obey this monition.

Can the Archdeacon compel them to obey his monition—on the ground that having care of the seats they ought not to have permitted Mr Atkinson to remove them into the Chancel at all?

92. To Bp Kaye from Haggard, Doctors' Commons, 26 April 1850 (K)

My dear Lord,

Unless the present Church Wardens of Stow were in office when the fittings of the Nave were transferred by Mr Atkinson into the Chancel, &, as it would seem, of his own motion, they are not responsible for that act: &, judging from the Archdeacon's note, I apprehend that Mr Atkinson is the wrong-doer, & that the monition should be directed to him: he is stated to have stripped the Nave without legal authority, & appears to me the person upon whom the law would fix to put it in statu quo.

Note: The last three words are in the bishop's hand; the remainder of the letter presumably dealt with another subject, and was filed elsewhere.

93. To Bp Kaye from Adn Stonehouse, Owston, 30 April [1850] (K)

My very good Lord

Accept my best thanks for Dr Haggard's opinion. Verily Mr Atkinson is a wrong doer—and concerning the election of Church Wardens he has made "confusion worse confounded—by going away to a funeral, and never returning—just when the election was about to commence—as they say—He says that he had nominated his man before he went.

I suppose that the end will be that I must take the declarations of all three and leave them to try the right—and that the expense of removing the seats, out of the Chancel, into the nave must be defrayed out of the subscriptions.

I hope to spread my prayer carpet next Monday in the Burghershe Chantry house, the day before my visitation at Lincoln.

P.S. Atkinson will be presented for refusing to read the burial service over a man on whom a jury have returned a verdict of accidental death—but I should think the Church Wardens can not support their presentments. . . .

94. To Adn Stonehouse from Atkinson, 30 April 1850 (K)

Dear Mr Archdeacon

I received, this morning, your note containing Dr Haggard's opinion as to fitting up of the Nave of Stow Church for Divine Service. From the tenor of Dr Haggard's opinion, it is quite clear that he has formed it upon a most erroneous impression of the real facts of the Case.

1. He has evidently been led to suppose that Divine Service was formerly

celebrated in the Nave—for he speaks of "the fittings of the Nave being transferred by Mr A. into the Chancel"; and again that "he is the person upon whom the law would fix to put it", i.e. the Nave—"in statu quo.

Now such was never the Case—neither the fittings now in the Chancel nor any others ever were in the nave, inasmuch as the Nave has always been vacant and unoccupied, as it is at the present time. Excepting for the removal of the hideous "singing gallery" which stretched across the Eastern extremity of the Nave just in front of the Western Arch of the Tower no change, beyond the taking off the decayed and falling plaster, has been made in the State of the Nave.

2. The seats under the Old Arrangement were situated chiefly under the Tower in the Centre of the Cross, there being a few extending into the North Transept but so decayed that *they were never occupied*—And perhaps 8 pews in the South Transept of which about 4 or 5 were occupied. The rest of the area of the South Transept was unoccupied, and had as at present no floor but the bare earth. Part of the area of the North Transept was also unoccupied, the rest occupied by the "lime house" a receptacle of rubbish. With the exception of some half a dozen or eight pews, not one of which could be called good, in the whole Church, all were in a State of extreme decay, some having no seats and others no bottom but the bare earth. These pews were chiefly formed out of the Old Oak open seats with which the Church had formerly been fitted, patched and made higher by deal boards nailed on to them.

So many of these benches as were found capable of repair, were repaired and placed in the Chancel. They could not be placed in the *Transepts* from the want of a floor, and the dangerous condition of this part of the fabric—nor could they be removed into the *Nave* on account of the unevenness of the floor, and because of there being three Doorways into it—two of them very large, with doors so ill-fitting and dilapidated as to admit strong draughts of air.

The seats &c were accordingly placed in the Chancel, as the only part of the Church fit to receive them. This was done in the year 1846 without a single objection from any quarter; and not only with the acquiescence of all at the time but with general satisfaction ever since, not a complaint of what had been done ever having been heard till the question of repairs was mooted by the Authorities. Now if the fittings ought to be restored to their former situation, they must be placed, not in the Nave, but in the Transept. But this is impracticable for two reasons.

1. The transepts are in a very dilapidated State, and stand in the most urgent need of repair. The Old South Tower Arch is in a dangerous condition and might fall any day—the walls, particularly the end walls, are seriously cracked and shaken, and a part of the area has no pavement, besides being occupied by building materials belonging to the parish—stone, lime, sand &c. The roof too of the South Transept is in a bad state.

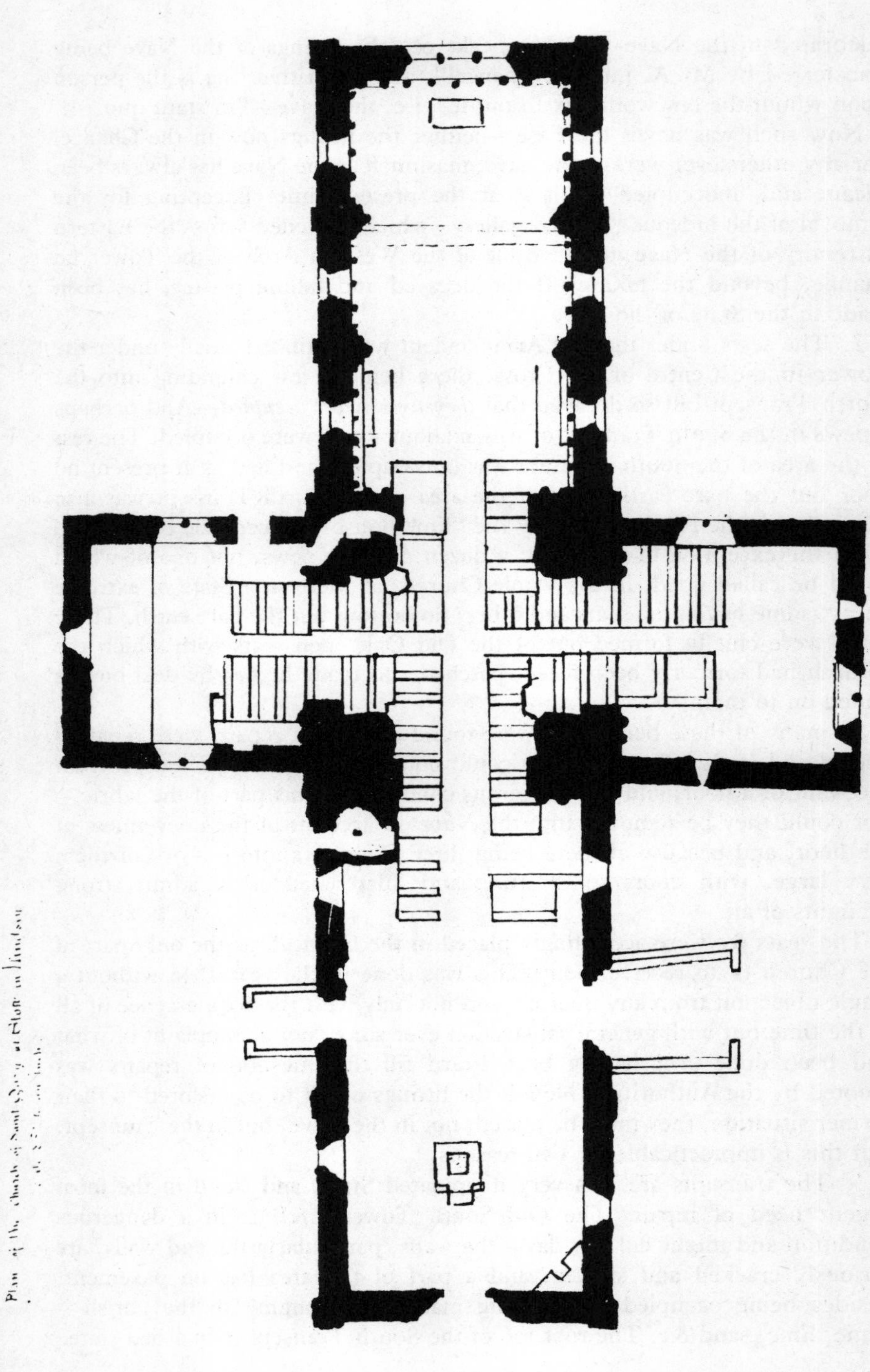

Plan of Stow Church, after Nattes (1793), amended in the area of the stair turret

2. Besides the obstacle arising from the state of the Transepts themselves, as above described, the only way of access to the Chancel is through the Transepts. There is not, and never has been any Doorway into the Chancel from the outside; consequently the workmen and all their apparatus and materials for the repair of the Chancel must pass through the Transepts. These causes make it impossible to have service in the Transept during the repairs. But as there is now a door opening from the outside into the Transept, and one or two others blocked up which might be opened if necessary, access could be had through the Transepts for the repair of the Chancel—without coming near the Nave, and thus leaving the latter entirely at liberty for Divine Service.

But at present the Nave is in an unfit state to receive the fittings now in the Chancel. The floor is so rough and uneven that the Benches would not stand—the doors let in every wind—the Tower Arch between the Nave and Transept must be temporarily built up, as the Architects say that some portions of the Transept walls will have to be taken down and rebuilt whenever the repair of them is undertaken—and the Chancel roof is to come off, and the glazing of all the windows out.

Your monition ordered the floor to be levelled—two of the doorways not wanted to be temporarily bricked up, and also the western Tower Arch. These are preparations which cannot possibly belong to me. Let these be made by those whose duty it is to make them—and then as to the mere removing of the fittings now in the Chancel, and the placing of them in the Nave, I will undertake it if any difficulty should be made about it.

I trust you will submit this statement of the Case to Dr Haggard in order that he may have the means of forming a correct opinion upon it, as his judgment must of necessity be governed by the statement of facts laid before him.

95. To Eccl. Com. from Hall, Kirk Ella, 30 April 1850 (EC)

Sir,

Referring to your letter, dated May 21st 1847—& addressed to me on the part of the Ecclesiastical Commissioners of England, I shall feel obliged, if you will inform me, how Mr Railton apportioned the amount at which he estimated my liability for the repairs of the Chancel of Stow Church between the two properties of which I was Lessee under the Prebendary.

Having lately sold Stow Park & its *Tithes*, I wish to know the sum I was to contribute towards the repairs in respect of the *latter* as distinct from the Rent Charge received in lieu of one third part of the Tithes of Stow, Sturton, Brandsby, & Normanby.

Note: The letter referred to is No. 31.

96. To Bp Kaye from Adn Stonehouse, 2 May [1850] (K)

My very good Lord

Atkinson as your Lordship said he would calcitrates violently at Dr Haggard—and demands that his statement should be laid before him—

I therefore send it with my statement—the facts of which as they regard the removal of the seats was taken from the Church Wardens statement to me.

97. To Hall from Eccl. Com. (Copy), 3 May 1850 (EC)

Sir

Stow Chancel

I have the honor to acknowledge the receipt of your letter of the 30th ultimo and in answer thereto to state that the sum of £200—at which your liability for the repair of this chancel was estimated by Mr Railton in respect of your Leases of Stow Park and its Tithes and of the Tithes of Stow, Sturton, Brandsby, and Normanby have not been apportioned between those Estates and that I am consequently unable to give the information you desire.

98. To Bp Kaye from Atkinson, 4 May 1850 (K)

My Lord

In the accompanying statement of facts connected with the funeral of the late W. Sargeant, I have refrained from making any observation on the Case, but I will now respectfully submit one remark upon it to your Lordship's consideration—It is this—that whereas the rubric before the Burial Office states that "the Priests and Clerks meeting the corpse at the entrance of the Churchyard, and going before it, either into the Church, or towards the grave . . ." it is left at the discretion of the Minister to go to the one or the other, as he may think fit—and that whichever way the Minister leads, it is the duty of the funeral procession to follow—that consequently when I led the way towards the grave, in this Case, and they instead of following me, turned another way to go into the Church, they disobeyed the order of the Church, and thus my accusers are the parties, and not I, who prevented the "burial service from being read" in the manner "set forth in the Book of

Common Prayer," and as such are deserving of your Lordship's censure. As Harrison the Churchwarden was actively directing and abetting this irregular proceeding, it is my intention to present him for so doing at the Archdeacon's Visitation.

Your Lordship will easily imagine the contrivances used to procure signatures to the memorial you have received. It has been carried about from house to house—some parties who refused to sign it have been threatened that mischief would be done them—others who refused have had their names put down—boys have signed it. And it has been taken to the Public House on a Saturday night to get the names of those who might be drinking there.

I was surprised this week to receive from the Archdeacon a copy of an opinion given by Dr Haggard as to the preparing of the Nave for Divine Service. The tenor of that opinion at once convinced me that Dr Haggard had been greatly misled as to the real facts of the Case. I had received a previous communication from Dr Stonehouse informing me that the Churchwardens had been to him and made some statements respecting the alterations I had formerly made, but he did not intimate that he was about to submit their statements to Dr Haggard. I wrote without delay to the Archdeacon correcting their gross misstatements, but unfortunately, he had not waited for my communication, but had sent that of the Churchwardens uncorrected to Dr Haggard. I wrote again to the Archdeacon another statement of the real facts of the Case, and requested him to submit it to Dr Haggard. He has informed me that he has done so—and I have requested him further to add my previous statement to the last in order to furnish Dr Haggard with a full view of the Case. I intend to present the Churchwardens at the Archdeacon's Visitation for not making the Nave ready for Divine Service.

Note: The accompanying statement recapitulated what Atkinson had written in No. 89.

The bishop, in his draft reply stated that it was his frank opinion that the option of preceding the corpse to the grave rather than to the church was given solely with reference to the danger of contagion during plague, and not with the aim of allowing the minister to make distinctions between his parishioners on the ground of religious opinion or moral character. This was the usual nineteenth century opinion, but Wheatly, writing in 1710, stated, "(if I rightly understand the words) if the corpse be to be buried within the church, he shall go directly thither; but if in the churchyard, he may first go to the grave . . ." (*A Rational Illustration of the Book of Common Prayer* . . ., ed. G. E. Corrie, Cambridge, 1858; p. 572.)

The Stow Burial Registers shows that Atkinson continued to refuse to bring the bodies of babies into church when they had received schizmatical, i.e. Methodist baptism, or, in one instance, had been baptised contumaciously outside the parish. Some 16 occasions are noted in the register.

Atkinson was not alone in making this stand. It was reported, for instance, that the vicar of Wrawby refused to have the bodies of dissenters brought into church (*Stamford Mercury*, 31 March 1854).

99. To Bp Kaye from Atkinson, 8 May 1850 (K)

My Lord

I received your Lordship's letter of the 6th Inst. last night on my return from the Visitation, and I must confess that I could not read it without some feelings of disappointment and pain, implying as it does—for so I fear I must understand it—a wish to discourage any attempt on the part of your Clergy to make the least differences in the administration of the rites of the Church in Cases even of the most flagrant wickedness.

I never supposed that the motive which actuated the framers of the rubric in question giving to the Minister the option of going towards the grave in the first instance, was that on which I acted in the Case of the late W. Sargeant—perhaps the reason your Lordship suggests may have been the true one—the only question with me has always been this—Does the rubric allow such an option to the Minister, and can he act upon it where he thinks proper without incurring the risk of a prosecution in the Ecclesiastical Court? This question I put to Dr Haggard and your Lordship conjointly at the Visitation dinner Table at Lincoln, the year I preached the Sermon. Dr Haggard's answer, in which your Lordship concurred, was most distinct in the affirmative.

I am aware that the prescribed course would be for me to present to your Lordship for correction and punishment such disobedient and criminous persons as the deceased in this Case, that you might, if need were, proceed to excommunicate them—but if the parochial Clergy abstain from pressing upon their Bishops the exercise of a discipline which they may be unwilling or unable to enforce, it surely is not too much to expect from the Bishops in return, that they will not discountenance their clergy in making it manifest to their Parishioners, in extreme Cases, so far as the letter of the law will enable or suffer them to do so, that the Church does not wish it to be supposed, as her enemies so often cast her in the teeth, that in her estimation there is one event to the evil and the good, and that to her the righteous and the wicked are both alike.

Note: This occasioned a stiff letter from the bishop: "My dear Sir" deleted in favour of "Reverend Sir". The deletions and interlinings make it impossible to know the terms of the rebuke, but the first paragraph is worth quoting: "You misapprehend my intention. I understood that the case that occurred at Stow was likely to be brought into the Ecclesiastical court; I wished, therefore, to prepare you for an objection which might be raised to your proceeding, and, in the present temper of the laity and their marked jealousy of anything which looks like an assumption of power on the part of the Clergy, was not unlikely to be raised."

100. To Bp Kaye from Adn Stonehouse, 9 May [1850] (K)

My very good Lord,

Accept my very best thanks for your kind consideration in sending Dr Haggard's opinion to the Burgersh Chantry—which arrived in tempore, just when it was wanted—

I got through the troublesome business of Stow tolerable well and I trust convinced Mr Atkinson that if he would engage in expensive Lawsuits about trifling things, he must do it at his own expense—

The presentation anent the burial I left to your Lordship—

Atkinson presented the Church Wardens—and the Church Wardens presented him concerning every presentable thing within the book of Articles—All this came to nothing

I exhorted the Church Wardens and Atkinson to peace—and they both promised to accede to any measures which I should propose to place the nave of the Church in a fit state for the celebration of divine Service—

I intend to propose to this effect—The Church Wardens to repair the great Western doors sufficiently to keep out the weather—and to make the floor sufficiently even for the seats to stand upon—this is nothing but a necessary repair which the Law would enforce at all times—Mr Atkinson having taken the seats out of the body of the church without any legal authority to replace them at his own expense—If it is necessary for the comfort of the parishioners during the time of divine service to brick up the great Western Arch of the Nave—when the roof is off the chancel. This expense must be defrayed out of the subscriptions—for repairing the Chancel—.

101. To Bp Kaye from Haggard, Doctors' Commons, 10 May 1850 (K)

My dear Lord

I return the Revd Mr Atkinson's letter to the Archdeacon, &, in reference to the Church, it does not enable me to think that the state of the Case is, legally, varied. Was your Lordship's prediction—with which the letter closes—fulfilled?

102. To Bp Kaye from Atkinson, 13 May 1850 (K)

My Lord

I trust your Lordship will permit me to offer a few words of Explanation and apology in reference to the letter which has given you so much offence. As that letter was founded upon a misconception of your Lordship's meaning, which I sincerely lament having fallen into, I ask your Lordship's forgiveness, and beg you to receive this my apology for whatever in that letter appeared unbecoming and undutiful.

With respect to the latter part of that letter at which your Lordship felt so much displeasure, I beg to assure you that the remarks in question were not intended to apply, in particular, to this Case, or to the administration of this Diocese. What I meant to say, however unhappily expressed, was merely to this effect—that as the Church certainly did not intend that her Ministers should be called upon to read the Burial Service over such characters as the deceased in this Case—and yet the direct mode of effecting that intention could not in these times be carried out by the rulers of the Church exercising the prescribed discipline—the Clergy might be allowed to avail themselves of the option given in the rubric, though not supposed to have been given with this view, to mark the Cases of such persons as had lived, and died without repentance, in extreme and notorious wickedness. I trust your Lordship has never had any cause, before now, to think that I felt or shewed less than due reverence for your person and office—and I trust also that in any future communication which it may be necessary for me to have with your Lordship I may never express myself in such a way as to incur your displeasure again.

I wish I could hope that in future I might have occasion to trouble your Lordship but seldom on matters connected with this Parish—but if such communications should prove more frequent than could be wished, I am sure your Lordship—even if you do not feel that you ought to overlook the offence I have given—will not suffer the remembrance of it to prevent you from rendering me such assistance as may be becoming my place to ask, and in your Lordship's power to give.

Note: The bishop in his draft reply confessed that he had been hurt by Atkinson's remarks but acknowledged himself completely satisfied by the explanation. He had not yet heard anything about the Sergeant Case coming before him.

103. Vestry Book

Stowe, May 25, 1850

A Vestry meeting was held in the church according to notice duly given by the churchwardens for the purpose of choosing a vestry clerk & for the purpose "of taking into consideration a letter from the Archdeacon wherein he recommends that we churchwardens are 'to repair the floor of the nave so as to make it sufficiently level to place the seats now in the chancel thereupon' &c."

Present: Messrs Harrison & Burton, churchwardens; Messrs. Ellis, Wilkinson, Credland, Palmer, Gelder, Walker, Hill, Taylor, Knowles, Robt. Harrison, Josh. Harrison &c.

Mr. Robt. Harrison proposed and Mr. W. Taylor seconded that William Ellis take the chair.

This being declared carried unanimously, Mr Taylor proposed and Robt. Harrison seconded "that Chas. G. Smith be Vestry Clerk for the year ensuing for the better management of business as it has been heretofore conducted in a disorderly manner". This motion having been put to the vestry the chairman declared it carried unanimously.

Mr. Gelder then moved that the letter of the Archdeacon be entered on the minutes of the meeting but it was not seconded therefore it was consequently lost sight of.

Henry Walker proposed and James Gelder seconded—"That as the Rev. George Atkinson minister of the parish had removed more than 12000 square feet of Plaster from off the walls of the interior part of the Church—had tore up and destroyed the family Pews and had converted them into long forms—had defaced the Pulpit, Reading Desk, &c and had removed them into the chancel—had removed a considerable portion of the stone pavement out of the floor of the nave and had taken it into the chancel also;—and that has he had also taken down and destroyed the singing and ringing galleries and the Royal arms which the Parishioners had but recently put up at a considerable expence;—and that has he had otherwise desecrated the sacred edifice without the consent of the Parish, and (according to the Archdeacon's letter) *without any legal authority*;—it is therefore the opinion of this vestry that he must replace them. That the Parishioners of Stow not wishing to avoid the responsibility of maintaining a parish church, but actuated by a sense of Justice to themselves, would humbly suggest to the Archdeacon the hardship under these circumstances of being put to any expense in repairing the interior of the church until the Rev. Gentleman has restored these dilapidations which he has so wantonly and illegally been the cause of. That the Parishioners of Stow are generally attached to the ordinances of the Church as by Law established when administered in a proper spirit, and they mourn the differences that exist between the Minister and themselves and they would rejoice to see *peace* again restored in their parish; yet they would wish that *peace* to be restored on fair and equitable terms only and not at the surrender of those privileges which they claim as their unalienable rights as freeborn Englishmen.

Signed in the vestry by

William Ellis — Chairman

George Burton, John Harrison — Churchwardens

William Wilkinson, James S. Gelder, Christopher Page, Joseph Harrison, Robert Harrison, William Hill, Henry Walker, Robert Credland, William Taylor — Parishioners

104. To Bp Kaye from Atkinson, 30 May 1850 (K)

My Lord

I was very happy to find on receiving your Lordship's last letter that my explanation of my former letter was satisfactory to you. I apprehend that your Lordship will have no further trouble about the Funeral Case. The Archdeacon at his late Visitation while noticing the presentment with respect to the funeral, and stating that this matter would be referred by him to your Lordship's decision, gave at the same time so clear an explanation of the rubric, that the Churchwardens and another chief agent in the agitation of this question, returned home quite discouraged and Crest-fallen, and so far as I can learn, very little is now said about the matter.

My object in writing to your Lordship now, is in reference to the Case of the election of Churchwardens. Howard my nominee, though named by me, in accordance with your Lordship's suggestion, to attend the Visitation did not attend—and has not been admitted to the Office—the other two attended and were admitted—and I am anxious that the Archdeacon should as was previously agreed upon, cite Howard with as little delay as possible, in order that further proceedings may be taken to try the right.

Your Lordship may have some idea of the utter disregard of truth shewn by these men, from the fact that when the Old Churchwardens went over to the Archdeacon at Owston, they declared to him that I had nominated no one at the Vestry meeting, and that in consequence the Parishioners had chosen Harrison and Burton. At the Visitation however they did not venture to repeat this statement to my face, but reluctantly acknowledged that I did nominate Howard.

105. To Bp Kaye from Adn Stonehouse, 4 June [1850] (K)

My very good Lord—

In answer to Mr Atkinsons letter I beg leave to say—that it is not the duty of the Archdeacon to cite Mr Howard—The party agrieved must apply to the Court of Queens Bench for a Mandamus to compel Howard to do his duty—So taught & ruled our Venerable Brother Archdeacon—Unless I am very much mistaken indeed—

When Mr Atkinson says his parishioners are chop-fallen he reckons his chickens before they are hatched—for he will receive today a letter which they sent to me—which will convince him of this great *fact*—and that when I speak of peace they make themselves ready for war". . . .

106. To Bp Kaye from Adn Bonney, Lincoln, 7 June 1850 (K)

My dear Lord

Whatever conversation I may have had with our friend Stonehouse respecting Church Wardens must have been to this effect. That the Archdeacon could not enter into the validity of a Church Wardens election—That the Archdeacon was a mere minister—in this case & whomsoever came before him, from a Parish, stating himself to be an Elected Churchwarden the Archdeacon must suffer to make the Declaration—otherwise the Court of Queen's Bench might send down a mandamus to the Archdeacon compelling him to let the Person qualify himself before him for the office.

The opinion of Dr Haggard I believe to be correct. And had the point been put to me in that shape by Stonehouse—I have no doubt I should have so expressed myself. Indeed until the Person have made the Declaration he is not in Law (I believe) a Church Warden, and the question of the Validity of his Election it would be fruitless to agitate, till that be done. . . .

107. To Bp Kaye from Atkinson, 12 June 1850 (K)

My Lord,

I wrote a letter to your Lordship. last Friday week I believe, with reference to Howard my nominee as Churchwarden being cited by the Archdeacon as was agreed upon before last Easter, and not having received any answer I begin to be apprehensive that the letter may not have reached your Lordship's hands.

I am happy to inform your Lordship that the National Society have promised a Grant of £25 towards the expense of fitting up our intended school. In the mean time we have begun to teach in the house which is the residence of the Mistress with prospects quite equal to what we expected. The Alterations in the future school have been begun.

108. To Bp Kaye from Adn Stonehouse, 12 June [1850] (K)

My very good Lord—

I feel it necessary to act with caution before I take any legal steps about citing Howard to take the declaration—owing to the *folly* of Mr Atkinson in going away to a funeral just at the moment of election—He says that he nominated Howard before he went—They deny it—and assert that Howard's name was never mentioned—Now this is the question—If Howard calcitrates against my citation on the ground that he never was appointed—How can Atkinson prove his assertion? I fear he had not one single friend there

Under this impression at the Visitation—I made Mr Atkinson deliver into court a protest—against the right of Election of both Church Wardens by the parish—in opposition to his nomination of Howard—This of course reserves his right to nominate next year—

I have Dr Haggards opinion He recommends after a long discussion pro & con—that the business should stand over until the next election—and I think as Mr Atkinson entered a protest—this business had better stand over until the next election—on account of the doubt that he ever nominated Howard at all—

Note: The bishop communicated the gist of this to Atkinson and requested him to correspond directly with the Archdeacon.

109. To Bp Kaye from Adn Stonehouse, 15 June [1850] (K)

My very good Lord

I rejoice greatly that you have requested Mr Atkinson to correspond directly with me about Howards citation, which I think he will not be very ready to do—

The fact is Atkinson in troubling your Lordship about this business has been practising a very artful Δοδγε—He thought you would know nothing about what had passed at the Visitation—and to what arrangement he then became a party—But what I am going to relate is a great fact—After hearing both parties at great length—anent this election of Church wardens & having great doubts in my mind whether Atkinson ever did nominate Howard I dehorted both parties from having any course to legal proceedings—and I proposed that Mr Atkinson should consent to deliver into the court a protest against the right of the Parishioners to elect both Church Wardens—so that his right to elect one next year might not suffer—He went out of court—drew up a protest—returned and delivered it to me—and I have carefully preserved it—

This is the arrangement which I think he did not wish your Lordship to know any thing about—and if he writes to me on the subject—I shall remind him of it—He shall not get off with "Non Mi recordo"; I shall calcitruo

I am going to London on Monday and if your Lordship should have occasion to write (which I hope will not be the case) direct No 38 Cross St Islington

I was perfectly aware that Dr Haggards opinion related only to last year—but I think it applies to this—it might be used as a precedent

110. Vestry Book

Stow, July 4, 1850.

A vestry meeting was held in the church this day according to notice duly given by the churchwardens for the purpose of selling a quantity of Lime, sand and mortar. Present;—The Churchwardens; Messrs. Rose, Ellis, Palmer &c.

The Sand was sold to Chas Smith for 2/6

A load of Lime and Mortar to Jonathan Rose 9/6

Also 2 loads of Lime at 11/3 per Ld to Josh Harrison 22/6

	George Burton	Chairman
Signed	John Harrison	Churchwardens
	William Ellis	
	Joseph Harrison	
	Robert Credland	

Note: These were presumably materials left over from the repairs noted by the Archdeacon (No. 149N). The following purchases were recorded in the churchwardens' accounts, 1849/50: 4½ tons of lime, 11½ tons of stone, 5 tons of sand. Mr Swift, the Gainsborough mason, was paid a total of £30.16.6 for stone, work, and lodging. Other expenses amounted to £8.13.6.

111. To Bp Kaye from Atkinson, 9 July 1850 (K)

My Lord

I beg to inform your Lordship that I received from Archdeacon Stonehouse a short time ago, a communication, enclosing an answer from the Churchwardens of Stow to his recommendation to them that they set about doing certain necessary things towards fitting up the Nave for Divine Service. This answer of theirs was of an evasive nature, and tantamount to a refusal to do anything whatever.

Under these circumstances the Archdeacon recommended that I should take the necessary steps to prepare the Nave for Service, and that the expense should be defrayed out of the subscriptions towards the restoration of the Chancel. He stated that the Archdeacon of Lincoln thought this would be the best course, in order to prevent further delay, and that unless something were done soon, the subscribers to the Restoration fund might begin to be dissatisfied.

I could not but feel the force of these reasons and having an opportunity of consulting Sir Charles Anderson shortly after receiving the Archdeacon's letter, I readily obtained his sanction, as a subscriber, to the course recommended. I intended, before beginning, to write and ask for your Lordships sanction also, but having some skilful and trusty men out of Yorkshire engaged upon the alterations of our school, and not doubting but that your Lordship would approve the plan of proceeding I set them to work the week before last first to remove the seats &c out of the Chancel into the Nave, and then to build a wall to stop up the Western Arch of the Tower. This was accomplished within the week, and all got ready for the Sunday.

I have, therefore, to ask your Lordship's sanction to this expense being placed to the account of the Restoration fund. It will not I think exceed £10, if it be so much.

As Mr Pearson had stated that it would be necessary to have the Chancel cleared before he should come down to make his final survey for the working plans, I wrote to him that we should be ready as last week, and accordingly he came down last Tuesday bringing with him an experienced Master Mason. In the course of the week they made a very minute and careful examination of the fabric of the Chancel from foundation to roof. The result was quite satisfactory as to its stability—and Mr Pearson thinks that the amount of our funds £1100 will be sufficient to cover the Cost of the proposed restoration, including the Salary of a Clerk of the works and the Architect's remuneration. The former will be about 2 guineas a week—his own Charges will be 5 per Cent. upon £1000, i.e. £50 and his travelling expenses (for five or six journeys which I suppose may average about £5 a journey) besides.

Mr Pearson does not recommend that the restoration of the Stone work should be done by *contract*—he is of the opinion that it may be executed better and at less cost by employing workmen under the direction of a Clerk of the works, whom it will be necessary to have on the spot to overlook the work in any Case. The roof had, perhaps, be better contracted for. I have a high opinion of Mr Pearson's uprightness, and of his ability as an Architect, and feel disposed, myself, to follow his advice as to this plan of proceeding—which would also have the advantage of saving time in beginning earlier than we could if contracts had to be entered into in the first instance—and should your Lordship agree with this view I will spare no pains, as being on the spot, to do all in my power to see the work brought to a satisfactory conclusion.

It will be necessary, now, to inform the Ecclesiastical Commissioners and Mr Hall that we are prepared to begin the restoration of the Chancel, and to settle with them about the mode of paying their respective proportions, that of the former being £300, Mr Hall's £200. I will write to Mr Hall on the subject and perhaps your Lordship will communicate with the Ecclesiastical Commissioners. If it could be so arranged the simplest way, perhaps, would be to have these sums paid to the account of the Restoration fund at Messrs Smith, Ellison & Co.

The next thing would be settle in what manner that fund is to be drawn upon to meet the Current Expenses for materials wages &c. If your Lordship thought it would not occasion you too much trouble, that the fund should stand in your name at the Bank, and payments be made by cheques signed by your Lordship to myself on account from time [to time], this would be a ready and satisfactory way—or otherwise some other subscriber might be joined with myself, and payments be made by the Bank on our joint application. In this Case it would be necessary to name some subscriber who is in the neighbourhood, and the subscribers most conveniently situated are Mr George Hutton and Sir Charles Anderson. Of the two the former is nearest, and he has property in the parish.

I will in any Case keep an account of all disbursements as well as receipts in order both to check the Clerk of the works or Contractor, and to be able to furnish the subscribers with a clear statement of the accounts when the work is completed.

All the Subscribers to whom I sent circulars have paid their subscriptions except Lord Yarborough and Mr Chaplin and I will write to them today. My late father's subscription will be paid on my sending for it. As some money must be retained to pay the Architect, and I shall shortly have to meet the Expense of the works at our National School which will be finished in about a fortnight, it will be convenient to myself to let a part of my subscription stand over to meet Mr Pearson's charges, and I will be responsible to him for their payment.

I have now mentioned so far as I can recollect all material points—

P.S. Since my letter was written I have heard of some Church meeting to be held at Lincoln on Thursday. I suppose it will be the meeting of the S.P.G. and will endeavour to attend—when perhaps your Lordship if present can spare me a few minutes conversation on the subject of this letter, and the trouble of writing be saved.

Note: The Bishop in his draft reply approved of all that had been done, but as he was likely to be absent frequently over the next few months thought it better that Atkinson and Mr George Hutton should jointly draw upon the Bank for the necessary sums. But see No. 126.

112. To Eccl. Com. from Bp Kaye, Riseholm, 12 July 1850 (EC)

My dear Sir,

The Commissioners have promised, in their capacity of Impropriators, to contribute £300 towards the reparation of the Chancel of Stow Church. The Repairs are now about to be commenced. May I therefore request you to obtain an Order for the payment of the money? It may be paid to Messrs Smith Payne & Smith, for Messrs Smith Ellison Ltd of Lincoln, to be placed to the account of the Stow Restoration Fund.

113. To Bp Kaye from Eccl. Com., 15 July 1850 (Copy) (EC)

My Lord

I have the honor to acknowledge the receipt of your Lordship's letter of the 12th Inst respecting the proposed reparation of the chancel of Stow Church with reference to which I beg leave to explain that the Ecclesiastical Commissioners for England have at present only agreed to defray their just proportion of the cost of the necessary works—upon the general terms of a Report made by Mr Railton three years ago.

The sum of £300 was merely an estimate and before any specific grant can be made it will be necessary that the Commissioners should see the plans, specification, and estimate, for the works now contemplated, and with these perhaps your Lordship will cause me to be supplied.

114. To Bp Kaye from Atkinson, 22 July 1850 (K)

My Lord

I have written to Mr Pearson requesting him to furnish Mr Chalk with whatever information he may require as to the proposed works.

I certainly have been under the impression ever since I received Mr Chalk's letter accompanying a Copy of Mr Railton's report that the Ecclesiastical Commissioners had agreed to pay the £300 which Mr Railton's report assigned as their share—just as Mr Hall agreed to pay the £200 assigned to him. Mr Chalk's letter, dated 21st May 1847 is thus worded.

"I am directed by the Ecclesiastical Commissioners for England to forward to you a Copy of Mr Railton's report on The Chancel of Stow Church and to inform you that they are ready to contribute their share of the expense accordingly."

I trust that Mr Pearson will be able to give such information and explanations to Mr Chalk that further delay may be avoided, as the summer is now so far advanced, and it would be a disadvantage to have the work begin nearer winter.

Note: See No. 29.

115. To Bp Kaye from Atkinson, 23 July 1850 (K)

My Lord,

By this day's post I have received a letter from Mr Hall informing me that he has paid to Messrs Smith Ellison & Co. his proportion of the Estimate for the substantial repairs of the Chancel, as Lessee, £200, and also his subscription of £20.

I believe I did not mention to your Lordship in my last letter that I have had kind letters from Lord Yarborough and Mr Chaplin, stating that their subscriptions should be immediately paid.

Mr Chaplin adds that the reason of his subscription not being paid at the time mentioned in the Circular of February last—was that observing from the papers the disposition shewn by the dissenting portion of the parishioners to evade their just liabilities, he was unwilling that any money of his should go to save theirs—and he is very express in his stipulation that no part of it shall be so employed.

I wrote in reply to inform him what we are proposing to do at present, and to assure him that his wishes will be strictly observed.

116. To Bp Kaye from Charles G. Smith, Stow, 4 Aug. 1850 (K)

My Lord,—

Knowing that your lordship is always anxious to patronize the Historical and Topographical accounts of places in your own Diocese,—and especially those whose antiquity is known to be a matter of fact,—I humbly solicit your Lordship's name as a subscriber to a "Topographical & Historical Account of Stow, The Ancient Sidnacester," situate in your own Bishopric, and since the seat of the venerated Bishops of Lindis or Lindsey, which I shall immediately publish on obtaining a sufficient number of subscribers to indemnify me from Loss.

May it please your Lordship also to favour me with a simple list of the Incumbents of Stow with their date of presentation, and by whom, as far back as your Lordship can ascertain, for I find it would give my volume a peculiar illustration.

117. To Bp Kaye from Atkinson, 7 Aug. 1850 (K)

My Lord,

In reply to your Lordship's enquiry respecting the individual who has solicited your patronage of his intended account of Stow, I beg to state that he is altogether unqualified for such an undertaking.

He is a person of most imperfect education—so much indeed as to be unable even to write English correctly, and he knows nothing of Latin, so that he can refer to none but the most common-place sources of information.

The person is a young man about 21 years of age who lives upon his father a poor shopkeeper and teaches a small school at Sturton in this Parish. He is the person who supplies the Stamford Mercury and the Lincolnshire Times Newspapers with the mis-statements which have appeared in them about the restoration of the Church, and other matters connected with the Church in this Parish, and has been all along a very active agent of the party who are most opposed to the Church.

118. To Bp Kaye from Atkinson, 12 Aug. 1850 (K)

My Lord

In the possible event of your Lordship not having heard further from Mr Chalk as to the business of the Stow Chancel, I beg leave to state that Mr Pearson has seen Mr Chalk, and he is to lay the plans and other documents before the Board at a meeting which is to be held on Thursday next. Mr Pearson apprehends that the whole business will have to be gone through afresh, as Mr Chalk does not seem to think anything settled by what took place on Mr Railton's survey in 1847.

119. To Eccl. Com. from Pearson, 13 Aug. 1850 (EC)

Memorandum of the Work required to be done in restoring the Chancel of St: Mary's Stow, Lincolnshire—

The present roof to be taken off and entirely reinstated, the old lead to be reused making good with new—

The upper part of the side walls to be taken down to the red line marked on the Elevation and the East End down to the window Sill. To restore a Norman East window; the present being a *Very* dilapidated early decorated one and of poor character—

To replace all the columns which have been distroyed of the arcade round the East End and sides of the chancel inside, as well as nearly all the bases and some caps—To restore in many places the sculptured arches and the ashlar work of the Walls—

The Side or lower windows and the clerestory windows require also reparation in many parts.—

The Stone bench round the chancel on which the bases of the small columns rest requires to be entirely restored and the whole floor and steps across it—

The Stone Vault also requires to be restored according to its original form now clearly shewn and with groined ribs similar to those which have been discovered built up in the upper part of the Walls—

The plinth moldings all round the Walls and part of the Wall above and below them on the outside surface requires to be renewed this dilapidation being caused by large accumulations of earth resting against it—

General repairs are also required to the Walls and stone work inside and out, that on the inside requiring also to be entirely freed from Whitewash and color—that on the outside careful pointing

The entire reglazing of the windows and gutters & spouts to carry off the water & drains also—

Estimated cost of the Whole of these works exclusive of Commission & superintendance

1350 £

John L Pearson
Architect

2 Delahay St.
Westminster

Six Plans received with this Memorandum; vizt—

1. Ground Plan.
2. East End—Elevation.
3. West End—Elevation.
4. South Side—Elevation.
5. Chancel and Nave—
   Transverse Sections.
6. Longitudinal Section.

[Above in another hand]

120. To Bp Kaye from Atkinson, Malham, 22 Aug. 1850 (K)

My Lord,

Your Lordship's letter of the 17th Inst. has been forwarded after me to this place, and I beg to thank your Lordship for this communication.

I considered it certain, as a matter of course, that your Lordship would have official information from Mr Chalk, without delay, of the result of Thursday's meeting, or I should have written to you on Monday morning before leaving Stow, to state that I had heard *indirectly*, that the Grant of £300 made in 1847, was confirmed and that the Money will be paid from time to time as the Architect shall certify the completion of such portions of the repair as the Ecclesiastical Commissioners are liable for.

I cannot quite see Mr Chalk's motive—for to him I must attribute it—in wishing to ignore or repudiate what everyone who sees the documents your

Lordship refers to must consider, "the distinct pledge" to pay £300 in 1847. I suspect however that Mr Chalk had a notion that the Commissioners might get off for a less sum if the question were re-opened. When Mr Pearson first saw him on the subject, he intimated that the whole business would have to begin afresh, but after he had seen the plans and specifications, and had perhaps taken the opinion of Mr Ferrey, who is now, I learn, the Commissioners' Architect, and who thought that the £300 was too little, he appeared, as Mr Pearson informs me, only too anxious to adhere to the arrangement of 1847.

When I left Stow I wished to be absent two Sundays, but I have written to Mr Pearson to say that I will return earlier rather than delay the commencement of the repair at this season of the year.

121. To Atkinson from Eccl. Com. (Copy) 24 Aug. 1850 (EC)

Dear Sir

Stow Chancel

The plans of the proposed restoration of Stow Church having been submitted to the Ecclesiastical Commissioners for England have been approved by them, and I am directed to acquaint you that upon the receipt from time to time of certificates from the Architect employed, of the amount due for the execution of works for which the Tithe owners are *strictly liable*, the Commissioners will make payments on account of the Commissioners' promised grant of £300 to the extent of three fifths of the amounts so certified—it being as you will see assumed that the remaining two fifths will in like manner be paid by the other Tithe Owner.

I have sent a copy of this letter to the Bishop of Lincoln and also to Mr Pearson the Architect, to whom I have returned the plans.

Note: Minute of General Meeting, 22 August 1850, refers.

122. To Pearson from Eccl. Com. (Copy), 24 Aug. 1850 (EC)

Sir

Stow Chancel

I return herewith your plans for the intended restoration of this Church which have been approved by the Ecclesiastical Commissioners for England, and I also forward a copy of a letter which I have written to the Incumbent with reference to the payment of the Commissioners' grant towards the Chancel.

You will have the kindness to send with each certificate a statement of the works to which it relates.

123. To Eccl. Com. from Bp Kaye, Henbury House, Bristol, 28 Aug. 1850 (EC)

My dear Sir,

I have received your Letter, inclosing a Copy of that which you have written to Mr Atkinson on the subject of Stow Chancel. I believe that Mr Hall, the Lessee of the Stow Prebendal Estate, has already paid £200, his share of the expense; and I doubt whether the Commissioners would have been gainers, if they had not abided by Mr Railton's Estimate. . . .

124. To Bp Kaye from Charles G. Smith, Stowe, 31 Aug. 1850 (K)

My Lord,—

It is now more than a month since I wrote to your Lordship, humbly soliciting a list of the Incumbents, Archdeacons, and Prebends of Stow from the earliest times with the names of their presentors; but to this day I have never received an answer either assenting or dissenting. Perhaps your Lordship did not receive my letter, but should you receive this, have the kindness to answer it forthwith.

Note: The bishop in his draft reply desired Mr Smith to apply to the Diocesan Registrar for the lists he required.

125. To Bp Kaye from Atkinson, 30 Sept. 1850 (K)

My Lord,

As I shall have occasion to draw upon the Stow Church Restoration Fund this week for money to pay wages and for other expenses, I shall feel obliged, in case your Lordship should not already have acquainted Messrs Elison &

Co with the proposed arrangement, if you will let them know that the Fund in their hands will be drawn upon from time to time by cheques signed by Mr G. Hutton and myself jointly or severally. As Mr Hutton is now at the sea side, I cannot obtain his signature this week, and it may sometimes happen that one or other of us may be absent, so that it will be convenient that one name should be sufficient.

As we are nearest to Gainsborough the cheques will generally be presented there, and when I go over to Gainsborough this week, I will shew Mr Wilkinson the Manager your Lordship's former letter in which this arrangement is approved.

Some progress has been made with the repair of the foundations and I will report further to your Lordship from time to time.

126. To Bp Kaye from James Inman, Lincoln, 4 Oct. 1850 (K)

My Lord

I have had the honor to receive your Lordships favor & as directed therein I will take care that cheques drawn by Mr George Hutton or by the Revd James Atkinson on account of the "Stow Church Restoration Fund" shall be paid either here or at Gainsborough. [*sic*]

127. To Bp Kaye from Adn Stonehouse, 9 Nov. [1850] (K)

My very good Lord,

. . . . .

Things are progressing well anent Stow Church—I will send you the letters I have received by the time you return to Riseholme

128. To Bp Kaye from Atkinson, 9 Dec. 1850 (K2)

My Lord,

The accompanying paper is a copy of a notice which appeared on the Door of Stow Church yesterday, and I think it right that your Lordship should be acquainted with the intended proceeding to which it refers.

There can be no doubt, I conceive, that a "public meeting" for such a purpose cannot legally be held in *the Church*, and I as the Incumbent having the legal custody of the Church, feel it my duty to object to this meeting taking place within it, the more especially at such a late hour, and consisting of such a profane rabble as I know will compose this assembly. If your Lordship concurs with me in this view, I should feel greatly obliged if you would signify to the parties whose names are attached to the notice—the acting Churchwardens—or to Mr Howard my nominee who has now made the declaration of office, that the proposed meeting cannot legally be held in the Church. I ask this because I am sure that the parties to this proceeding would disregard any expression of opinion from myself on the subject.

I suppose from a knowledge of the party in the Parish, who are the chief movers in this matter that a charge may eventually be made of "Romanizing practices" in my Church. Should such a charge or any other into which your Lordship may deem it necessary to enquire, be laid before you, I shall, as in duty bound, cheerfully make answer to it—but I must, in conscience, object to this mischievous and unauthorised interference of the "National Club" between the Clergy and their Parishioners—which is, I presume, only a prelude to the further assumption over us of a power which belongs only to our Bishops.

I will only add that the most active promoter of the intended meeting is an avowed infidel.

129. To Bp Kaye from Atkinson, 10 Dec. 1850 (K2)

My Lord,

I wrote to your Lordship yesterday, a letter directed to Riseholme, containing a copy of a Notice of a Meeting to be held in the Church at Stow on Thursday Evening next, requesting that you would state your opinion whether such a meeting could legally take place in *the Church*.

Having since heard from Mr Richter who is here that your Lordship was then in London, and would probably leave Town for Riseholme today, I fear my letter may cross you, and I therefore send this note enclosing another Copy of the Notice which is now on the Church Door—in order that your Lordship's answer may be received in time, in the event of the former letter having missed you.

P.S. A letter put into the Post Office at Lincoln on Wednesday would reach Stow the next morning.

129A.

Copy.

We the undersigned Churchwardens of the Parish of Stow have received a note enclosing copies of suggestions from the Secretary of the Committee of the National Club, on the best mode of putting a stop to Romanizing practices within the Church of England.

They the Committee request that we take the suggestions into our immediate consideration and communicate the result to them as soon as possible.

We therefore hereby give notice that a public meeting of the Inhabitants of this Parish will be held in the Church at Stow on Thursday Evening next the 12th Inst. at 6 OClock.

(Signed) John Harrison } Churchwardens.
George Burton }

Note: The bishop's draft reply, dated 11 December, stated that there could be no doubt of the illegality of holding such a meeting in the church. He advised sending for Mr Howard (the legal churchwarden) to tell him that all parties concerned with the meeting would render themselves liable to the penalties of the law. The bishop discounted the likelihood of any charges of Romanizing practices being brought upon Atkinson; he knew very little about the National Club.

130. To Bp Kaye from Atkinson, 17 Dec. 1850 (K2)

My Lord,

In returning my sincere thanks for your Lordship's kind letter of the 11th Inst. I have also the satisfaction of stating that the meeting proved a complete failure, and instead of furthering the views of the Agitators has covered them with ridicule and confusion.

In accordance with your Lordship's suggestion I sent for Mr Howard, who communicated the necessary instructions to the Parish Clerk that he might inform the promoters of the meeting that it could not legally be held in the Church—Mr Howard himself being unwilling to come into direct contact with the parties.

It appears that they had previously expressed their fears that they might not be permitted to meet in the Church—and they assembled quietly in the Old Schoolroom.

Mr Spencer, a Quaker, was the only person of consequence in the Parish who was present, and the small attendance did not include a single Churchman. No one could be prevailed on to take the Chair, and the meeting eventually broke up without having done anything whatever.

Your Lordship did me but justice in believing that no charge of "Romanizing Practices" could be justly brought against me. I was well assured however that it was the object of the promoters of this meeting to get up such a charge, but when challenged at the meeting, by some of the well-affected working people who had gone in from curiosity, to specify anything of the kind in our service they were silent.

I had hoped er'e this, to have sent to your Lordship a proper report from Mr Pearson as to the progress of the works at our Chancel, but his coming has been prevented by illness. The report shall be sent when the Architect has been, and in the mean time I am glad to say that the Restoration is going on steadily, and I think on the whole in a very satisfactory manner. The weather has been most propitious.

131. To Eccl. Com. from Atkinson, 29 Jan. 1851 (EC)

Dear Sir,

I enclose herewith the Certificate of Mr Pearson, our Architect, in regard to our Chancel Repairs, in accordance with the directions contained in your Letter as to the mode of payment.

Messrs Smith, Ellison &Co, Bankers Lincoln are the Treasurers to the "Stow Church Restoration Fund", and if you will pay the Amount certified for, to that account at Messrs Smiths, Payne & Smiths, in London or if more convenient, to myself, or to Messrs Smith, Ellison &Co Lincoln, you will oblige

131A.

St:Mary's Stow—Lincolnshire
No. 1.

2 Delahay St Westminster
January 20th 1851.

I hereby beg to certify that the *substantial repairs* to the Chancel of this Church are now going on & that considerable progress has been made & work done to the

£200.0.0 Value of 300£s, 200£ of which I conceive to be a proportion to be paid by the Ecclesiastical Commissioners of England

John. L. Pearson.

James J Chalk Esqre
Assistant Secretary.

132. To Pearson from Eccl. Com. (Copy), 11 Feb. [1851] (EC)

Sir

Stow Church

With reference to a certificate signed by you respecting the progress of the repair of the Chancel of this Church which has been forwarded to me by the Revd G. Atkinson, I beg leave to call your attention to a communication which on the 24th August 1850 I addressed to you and to request that you will furnish me with an amended certificate in accordance with it.

Note: See No. 122.

133. To Eccl. Com. from Pearson, 2 Delahay St, 18 Feb. 1851

Sir,

My absence in the country has prevented me before this sending you the enclosed which I trust is what you require.

133A.

St Mary's, Stow, Lincolnshire

2 Delahay Street
February 18th 1851

No 1

I have to certify that the repairs and restorations of the Chancel of this Church are now going on, and that considerable progress has been made, and work done to the value of four hundred and fifty pounds, three hundred and fifty pounds of which sum I consider has been expended upon the substantial repairs.

Viz: In taking up and rebuilding the foundation walls to the depth of two feet all round the Chancel, which from the absence of Drains, and the drip of the roofs had become seriously impaired;—the refacing of the Walls to the average height of four feet above the ground line, this portion of them having been destroyed by an accumulation of soil and damp against them—The rebuilding and renewing of the flat buttresses, which had become detached, and were decayed, and in renewing and replacing the base mouldings.

Throughout the chancel, on the inside and out, repairs have been made to the walls where fractures and decay existed, the East Gable has been taken down in consequence of its imperfect state from fractures and other causes, and is now partly rebuilt, and the new East window incerted.

The dilapidated stone bench all round the inside, and the ruined columns, bases, and arches have been renewed and repaired.

A portion also of the Timber and Boarding for the new roof is on the site, as also stone and other materials for more advanced works.

John L Pearson.

134. To Eccl. Com. from Atkinson, 19 Feb. 1851 (EC)

Dear Sir,

Stow Chancel

Not having had an opportunity of calling at Messrs Smith, Ellison &Co's bank at Lincoln since I sent you Mr Pearson's certificate for £200 of the proportion to be paid by the Ecclesiastical Commissioners towards the Repairs of Stow Chancel, I am not aware whether the Amount certified for has been paid into the Treasurers' hands. Will you have the kindness to inform me? And in the Event of the money not having been paid, will you have the goodness to cause this to be done at your earliest convenience. My letter to you was dated January 29.

135. To Atkinson from Eccl. Com. (Copy), 24 Feb. 1851 (EC)

Dear Sir

Stow Chancel

I duly received your communication of the 29th ultimo but as Mr Pearson's certificate which you sent did not accord with the instructions which I gave to him on the 24th August last, I referred it to him for amendment and having now received his answer to my application, I will now submit the case to the Commissioners without delay.

136. To Ewan Christian from Eccl. Com. (Copy), 4 March 1851 (EC)

Dear Sir

Stow Chancel.

Before the Commissioners make any payment in this case they are desirous that you should report as to whether the works now in progress are carried on in such a manner as to effect the object which it appears by the accompanying file of papers, the Commissioners had in view in contributing towards them.

The Incumbent is the Revd George Atkinson, Stow, whom I have requested to render you any assistance.

Note: Minute of Estate Committee, 26 February 1851, refers.

137. To Atkinson from Eccl. Com. (Copy), 4 March 1851 (EC)

Sir

I have by direction of the Ecclesiastical Commissioners for England instructed Mr Ewan Christian of Bloomsbury Square, London, to inspect the works now in course of progress in the Chancel of Stow Church and to report to them on the subject—You will I doubt not be kind enough to procure for his inspection the plans & specifications which were approved by this Board.

Mr Christian will I believe be with you next week.

138. To Eccl. Com. from Atkinson, 5 March 1851 (EC)

Sir,

I have received your Letter of yesterday's date stating that Mr Christian of London is to inspect the works going on in our Chancel. I have written by this Post to Mr Pearson, in whose possession the plans and specifications are, to request that he will shew them to Mr Christian. I should suppose he had better see them before he comes down from London. Will you arrange for this? Mr Pearson's address is 2 Delahay Street Westminster.

I trust that as much more than Mr Pearson has certified for has been expended in substantial and necessary repairs—the Cost of which has been already paid out of the Subscriptions raised in the County and from the Proportion paid by Mr Hall, no unnecessary delay will take place in regard to the payment of the proportion due from the Ecclesiastical Commissioners.

I shall be glad to afford Mr Christian every facility for inspecting the works, and I doubt not that his report will certify that they are well done. They have not been done by contract, and so far from anything like slighting or insufficient work being the Case, my great anxiety and labour has been to prevent a wasteful expenditure of our funds in overmuch care and exactness.

Note: The secretary to the Commissioners sent a copy of this letter to Mr Ewan Christian.

139. To Eccl. Com. from Ewan Christian, 6 Bloomsbury Square, 19 March 1851 (EC)

Dear Sir,

Stow Chancel

Having in compliance with the instructions received from you dated the 4th March last, surveyed the Chancel of Stow Church; I beg now to report to you thereon.

The works necessary for the repair of this structure have up to the present time been carefully executed.

A considerable part of the East wall has been rebuilt and the base together with the buttresses, and other essential portions of the side walls both internal and external as high as the capitals of the pillars, have been restored with new Masonry where necessary.

The large dilapidated East window has been removed, and two new ones harmonizing with similar features in the side walls, have been introduced instead of it.

With very little exception all the work that has been done hitherto has been strictly of the nature of substantial repairs, no new ornamental stonework having been introduced except in the East windows mouldings &c.

There yet remains to be done, the completion of the East wall; the repairs or partial rebuilding of the North and South walls above the level of the capitals of the pillars, and the renewal of the Roof. It is also intended to restore the groined ceiling—with regard to the latter, I think it right to say, as it is a matter which will affect the stability of the structure, that I have doubts in my own mind whether this part of the work can be soundly and satisfactorily executed on the construction proposed as explained to me on the spot; and I think that it is a question worthy of the most careful consideration of the Architect whether such construction may not be amended.

With regard to the cost that has been already incurred in the works of reparation; I may report, that there is every evidence of careful supervision having been exercised during the progress of them; that I have seen Mr Atkinson's account book, and have examined his statements; and I find that exclusive of the cost incurred in the preparation of work for the groined ceiling, exclusive also of Clerk of works salary (£56) the sum of £444 has been expended in labour performed, materials used or on the ground, and carriage of the same to the site; and as the value of the materials upon the ground not yet used is probably about £20, it follows that £424 is the value of the work now actually executed in the repair of the building—I return you the several papers relating to the business and— [&c., &c.]

140. To Atkinson from Eccl. Com., 26 March 1851 (EC)

Sir

Stow Chancel.

The works in progress in the repair of this Chancel having been surveyed by the Architect employed by the Ecclesiastical Commissioners for England, I am directed to acquaint you that in his report he states that he doubts whether the groined ceiling can be soundly and satisfactorily executed on the construction proposed, as explained to him on the spot.

As this point materially affects the stability of the structure, the Commissioners would suggest that the attention of the Architect employed on the building should be directed to the consideration of whether such construction may not be amended.

141. To Eccl. Com. from Atkinson, 28 March 1851 (EC)

Sir,

Stow Chancel

I have to acknowledge the receipt of your letter of the 26th Inst. in which you state that Mr Christian in his report to the Ecclesiastical Commissioners for England, respecting this Chancel expresses a doubt whether the groined ceiling can be soundly and satisfactorily executed on the construction proposed.

It is obviously a matter of the highest moment that the stability of this part of the works should be placed beyond reasonable doubt, and I have written to Mr Pearson our Architect to call his particular attention to the subject.

In justice, however, to Mr Pearson I must state that I know this point has already received his most attentive and anxious consideration during several visits of inspection to the Church; and that in June last, particularly, when we were making arrangements for commencing the restoration, he came down from London on purpose to make a full and final investigation of this matter. On that occasion he brought with him from London an experienced Master Mason one who has had as much practice in the construction of groined roofs, as any man perhaps of the present day, and while here he entirely agreed with Mr Pearson that the groining might be constructed on the plan proposed by him with perfect safety.

It so happens that the same individual is now here superintending the construction of the springing of the vaulting on the plan proposed by Mr Pearson. Before he was aware of Mr Christian's doubts he several times incidentally remarked that the vaulting would be on this construction very strong. When I mentioned Mr Christian's report, he said there was no cause for fear, for that there would be strength to carry a groining three times the weight of that intended to be put up.

Mr Ashton will be prepared on his return to London, in conjunction with Mr Pearson to give any explanation which may be desired.

I should feel obliged if you would furnish me with a copy of Mr Christian's report entire.

142. To Eccl. Com. from Atkinson, 28 March 1851 (EC)

Sir,

Stow Chancel

I must beg leave to recal your attention to the request I made in a former letter that the sum of £200 certified by Mr Pearson as due from the Ecclesiastical Commissioners for substantial repairs to this Chancel executed and paid for, might be paid without any unecessary delay.

I must confess my inability to conceive why this payment, called for two months ago, should still be withheld. The question which has been raised about the construction of the vaulting can be no reason for further deferring the payment.

The works have now been in progress 7 months—nearly the whole amount expended has been on account of substantial and necessary repairs—and the Cost of these has been defrayed out of the funds furnished by subscription and from the proportion of the Estimate contributed by Mr Hall, the Prebendary's Lessee, while not a shilling has yet been received from the Ecclesiastical Commissioners.

Having been intrusted, as the resident Incumbent, with the charge of looking to the proper application of the money subscribed towards restorations other than those of a strictly legal and necessary kind, I could only permit the cost of these latter to be defrayed in any degree from the subscribed funds as a temporary measure of convenience, to be repaid as the Architect, should, according to your instructions in August last, give his certificate to enable us to receive the Amount due from the Ecclesiastical Commissioners.

I feel myself now in a very unpleasant position in respect to these funds, and I trust the Board will at once order payment of the money, as I cannot venture any longer on my own responsibility to carry on the works without explaining these financial matters to the Bishop and the Lord Lieutenant under whose patronage this restoration was commenced.

143. To Atkinson from Eccl. Com. (Copy), 5 April 1851 (EC)

Sir,

Stow Chancel

I have submitted to the Ecclesiastical Commissioners for England your letters of the 28th ultimo and am directed to explain to you that when the plans were submitted to and approved by them, it had not been determined that the groining should be executed, but being now informed, not only that it is to be done, but that doubts are entertained by their Architect as to the principle of construction, the Commissioners feel it to be incumbent on them to inquire fully into the matter, for it must be borne in mind, that should any accident occur by reason of any defect in this respect, not only would the money expended in the restoration have been thrown away, but the Commissioners might as Tithe Owners be called upon to rebuild a considerable portion of the edifice.

Under these circumstances the Commissioners consider that they would not be justified in making any payment until all doubts shall have been set at rest, and to this end I am to request that you will instruct Mr Pearson to forward the plans and specification of the groining to me in order that they may be submitted to Mr Christian.

Note: Minute of Estates Committee, 2 April 1851, refers.

144. To Eccl. Com. from Atkinson, 14 April 1851 (EC)

Sir

Stow Chancel

In compliance with the request contained in your letter of the 5th Instant, I enclose the plan of the groining, together with a paper of Notes—on the other half of this sheet—by the Clerk of the works on the spot, which will shew the manner in which the springers have been put in so far as this part of the work has proceeded. Two sets of these main groins have been completed, viz, those on the Eastermost pair of vaulting piers—the two westermost have not yet been commenced.

It must be obvious that no other person can have so great an interest in the stability of the structure as myself who may have to minister in this Chancel—and I trust that from this fuller explanation Mr Christian will see reason to agree with Mr Pearson as to the safety of the construction: indeed, except as to the taking down of the Clerestory windows, it is exactly the same plan as was suggested by Mr Christian when here; for the whole of the upper portion of the wall will have been rebuilt with the exception of just the windows, and a small portion of the wall on each side of them, no more than was necessary to keep them up.

I shall not on the present occasion enter into any remarks on the explanation contained in your letter further than to observe that it was distinctly understood between Mr Pearson and myself before the plans were submitted to the Ecclesiastical Commissioners that the groining was to form part of the restoration: and it will appear from the enclosed tracing of the interior taken from the plans approved by the board, as well as from the enclosed Copy of the memorandum sent in with the plans that the statement as to the groining not being then determined on must be founded in mistake.

Note: The memorandum referred to in the last paragraph was dated 13 August 1850 and is No. 119.

144A. (Copy)

Notes on the actual construction of the Springing of the Groining—

abutment The thickness of the wall at the back of the Transverse Arches on the level of the highest springers is 7 Ft and the width along the wall of the new work is about the same increasing in width upwards according to the red lines as shewn on the elevation. The depth of work shewn on the plan as being in *cement* cement (A) is less than what has been actually so executed, the cemented work through the thickness of the wall being from 2 ft 9 in to 3 ft in depth. In addition to the strength given *Iron ties* by the cement a course of hoop iron ties 6 in or 7 in apart has been laid across the wall on the top of the old work the old work being found in a very sound state.

Another similar course of ties on the top of the cemented work, and a third on the top of the springers, these last like the others being laid in cement to prevent their corroding.

The precaution was further taken to insert dowels in the following manner

dowels 1st the Abacus was dowelled to the cap of the main vaulting pier, then the first springer which consisted of one solid stone with the two diagonal ribs and the transverse rib all worked upon it was dowelled to the abacus each succeeding course of springers (which consisted of two stones only, one with the transverse and one diagonal rib, the other with the remaining diagonal only, placed alternately on the east and west side so as to cross joint and bond) being dowelled into the course below with four strong hard stone dowels these as well as the beds being run in with Portland Cement.

Stow April 14th 1851
Joseph Emery
Clerk of Works

N.B. in setting the springers of the first groin as above detailed the Clerk of the works had the assistance of Mr Ashton, an experienced Master-Mason from London, sent down by Mr Pearson for this purpose. *G. A.*

145. To Ewan Christian from Eccl. Com., 16 April 1851 (EC)

Dear Sir

Stow Chancel

I forward herewith a file containing some correspondence which has taken place between Mr Atkinson and myself since the date of your Report of 19th March upon this case, and I have to request that you will consider the papers and also the enclosed plans with reference to the views expressed in your Report respecting the security of the roof as proposed to be reconstructed and that you will report further to the Ecclesiastical Commissioners on the subject.

You may perhaps find it convenient to communicate with Mr Pearson of Delahay Street, Westminster, who is the Architect employed in the superintendence of the works.

146. Vestry Book

Stow, April the 21, 1851.

A vestry meeting was held in the church according to notice duly given "for the purpose of electing Churchwardens and a Vestry Clerk for the year ensuing." Present the Rev. G. Atkinson in the chair, the churchwardens (Messrs Harrison and Burton) and the following parishioners viz Messrs. Spink, Taylor, Marshall, Walker, Josh. Harrison, Gilbert, Ellis, T. Spencer, Jas Spencer, Jollands, Coultas, Howard senr., &c.

Moved by William Ellis and seconded by Henry Walker that John Harrison and Robert Gilbert be the churchwardens for the ensuing year.

It having been moved by William Ellis and seconded by Henry Walker that John Harrison and Robert Gilbert be Churchwardens for the ensuing year, the Minister of the parish who was present and in the chair, stated that he could not agree in this choice, and that therefore proceeding according to the Canon in this case, he should himself choose one Churchwarden and call upon the Parishioners to choose another.

Henry Walker moved and William Ellis seconded that whereas the Chairman (The Rev. G. Atkinson) declines to have the propositions of the parishioners inserted in due course in the Vestry book—William Taylor take the Chair. This motion was carried unanimously.

It was then again moved by Henry Walker and seconded by John Jollands that, whereas the Incumbent, the Rev Geo Atkinson procured a person named Edward Howard during the last year to be inducted Churchwarden in the proper court contrary to the custom and privilege of the parish of Stow, this vestry hereby enters its solemn protest against such violation of its ancient right to choose both Churchwardens independent of the Incumbent.

The motion made by William Ellis and seconded by Henry Walker that John Harrison and Robert Gilbert be the churchwardens for the ensuing year was then put to the meeting by the Chairman and on a show of hands being taken it was declared to be carried unanimously.

It was then moved by Joseph Harrison and seconded by George Sergeant that Chas. G. Smith be Vestry Clerk for the year ensuing.—This motion was then put to the meeting and by a show of hands it was declared to be carried nem. con.

Mr Thos Spencer then moved and Wm Ellis seconded the following resolution:—Resolved that this Vestry deeply regrets that the Minister of the Parish should year after year hold himself hostile to his Parishioners and scarcely ever meet them in vestry assembled without perpetrating some act of harshness or oppression. This was carried unanimously.

Signed: William Taylor, Chairman

John Harrison
George Burton } Churchwardens

Joseph Harrison, Robert Gilbert
Henry Walker, William Ellis
George Sergeant, William Hill
George Harrison James Spencer } Parishioners

"Turn over"

Thomas Spencer

Note: The first three paragraphs were written by Atkinson, the remainder by Charles G. Smith.

147. To Eccl. Com. from Ewan Christian, 6 Bloomsbury Square, 22 April 1851 (EC)

Dear Sir,

Stow Chancel

I have carefully examined and considered the enclosed papers and drawings, and have communicated with Mr Pearson thereon; and beg to report that the construction proposed for the groining and walls as explained by that Gentleman is in my opinion sound and sufficient, and calculated to meet the difficulties which occurred to my own mind when considering the scheme of construction described to me at Stow—Too much care cannot however be exercised in rebuilding the flank walls, the progress of which should be very slow and regular, but on this point the Architect's views are in entire accordance with my own and his instructions have been given to that effect. It may not however be superfluous to reiterate them.

148. To Atkinson from Eccl. Com., Accountant (Copy), 25 April 1851 (EC)

Sir

I have on behalf of the Ecclesiastical Commissioners for England to inform you that the sum of £200 on account of their grant towards the repair of the Chancel of the Church of St Mary, Stow, Lincoln, will be paid on the presentation at this office through a Banker of a receipt signed by the Treasurer of the "Stow Church Restoration Fund."

149. Vestry Book

Stow, May 22, 1851

A vestry meeting was held in the church this day at six o'clock in the afternoon according to notice duly given "for the purpose of passing (if found correct) the accompts of the last year's churchwardens and for the purpose of laying a rate for the necessary repairs of the church; and also for the purpose of taking into consideration the propriety of reletting those Church-gardens whose occupiers have not paid their rent on or before this day"—Present Messrs Harrison & Gilbert churchwardens, Messrs Burton, Ellis, Howard, Palmer, Wilkinson, Thos Smith &c, &c.

Mr Churchwarden Harrison was called to the chair.

Mr Ellis proposed and Mr Josh Harrison seconded that a 2½d rate be granted for the necessary repairs of the church.

On this motion being put to the meeting it was carried unanimously.

Mr. Wilkinson proposed that Thos. Otter Geo. Kennington & Josh Bains's garden should be relet and the parties put into the court for the recovery of the rent in arrears if it were not paid on or before the 2nd day of June and others also who are in arrears. This was seconded by Geo. Harrison and carried unanimously.

Signed: John Harrison Chairman
Robert Gilbert Churchwarden
Geo Burton
William Wilkinson
Robert Credland
George Harrison
William Ellis
Thomas Smith
} Parishioners

Note: This church rate arose from the Archdeacon's parochial visitation of 3 May 1851, the minute of which he reported to the Bishop on 12 May: "The restoration of the chancel of Stow Church is going on in a very satisfactory manner, and when finished it will be a perfect specimen of the original architecture. The foundations of the nave and transepts have been repaired for the most part well, but with one exception, which is not done so efficiently as it ought to be. Divine service is now performed in the nave.

"It is my opinion that when the chancel is finished, and a sufficient space railed off for the administration of the Holy Communion, the accommodation for the parishioners will be very small. We must therefore endeavour to get the transepts repaired, which will provide sufficient accommodation, and this is the utmost which I think we shall ever be able to accomplish, for many years to come." (*A Stow Visitation. Ven W. B. Stonehouse, 1845*, edited Canon N. S. Harding, 1940, p. 93.) The Archdeacon's threats of February 1849 (No. 61) seem to have been effective.

150. Architect's Certificate forwarded to Eccl. Com. by Atkinson, 28 May 1851 (EC)

St Mary's Stow Lincolnshire
Chancel
No 2.

2 Delahay St
May 24th 1851

I have to certify that the Substantial Repairs to this Chancel have continued to progress since the 18th of February the date of my last Certificate and that six hundred and thirty pounds have up to this date been expended upon *them alone*; four hundred pounds of which sum has been paid into the hands of the treasurer The Revd Geo: Atkinson Viz: two hundred pounds by the ecclesiastical commissioners of England and two hundred pounds by the Prebendary's Lessee.

The works to which this certificate refers as having advanced are the rebuilding of the East End with its windows the continuation of the repairs to the buttresses, the repairs to Walls & stone work generally inside & out, to the arches window jambs string-courses renewing of the ashlar work inside and the rebuilding of portions of the Side Walls;—scaffolding & materials Superintentants Salary & a proportion of Architects commission & expences included

John L Pearson Architect

To the Ecclesiastical Commissioners
of England.

151. To Atkinson from Eccl. Com. (Copy), 5 June 1851 (EC)

Sir

Stow Chancel

In answer to your application of the 28th ultimo for a further payment on account of this Chancel, I am directed to point out to you that, although £630 may have been expended in substantial repairs alone, these repairs are being done on a scale of expense exceeding that which is necessary, or with which the Commissioners as Tithe Owners are legally chargeable; and that as there is no guarantee for their completion and it is quite possible that the means for meeting the extra expenditure may fall short, and an outlay which they never contemplated might thereupon be required of the Commissioners, I am to acquaint you that they do not feel that they would be justified in making any further payment until the whole of the substantial repairs of the Chancel shall have been completed.

Note: Minute of Estates Committee, 3 June 1851, refers.

152. To Eccl. Com. from Atkinson, 7 June 1851 (EC)

Sir,

Stow Chancel

I have to acknowledge the receipt of your Letter of the 5th Inst. in which you state as a reason for refusing to make a further payment on account of the substantial repairs of this Chancel that "these repairs are being done on a scale of expense exceeding that which is necessary, or with which the Commissioners . . . are legally chargeable."

As I have made it my constant care, ever since the works were begun, to watch most vigilantly over the expenditure incurred in doing the substantial repairs, and to prevent any of the old work from being unnecessarily disturbed, I must request that you will have the goodness to furnish me with the Evidence or authority on which the statement quoted from your Letter is made.

I also take this opportunity of renewing the application which I made in a former letter—but of which no notice was taken—that you would furnish me with a copy entire of Mr Christian's report made after his inspection of the works.

Note: For Mr Christian's report, see No. 139.

153. To Atkinson from Eccl. Com. (Copy), 14 June 1851 (EC)

Sir

Stow Chancel

I have submitted to the Ecclesiastical Commissioners for England your letter of the 7th Instant and am directed to point out to you in answer thereto that no other evidence than the communications made to this Office either by you or your direction is necessary for establishing the fact that the repairs of this Chancel are "being done on a scale of expense exceeding that . . . which is necessary or with which the Commissioners are legally chargeable". In explanation of this I am to instance the putting up of a stone roof and the consequent additional strengthening of the side walls—both works being clearly in excess of what could be deemed "necessary".

With reference to your request for a copy of Mr Christian's Report to the Commissioners I am to state that the substance of such portion of it as was considered necessary having been communicated to you by my letter of the 26th March last, the Commissioners do not consider it expedient to furnish a copy.

Note: Minute of Estates Committee, 13 June 1851, refers.

154. To Eccl. Com. from Atkinson, 25 June 1851 (EC)

Sir,

Stow Chancel

Before I proceed to notice the statements contained in your Letter of the 14th Inst I beg to state that the Tenor of the Communications lately received from the Ecclesiastical Commissioners for England through you, in reference to the repairs of this Chancel, renders it necessary to suspend the progress of the works for the present, and that accordingly all operations will be discontinued, and the workmen discharged at the End of this week.

Your Letter of the above date alleges "that no other Evidence than the Communications made to this Office either by you or your direction is necessary for establishing the fact that the repairs of this Chancel are being 'done on a scale of expense exceeding that which is necessary or with which the Commissioners are legally chargeable.'"

On this I must beg to remark that I am quite at a loss to conceive what, or how any, communication directly or indirectly proceeding from me on this subject, can be capable of such an interpretation,—but you proceed in explanation of this to "instance the putting up of a stone roof, and the consequent additional strengthening of the side-walls—both works being clearly in excess of what could be deemed *necessary*"

Now, in the first place, as to the stone roof, I beg to state, what indeed I thought I had already sufficiently explained, that not one shilling of the Cost of this part of the works has been, directly or indirectly, charged to the Tithe Owners, or expected from them. On the contrary, I beg to point out, that the Tithe-Owners are great gainers by the putting up of the Stone-roof because the Timber roof being thereby hidden, the new timber roof required as part of the substantial and necessary repairs, will be of a much plainer and less Costly construction than it could have been, had it been open to view. I am informed by an experienced person that in this way a very considerable sum will be saved to the Tithe-Owners.

Next, as to the "Consequent Additional strengthening of the side-walls," I have to state that there has been *no such strengthening* out of the funds provided by the Tithe-Owners, nor indeed *any strengthening has been* done to the side walls, except the necessary repair of the foundations and buttresses where they were decayed and insecure, precisely what must have been done had no stone roof been put up. With this necessary repair, and with this only have the Tithe-Owners been held chargeable, and charged accordingly. What your Letter refers to as "additional strengthening of the side walls" must I conceive be the taking out and rebuilding those portions of the side walls which intervene between the Arches of the Stone-roof inside, and the external buttresses in order to obtain a more solid and firm abutment to those Arches. This was necessary only at the four principal points of support, from the level at which the Arches spring upwards—and this strengthening has been done as *part of the groining, and wholly without expense to the Tithe Owners*.

I must, therefore, respectfully submit to the Commissioners that the instance alleged in your Letter does not in any wise bear out the statement in support of which it is adduced, but, that, on the Contrary, the Tithe Owners will be saved a considerable sum in the timber roof by means of this very stone groining.

As to Mr Christian's report, I am sorry that the Commissioners refuse me a copy of it. As that portion of it which seemed to make against us, was communicated, it did not seem to me unreasonable to ask for the advantage of anything in it which might be in our favour, as I ventured to hope, from remarks which fell from Mr Christian during his inspection of the works, that it would be generally favourable, and I feel that I am entitled to assume that it is so, from its being withheld.

But however that may be, I will venture to say this much, that a fair report by any Architect who should inspect the works, *must* be in our favour, not only as to the work itself, but as to the *Cost* of doing it. I beg to assure the Ecclesiastical Commissioners that I feel very reluctant to appear in any way as occupying an antagonistic position towards them in this matter. Being entrusted by the subscribers towards the restoration and also by Mr Hall the Prebendary's Lessee with the duty of looking to the Expenditure of the funds contributed by them, I felt there was a great responsibility devolving upon me in consequence, and to the utmost of my power I have endeavoured to discharge it. I have been as careful over the Expenditure of the funds as if the money had to come out of my own pocket. I have kept accounts of every shilling expended, which I am ready to shew, and which I wish to have audited when the work is concluded. I have spent almost every hour I could spare at the Church ever since the works were begun. I explained both to the Architect, and to the Clerk of the works, *at the very first*, that nothing must be ordered without my approval, and that I should feel it my duty to prevent the outlay of a single shilling unnecessarily. I have all through interfered whenever I saw occasion to prevent Old work being pulled to pieces without absolute necessity, and have in fact prevented much from being done which the Architect as well as the Clerk of the works judged necessary. I have borrowed from gentlemen in the neighbourhood and others, scaffold poles, carriages for stone &c ropes and many other things necessary which must otherwise have been bought at a great expense—I obtained a gift of all the sand from Lord Brownlow, and have, in every way I could think of, laboured to save and to keep down expense, and I am confident that the Tithe Owners could not have got the necessary and legal repairs done so economically in any other way.

But the truth is, as during the progress of the works became manifest, that the Estimate made by Mr Railton was altogether inadequate, and no Care or Economy could possibly have made it adequate to do the necessary repairs "well and sufficiently". A further provision, therefore, will have to be made by the Tithe Owners, in addition to the Amount already expended before the necessary repairs can be proceeded with. I am aware that the stopping of the works will be a great disadvantage, and will eventually cause increased expense both to the Tithe Owners and to those who have to provide for other restorations, but as these latter including the groined roof have been carried as far as they can be until the present roof has been taken off and replaced, no alternative is left but to suspend all further operations until some arrangement is come to.

155. To Atkinson from Eccl. Com. (Copy), 3 July 1851 (EC)

Sir

Having laid your letter of the 25th ulto before the Ecclesiastical Commissioners for England, I am desired to inform you in reply, that the Commissioners have learnt with surprise and regret, that you are about to suspend the works for the repair and restoration of the Chancel of Stow Church.

I am further directed to refer you to our former correspondence on this subject, and especially to my letter of the 24th August last, from which you will perceive, that upon approving your plans for the *restoration* of the Chancel, the Commissioners strictly and distinctly limited their contribution to £300, the sum originally determined upon as their portion of the cost of *repairing* the Chancel as estimated by their Architect.

"*Within the limits of this amount*" I then informed you, "that the Commissioners would make payments on account from time to time, upon certificates from the Architect employed of the amount due for the execution of works for which the Tithe Owners are strictly liable".

The cost to the Commissioners having been thus limited to £300 in the whole, whilst on the other hand they continue liable for repairs not yet completed, it follows that they cannot consistently with the engagement between them and yourself, or with safety to the funds entrusted to their charge, pay over the last instalment until the entire completion of those parts of the "works for which as Tithe Owners they are liable".

The intimation in your letter of the 25th Ultimo proves the necessity of this precaution.

If unhappily the funds at your command prove insufficient to carry on the work, and you are consequently obliged to abandon it, its completion may devolve upon the Commissioners at an expense beyond the reserved £100 and to be defrayed from funds applicable by law to other and even more important objects.

I am further to inform you that the Commissioners, having approved of the plans, have been throughout most anxious to aid you in their completion; and that the small sum now retained by them is not more than would have been reserved until the entire completion of the work, had it been executed under their own direction and which in that case would have been limited to those necessary repairs, for which alone they were liable.

Should you unhappily be compelled to abandon the work which you have undertaken, I am desired to request, that you will give the Commissioners immediate notice, that they may proceed to take such steps as may appear to them necessary, under so unfortunate and unexpected a contingency.

Note: A draft of this letter, endorsed "Fair off" is in the file. The letter of 24 August 1850, quoted above, is No. 121.

156. To Eccl. Com. from Atkinson, 7 July 1851 (EC)

Sir,

Stow Chancel

In reply to your Letter of the 3rd Instant I beg to state that in accordance with the intimation I had given in my letter of the 25th Ultimo to the Ecclesiastical Commissioners for England, the works connected with the repair and restoration of this Chancel were suspended at the End of that week, and the whole of the men employed have since left the Parish.

It was not without the greatest reluctance that I carried into effect this measure, but I felt that to carry on the works further under existing circumstances might involve me individually in most serious pecuniary responsibilities.

The Amount raised by subscriptions for the purpose of effecting such restorations as the Tithe Owners were not legally liable to—this Amount being at the utmost barely sufficient to complete those restorations—had previously through the long delay in payment on the part of the Ecclesiastical Commissioners, become involved in carrying on the substantial and necessary repairs to the extent of at least £400, in addition to the £200 provided and paid by Mr Hall the Prebendary's Lessee, which had been wholly expended, so that I felt myself, as former Letters of mine to the Board had given intimation, in a very embarrassing position in regard not only to the Cost of the remaining repairs, but also as to the subscribers, whose funds, entrusted to my administration, had been thus expended on works for which they were not intended.

My anxiety was in part relieved by the payment about the middle of May, which was more than 8 months after the Commencement of the works, of the sum of £200 by the Ecclesiastical Commissioners, enabling me so far to replace what had been in fact borrowed from the subscriptions. But when I found that the Ecclesiastical Commissioners declined to make any further payment, either to enable me to replace the remaining portion of that which had been expended out of the subscriptions in effecting necessary repairs, or to meet the Cost of such repairs still requiring to be done, until all the works were completed, I felt, with every desire to work together with the Tithe Owners, as having indeed one interest with us, that in justice to the subscribers and to myself I could not proceed further.

With reference to the Commissioners having "strictly and distinctly limited their Contribution to £300, the sum originally determined upon as their proportion of the Cost of repairing the Chancel as estimated by their Architect", for which you refer me especially to your Letter of the 24th August 1850, which letter is now before me—I find that letter, after stating that the plans had been approved by the Commissioners, to run in the following terms—"I am directed to acquaint you that upon the receipt from time to time of certificates from the Architect employed, of the Amount due for the execution of works for which the Tithe Owners are strictly liable the Commissioners will make payment on Account of the Commissioner's grant of £300 to the extent of three fifths of the Amounts so certified"—but I do not find in that letter the words—"*Within the limits of this Amount*" which, in your letter of the 3d Instant, are marked as a quotation from it, and underlined. Though it may be inferred from the terms of that letter that the Commissioners did not contemplate an expenditure on their part beyond the £300 it can scarcely be said, on consideration, I think, that the Commissioners "strictly and distinctly limited their contribution to that Sum". The Expression in that letter of "Certificates from the Architect employed of *the Amount due for the Execution of works for which the Tithe Owners are strictly liable*", appears to meet both the law and the equity of the Case. I should have felt most happy if the Cost of the execution of the works in question could have been brought within the Estimate of Mr Railton—I have spared no pains to that End—but after all it has been found impracticable, and the Estimate must of necessity be increased. That the sum of £500 might be too much or too little to defray the Cost of the necessary repairs must probable have occurred to the Commissioners. From a letter addressed by you to the Bishop of Lincoln of the date July 15th 1850 in answer to one from his Lordship in reference to the mode of payment of their proportion of the Estimate, I infer that such must have been the Case. That letter, now before me, says "With reference to the proposed reparation of the Chancel of Stow Church . . . I beg leave to explain that the Ecclesiastical Commissioners for England have at present only agreed to defray their just proportion of the Cost of the necessary works upon the general terms of a report made by Mr Railton three years ago. *The sum of £300 was merely an Estimate* and before any specific grant can be made, it will be necessary that the Commissioners should see the plans, specification and Estimate of the works now contemplated".

Upon this general principle that the Tithe Owners should provide for the necessary repairs and no more, and that the Cost of all other restorations should fall on the subscribers the work was begun, and has been carried on.

The Commissioners did not think proper to pay the Amount certified at the end of January by Mr Pearson the Architect employed without first sending down an Architect on their part about the middle of March to inspect the works and report to them. What may have been the general tenor of Mr Christian's report I have not had an opportunity of knowing, but that gentleman on preparing to commence his inspection of the works at the Church, stated to me, that as the Commissioners made "a distinction between substantial repairs, and ornamental restorations for the former of which only they held themselves liable, he must request me to point out to him what had been done of both kinds." I replied that I would point out to him all we had done, and then he could judge for himself what came under each class—When I had done so—setting aside the preparation of Arch stones for the groining—Mr Christian's remark was "*All this I consider substantial repair.*"

By this principle we are willing to abide, and, if the Tithe-Owners think fit to co-operate with them in completing the necessary repairs still required in conjunction with our restorations in the most economical manner consistent with sufficiency and stability, otherwise we must leave the completion of the necessary repairs in the Tithe Owners' hands.

It is very important that this business should be attended to without delay, as from the exposed condition of the tops of the walls, and the church being open to the weather in various places together with the insecure state of the roof, the fabric might sustain serious damage if the repairs were not completed before winter.

Note: Atkinson quotes from letters, Nos. 121 and 113.

157. To Ewan Christian from Eccl. Com. (Copy), 19 July 1851 (EC)

Dear Sir

Stow Chancel

The Ecclesiastical Commissioners for England and the Prebendary of Stow are as you are aware liable as Tithe Owners to the sustentation of the above Chancel; and in the year 1847 application was made to them to put it into repair.

Mr Atkinson, the Incumbent, to whom reference was made, being desirous that the Chancel should be completely restored, suggested that the amount which the Tithe Owners would have to expend in the necessary repair should be ascertained and that subscriptions should then be raised in the neighbourhood for completing the restoration.

To this end a survey and estimate were made by Mr Railton by direction of the Commissioners, and he having estimated the necessary repairs at £500, Mr Atkinson was informed that the Tithe Owners were prepared to expend that sum; I am not aware of the steps thereupon taken by Mr Atkinson towards raising subscriptions, but the works were sometime after commenced under his direction and after considerable progress, they have been stopped for want of funds. A correspondence of some length has recently taken place between Mr Atkinson and the Commissioners in which inter alia a question is raised as to the sufficiency of Mr Railton's estimate; and I am therefore directed to request that you will report to the Commissioners whether after the examination of the works which you have already made you are of opinion that the necessary repairs to which the Tithe Owners were liable, were properly estimated at £500 and if you should think that they were not, that you will state what you consider the estimate should have been, giving in that case the grounds on which your opinion is based.

158. To Eccl. Com. from Ewan Christian, 6 Bloomsbury Square, 26 July 1851 (EC)

Dear Sir,

Herewith I transmit to you my report on the plans of Bywell St Peters parsonage, and upon the case of Stow Chancel.

I regret that I have not been able to send you the latter sooner, but just after I received your instructions I had to leave for Staffordshire on business which completely absorbed my attention whilst absent.

I have prepared the report as soon as possible after my return.

I may perhaps say in reference to Stow Church that I always considered Mr Atkinson had accepted £500 as a final sum from the Commissioners intending to find the remainder of the Cost whatsoever it might be by subscriptions. In any other view of the matter Mr Railton's calculations should have been tested by his Architect.

158A.

Dear Sir,

Stow Chancel

I beg to acknowledge the receipt of your letter dated 19th July, requesting me to report to the Ecclesiastical Commissioners; "whether after the examination I have already made of the works at Stow Chancel, I am of opinion that the necessary repairs to which the Tithe Owners were liable were properly estimated at £500, and if I should think they were not, that I will state what I consider the estimate should have been, giving in that case the grounds on which my opinion is based".

I will endeavour to put you in possession of my views upon this subject briefly and clearly—

The difficulties attendant upon making an estimate of the cost of repairing a dilapidated edifice of the extent and character of the Chancel at Stow are very considerable, and cannot be overcome except by much patient and skilful labour—Whatsoever care also may be exercised in the preliminary survey and after calculations, these are always liable to be falsified by the actual condition of the fabric, as exhibited when more closely examined by the workmen.

The only estimate upon which in such a case dependance is to be placed, (and this with a considerable allowance for contingencies) is such as a Builder would make, when about to contract for the necessary works from carefully prepared drawings and specifications. Whether such elaborate calculations formed the basis of the estimate upon which the Commissioners have proceeded I cannot say, but certainly the result has not proved its accuracy—

I do not think that the cost of the works was properly estimated at £500.0.0

My reasons for thinking so, are as follows—

When I visited Stow in March last, a considerable portion of the work for the reparation of the walls was still incomplete; probably rather more than a fourth part yet remained to be done, and the roof had not been touched. Exclusive of the Clerk of Works salary, exclusive also of the cost of preparation for the groined ceiling and of the value of materials upon the ground, the sum of £424 had been actually expended upon the works then executed, and evidently under careful supervision.

If then to £424, be added one fourth £106.0.0, and 10 per Cent for contingencies £53, the whole sum required to be expended on the walls would amount to £583, and at a less sum than this I think the repairs ought not to have been estimated, and this exclusive of the necessary reconstruction of the Roof.

With regard to the latter I have not sufficient data to enable me to estimate with accuracy the cost of its repair—The roof is a badly constructed one, but it is covered with lead and has some sound timbers remaining in it—The lead must be recast, and the roof reframed with new principal trusses, and this may probably be done with solid plain carpentry for about £200.

This however might be exactly ascertained by obtaining a Contract for the work. I may perhaps be allowed to add that with regard to the completion of the repair of the walls, no better course can be followed than that which has been hitherto pursued under Mr Atkinsons direction, requiring from him exact accounts of the cost of the works.—

Repairs of the nature required can only be properly executed by careful men under vigilant superintendance; this has been done hitherto, and I can only recommend that it should be carried on in like manner to the end—

159. To Atkinson from Eccl. Com. (Copy), 29 July 1851 (EC)

Sir

Stow Chancel

The Ecclesiastical Commissioners for England having on receipt of your letter of the 7th inst again referred to Mr Christian have directed me to acquaint you, without prejudice, and subject to the conditions hereinafter mentioned, that they are prepared to consider the estimate for the substantial repairs to which the Tithe Owners are liable as £583 exclusive of the reconstruction of the roof and that they are willing to contribute 3/5ths of the increase, together with the like proportions of a contract to be entered into for the reconstruction of the roof, with solid plain carpentry provided that the Lessee of the Prebend will contribute the remaining 2/5ths in each case and provided that you will then undertake the entire completion of the Chancel including the groined roof and that they shall not be required to make any further payment (except their proportion of the roof) until the whole of the works shall have been completed.

Note: Minute of Estates Committee, 29 July 1851, refers.

160. To Eccl. Com. from Hall, Wolfreton House, 7 Aug. 1851 (EC)

Sir,

Mr Atkinson has furnished me with copies of letters which have passed between him, & you on behalf of the Ecclesiastical Commissioners for England, relative to the repairs of Stow Chancel.

This correspondence has disclosed to me a state of affairs which has not a little surprised me, & it also brings under my notice an application for further assistance towards those repairs, for which I was wholly unprepared. I considered my responsibility to have been limited to the amount fixed by the estimate of Mr Railton, & with any other understanding I should neither have advanced the whole of the money before the commencement of the works, nor should I have contributed to the restoration fund.

Since however the Commissioners, influenced, as it appears by the report of Mr Christian, have consented to an increased estimate, I know not on what grounds to resist their appeal to me.

But I venture to hope that they will not insist upon a pledge from me to contribute my proportion of an undefined amount. If such an arrangement can be made, I should greatly prefer to pay to them at once, what may be considered a fair & reasonable sum, on being idemnified against further demands. At the least, if this cannot be done, I trust that the Commissioners will favour [me] with their estimate of the cost of the reconstruction of the roof, so as to enable me to form some idea of the liability I should incur by acceding to their proposal.

161. To Hall from Eccl. Com. (Copy), 8 Aug. 1851 (EC)

Sir

Stow Chancel

In answer to your letter of yesterday's date I beg leave to explain to you that the Ecclesiastical Commissioners for England entertained the opinion expressed by you that the amount which they and you agreed, on the Report of Mr Railton, to place at Mr Atkinson's disposal was to cover their and your liability as Tithe Owners—but from the statements they have recently received from Mr Atkinson, they felt that whatever might have been the understanding originally, they could not in justice to that gentleman, now that better means of forming an opinion existed, refuse to refer to Mr Christian, whose report, of which I enclose a copy, satisfied them as I trust it will you that something further should be done, and they accordingly directed me to address to Mr Atkinson the letter of the 29th ultimo, of which I also enclose a copy.

With regard to the roof, you will see that Mr Christian estimates the cost at about £200: but as this part of the work is of a character to form the subject of a distinct contract, and would under any circumstances have to be provided wholly by the tithe owners, the Commissioners thought it more expedient to keep it separate from and more immediately under their control than the other works, and if you should see fit to co-operate with them I will take care that no Contract for it is entered into without your sanction and approval.

I shall be happy to give you any further information and am &c.

162. To Eccl. Com. from Hall, Scarborough, 11 Aug. 1851 (EC)

Sir

Your letter of the 8th Inst with the other papers enclosed has been forwarded to me at this place. While admitting, that confirmed as the statements of Mr Atkinson are by Mr Christian's report, he has a strong case for further assistance, I do not consider that I ought to contribute in the same ratio as before.

Nearly two years ago on selling to Mr Ashton Cox the Stow Park Estate, I at the same [time] transferred to him the lease of the tithes of that property, which, I believe, were commuted at something more than £100. By an arrangement between us, I was to pay the whole of Mr Railton's estimate, but it appears to me no more than reasonable that Mr Cox should bear his proportion of any additional sum required for the completion of the repairs of the chancel. I can hardly have any liability in respect of that which is no longer mine.

I shall be glad to be informed whether the Ecclesiastical Commissioners coincide in this view & am [&c., &c.]

163. To Hall from Eccl. Com. (Copy), 19 Aug. 1851 (EC)

Sir

Stow Church

I beg leave in answer to your letter of the 11th Instant to point out to you that the further payment of the Ecclesiastical Commissioners towards repairing of the Chancel of this Church was in my letter to Mr Atkinson dated the 29th ulto made dependant on further proportionate contribution from the owner of the other Estate to which a share of the liability in this respect attaches.

You will I think agree with me that it is not within the province of the Commissioners to determine on whom under this view of the matter the burden should fall, but simply to be assured that the rateable contribution in respect of the property is made by some one.

Aug. 30—1851—This letter was returned by the Dead Letter Office marked "Not Known" B

Note: This letter was forwarded to Mr Hall at Wolfreton House on 4 September 1851.

164. To Eccl. Com. from Atkinson, 21 Aug. 1851 (EC)

Sir,

Stow Chancel

On the receipt of your Letter of the 29th Ultimo I sent a copy of it, and of a portion of the previous correspondence which had taken place between the Ecclesiastical Commissioners and myself, to the Revd S. W. Hall, the Lessee of the Prebendary of Stow. On the 9th Instant I received an answer from Mr Hall in which he said, that he did not see on what ground he could decline to accede to the proposition made by the Ecclesiastical Commissioners, but that he had written to you on the subject, and after he had received your reply, he would write further to me.

I have since been waiting in expectation of hearing further from Mr Hall, but not having done so, and as the summer is rapidly passing away, I will not lose more time in communicating directly with you on the subject of your Letter of the 29th Ultimo.

I must observe that besides the roof and those parts of the walls on which it will immediately rest requiring reconstruction, there are various other substantial repairs still wanting to different portions of the Chancel, but without taking these into the Account, Mr Pearson estimates the Cost of a new flagged floor, the glazing, and the drains outside the Chancel—none of which are provided for—at £100.

Notwithstanding these deficiencies however, I feel disposed, both to save delay, and in order to meet the Tithe-Owners in a liberal manner, though I am aware not without risk to myself, to accept the proposition contained in your Letter of the 29th Ultimo, provided that a fair arrangement can be made between the parties in respect to the Cost of the reconstruction of the roof, and the parts necessarily belonging to it, and with some modification of the terms specified in your Letter as to the payment of the money.

On these conditions I would give the Tithe Owners a guarantee to complete the whole of the works including the groined roof. As to the £100 of the original Estimate still retained by the Commissioners, that sum and at least as much more having been expended, out of the subscriptions, in strictly substantial repairs, and Mr Hall's £200 having been wholly paid, I think the Commissioners' £100 ought likewise to be paid before the recommencement of the works and this I should expect. The cost of the re-construction of the roof to be paid on the Contract being signed by me.

As we should wish to have a good tiled floor and this would probably be some length of time unfinished, I should be willing to leave in the Commissioners' hands as security for its completion, their proportion of the £83 which would be quite sufficient to cover their share of the Cost of an ordinary floor.

I have asked Mr Pearson to prepare a plan, specification and Estimate for a roof of plain solid Carpentry and I hope to be able to submit them shortly to your inspection.

165. To Eccl. Com. from Atkinson, 26 Aug. 1851 (EC)

Sir,

Stow Chancel

I have the honour to acknowledge the receipt of your Letter of the 23d Instant—and have now inclosed Mr Pearson's plan, specification and Estimate for the re-construction of the roof—of which, as the season is now becoming so far advanced, I beg to request the favour of your early consideration.

Mr Pearson informs me that in making the accompanying Estimate he has not included any charge for the Architect or the Clerk of the works—and as I mentioned in my letter of the 21st Instant the floor, the glazing and the drains outside which are also unprovided for, will occasion an expense of about £100, besides many other smaller repairs.

Note: A copy of the letter acknowledged by Atkinson is missing from the file.

165A.

Specification of Works required to be done to complete the Substantial Repairs to the Chancel of St: Mary's Church, Stow Lincolnshire.

To construct a new Roof over the Vaulting, according to the Drawing, in the best manner, with the best Memel deal, free from sap wood, dead knots, and shakes,—Wrot iron bolts and straps where shewn, The Roof to have 5 pairs of Principals, one over each of the Transverse Ribs of Groining, and one over each of the intersections of the Diagonal Ribs, the tie beams of the latter to be raised as shewn, to clear the stone-work in the centre. The Purlins to continue on into the walls at each end of roof and properly bedded on these. The boarding under the lead to be of inch yellow deal, listed free from sap wood, and laid close jointed, inch gutter boards and bearers, and inch deal to side of gutters. The gutters to have a fall of 2in in ten feet, and 2in drips, a cistern over the head of rain water pipe next the Tower on each side of roof;—A trap door also 2 ft by 3ft, to be constructed with proper rebates and fillets, for access on-to the roof and to gutters.

Waller,—

To rebuild the side walls above the top of the Clerestory windows with walling to correspond with the old work below, properly bonded with large flat bedded stones,—the East Gable to be built in a similar way, and according to the drawings. The Mortar to be composed of 2/5ths Wounsworth or Doncaster lime, and 3/5ths of clean sharp sand. To point the new work in a careful manner, and to dash over the joints with some sharp sand,—the old walls also to be repointed throughout, and dashed in the same way.

Plasterer,—

To plaster the walls of the Clerestory above the level of Caps to Vaulting shafts on both sides, and in the recesses of the Arcading round the lower portion of the walls inside, with 2 coats work, finished with a float and some sharp sand.

Mason,—

The Parapet; the Corbel Tables and Strings; the Coping to the Gable; the Tops of Buttresses at the East end; the Weathercourse at the Tower, over the Roof; the Cross; and the [two (*del*)] loop-holes in the Gable;—to be got out of the best Ancaster *weather* stone, properly laid on its natural bed.

The Corbels to be spaced as shewn, in each of the Bays, on each side of Chancel.

[The Centre Buttress at the East end to be carried up within 5 feet of the point of the Gables, faced with dressed stone like the old work (*deleted*)] The Coping 4in thick, with solid Foot stones and top stones and two intermediate ones. The Weathercourse at the Tower to be 4″ × 6″, chamfered on the top and fitted in with cement.

The two courses of the Parapet to be dowelled or plugged with Yorkstone dowels, run in with Portland cement, the whole of the Masonry, to be carefully bedded and jointed, and truly worked

The Cross to have a Copper dowel 10 inches long, let in and run with Portland cement.

Plumber,—

To cover the whole of the Roof with the best milled lead, of 7 lbs to the foot, to turn up at each end 6 inches, and let in under the stone-work 2 inches, properly fixed, and pointed up with Cement. To turn up 6 inches at each of the rolls, which are to be of lead only (no ridge roll) the overlappings of the sheets not to be less than 6 inches, and these to be arranged as indicated, the ends of the rolls to be bossed and soldered. The sheets to be fixed with lead headed nails

To lay the gutters with 7 lbs lead, with a fall of 2 inches in ten feet, properly dressing the same to the drips and rolls, turning up 9in against the Parapet, and up under the lead of Roof. Put flashings of 5 lbs under the Coping of Parapet, 8 in wide, similar flashing and apron pieces to trap door in Roof. Form proper Cesspool in each gutter, at the Tower end, with proper 4 in: lead socket pipe thro' the wall into rain-water pipes, properly soldered at the Cesspool;—a strong Rose to be put over each of the rain-water pipes, of a hemispherical form, to prevent any matters stopping up the pipes.

To provide and fix a cast iron rain-water pipe, with proper shoes, to communicate with the drains,—to each side of the Chancel.

The Contractor to provide all materials and workmanship required to perform the above works in the best and most substantial manner, and to the entire satisfaction of the Architect.

The old lead to be reused, and recast if necessary. The Contractor is required to state the price per cwt he will allow for the old lead, weighed at the time it is taken off the old roof, the Contractor providing the means for doing so, and the amount of which to be deducted from the Contract.

All old materials that are sound and good, such as walling stones, free stone, and Timber, may be reused where directed by the Architect.

J. L. Pearson
2 Delahay St
Aug 15, 1851

165B.

August 1851

St Mary's Stow Lincolnshire
Chancel

The estimated expense of the new roof gutters &c according to plan & specification	660. 3. 6
The deduction for old lead and other materials	166.18. 6
	£493. 5. 1

166. To Atkinson from Eccl. Com. (Copy), 28 Aug. 1851 (EC)

Sir,

With reference to your letter of 26th instant I am directed to inquire whether the specification and estimate of the repairs for the Chancel of the Church of Saint Mary Stow, transmitted by you, have reference to the reconstruction of the roof only, or are intended to include the whole of the repairs. Your letter refers to the Estimate as that for the reconstruction of the roof while the specification is "of the Works required to be done to complete the substantial repairs to the Chancel."

167. To Eccl. Com. from Atkinson, 29 Aug. 1851 (EC)

Sir,

Stow Chancel

In reply to the enquiry in your letter of yesterday as to whether the specification and Estimate sent by me have reference to the reconstruction of the roof only, or are intended to include the whole of the repairs, I beg to state that my impression is, that they have reference to the Reconstruction of the Roof only. My instructions to Mr Pearson were to make a specification and estimate for the roof including only such stone work, as must, from its nature and position, of necessity be considered as forming part of the roof—suggesting that, at the same time—as there are many other repairs of a substantial nature requiring to be done—they might be mentioned in the specification *separately*, but must not be included in the Estimate.

I observed in the specification itself only one item of such other repairs—viz the plastering of a portion of the interior walls. And this, besides the Title, struck me as giving rather an air of ambiguity to the specification. I kept the specification by me a few days in expectation of a visit from Mr Pearson in order that I might confer with him before sending it—but as I found he could not come so soon as I had hoped, I thought it better to send it.

I am writing by this Post to Mr Pearson for his explanation on the point in question, and in order to save time I will request him to communicate immediately with your Office on the subject.

168. To Eccl. Com. from Pearson, 2 Delahay St, 3 Sept. 1851 (EC)

Stow Chancel

Sir,

Mr Atkinson has written to me to say that some doubts are entertained from the title of the specification which he forwarded to you as to whether it has reference to the roof only or to the whole of the repairs and this same also with reference to the Estimate. I beg to inform you that that in each case the works connected with the roof only are included. I regret that my absence in the country has prevented me writing to you upon this subject earlier

169. To Eccl. Com. from Hall, Wolfreton House, 6 Sept. 1851 (EC)

Sir,

I am sorry for the delay which has taken place in my receipt of your letter of the 19th Ultmo. In reply to the proposal of the Ecclesiastical Commissioners, I will thank you to inform them that, of the two fifths remaining after their contribution towards the additional sum needed for the repairs of Stow Chancel, I am willing to pay my just proportion to be estimated in respect of the tithes which are held by me.

170. Specification from Pearson, 2 Delahay Street, 8 Sept. 1851 (EC)

Specification of the works required to be done in constructing and in putting on a New Roof to the Chancel of St Mary's Church, Stow Lincolnshire.

Note: There followed the first paragraph of No. 165A, the Plumber's Work, and the last three paragraphs, with minor variations of wording, and omitting the words, "The contractor is required . . . from the Contract" from the penultimate paragraph.

170A.

Sep 8/1851
St Marys Stow Lincolnshire
Chancel—

The Estimated expence of the new roof covered with lead and the gutters but without any parapet or other stone work that is connected with it	484. 10. 0
add for incidental Expences 5 per ct	24. 4. 6
	£508. 14. 6
The deduction for old lead & other materials	166. 18. 5
	£341. 16. 1
Proportion for Architect & clerk of works	35. 0. 0
	£376. 16. 1

171. To Ewan Christian from Eccl. Com. (Copy), 9 Sept. 1851 (EC)

Dear Sir,

Stow Chancel

I send you Mr Pearson's plans, specification and estimate for a new Roof and am to request your report thereon having reference to the estimate of £200 mentioned in your report of the 26th of July last.

172. To Atkinson from Eccl. Com. (Copy), 10 Sept. 1851 (EC)

Sir,

Stow Chancel

I send you copies of two letters from Mr Hall on the subject of these repairs from which it would appear that as he contemplates contributing for only in proportion to the amount of Tithe Rent Charge now held by him it will be necessary that you should apply to Mr Ashton Cox for the remainder of the two fifths of the whole further cost.

Mr Pearson has revised his specification and estimate reducing the latter to £376. 16. 1 and they are now before Mr Christian.

173. To Eccl. Com. from Atkinson, 16 Sept. 1851 (EC)

Sir,

Stow Chancel

I have the honour to acknowledge the receipt of your Letter of the 10th Instant enclosing copies of two Letters from Mr Hall in reference to the proportion of Tithe Rent Charge transferred by him to Mr Ashton Cox.

Mr Hall having paid me a visit last week mentioned the subject of his letters to you, and stated the substance of them to me. He acknowledged that the question between himself and Mr Cox is one on which different views might be taken, and that Mr Cox in all probability would demur to paying any proportion of the increased Estimate—and he further agreed with me that it would not by any means be proper, under the circumstances of the Case that any application should be made by me to Mr Cox, a step which could hardly fail to bring me as the Clergyman of the Parish into collision with Mr Cox as my parishioner, and it was agreed between Mr Hall and myself that I should leave the matter in his hands, as I am content to do.

I trust that the result of Mr Christian's consideration of the Estimate now before him will be such as may leave it in my power to undertake the completion of the repairs—and that in determining the Amount to be granted, the shortness of the days in which the work will have to be done will not be lost sight of.

174. To Eccl. Com. from Ewan Christian, 6 Bloomsbury Square, 18 Sept. 1851 (EC)

Dear Sir,

Stow Chancel

In reply to your letter of the 9th Sept. requesting me to report upon Mr Pearson's design and estimate for the New Roof with reference to the estimate in my Report of the 26th July last;—I write to say, that I have examined the Design and Estimate in question, and have calculated from them the cost of the New Roof as proposed therein, and find that my valuation differs but little from that of Mr Pearson—I value the timber framing and boarding including ironwork

	at 131. 0. 0	
and the new lead covering	at 338.15. 0	
		469. 15. 0
From which has to be deducted the value of old lead and timber		135. 15. 0
giving a Builder's cost of		334. 0. 0
To which should be added for the contingent expences of Architect and Clerk of Works 10 per cent on the former amount or		46. 10. 0
		£ 380. 10. 0

If you refer to my report of the 26th July last, you will perceive that I stated I had not sufficient data to enable me to estimate with accuracy the cost of the repair of the roof, but that I thought that it might be reframed with new principal trusses and covered with the old lead, newly cast, probably for about £200. 0. 0. In making that statement I had in view a reconstruction of the present roof on better principles, but with the same pitch; and for such a roof, only a small quantity of new lead would have been required; and my present calculations prove that for the amount of work to be done under such circumstances, £200 would have been nearly sufficient—

This may be made clear in the manner following—

Namely: . . . Amount of Estimate as before stated		334. 0. 0
Deduct for 5 Tons less of lead—	125. 0. 0	
Ditto for one fourth less new timber and boarding	32. 0. 0	157. 0. 0
		177. 0. 0
Add for contingencies 10 per cent on £177 + Value of old materials deducted from former estimate £135 = £312 =		31. 0. 0
Total £		208. 0. 0

Mr Pearson's design for the New Roof is unquestionably very superior to the old one, is a necessary part of his design in the restoration of the East front, and has I believe been approved by the Commissioners; but as a matter of repair so high a pitch would of course be unnecessary.

Relying therefore upon observations made whilst at Stow, and the tenour of former instructions, I considered that for the purposes of the Ecclesiastical Commissioners a repairing estimate was that which ought to form the basis of any calculation of the required expenditure, and upon this consideration my opinion as before expressed to you, was formed—

The construction proposed for the New Roof in Mr Pearson's design is sound and substantial, and will in my opinion be a great improvement upon any modification of the old one—I return you the tracings and estimates &c which I would not have retained so long, but that I have been absent from town on a distant journey.

[*Enclosures*] 2457/51.4b *and* 2537a/51.2a & 2b.

175. Eccl. Com., Estates Ctee, Minutes (Copy), 23 Sept. 1851 (EC)

Stow Church

Read

A Report (No. 2597/51) from Mr Christian with reference to a further plan, specification, and Estimate (Nos: 2457/51(4b)—2537a/51 (2b) and 2a.) relative to the restoration of the Chancel of Stow Church under the superintendance of Mr Pearson the Architect hitherto employed on it.

Resolved

That in addition to the arangements agreed on by the Committee of the 13th June last the Commissioners will be prepared to contribute for the purpose of reconstructing the roof 3/5ths of the sum of £376. 16. 1 at which the cost is estimated by Mr Pearson

176. To Eccl. Com. from Atkinson, 24 Sept. 1851 (EC)

Sir,

Stow Chancel

I beg to state that I received yesterday a letter from Mr Hall in reference to the subject of the proportion of the increased Estimate for the repair of this Chancel to be paid by the Lessees of the Rent Charge belonging to the Prebend of Stow—the determination of Mr Hall on the question between himself and Mr Ashton Cox, he has authorized me to communicate to the Ecclesiastical Commissioners for England, and it is so honourable to him that I cannot forbear to give it in his own words—

"Since the receipt of your Letter the subject of my proportion of the increased Estimate has occupied much of my thoughts, and though I still adhere to that view of my strictly legal obligations which was made known to the Commissioners I must admit the probability that the enforcing of any claim against Mr Cox might be attended with no little difficulty and delay, as well as be productive of hostile feeling towards you, his Pastor.

"In the alternative you mentioned, I cannot think of acquiescing, for it would be little short of injustice towards a Friend, did I permit a burden to devolve upon him, which, even were he better able than myself to bear it, certainly ought not to rest upon his shoulders.

"I therefore authorize you to inform Mr Chalk that I will be responsible for 2/5ths of the increased Estimate under the conditions proposed to you by the Commissioners.

"It will give me pleasure to find that by consenting to this, any obstruction has been removed in the way of an early resumption of the works at the Chancel, which have been so unfortunately interrupted."

Mr Hall enclosed for my perusal the Copy he had received from your Office of Mr Christian's report of the 26th of July in which I observe that the sum of £583 is exclusive of the Clerk of the works' salary and also of the Architect's charges, but as these expenses are as indispensible a part of the Cost as any other I beg respectfully to submit to the Ecclesiastical Commissioners that the Tithe Owners ought to share with the subscribers in their just proportion of this burthen.

177. To Hall from Eccl. Com. (Copy), 29 Sept. 1851 (EC)

Sir

Stow Chancel

By a letter from Mr Atkinson I learn that you are prepared to contribute 2/5ths of the increased estimate for these repairs, but as the precise amount of such estimate has not up to this time been named, I deem it right in order to avoid any misunderstanding hereafter to communicate it to you. The estimate for the general repairs, exclusive of the roof, has in accordance with Mr Christian's Report of the 26th July, of which you have a copy, been taken by the Commissioners at £583, and for the roof Mr Pearson's estimate of which I enclose a copy, amounting to £376. 16. 1 has been adopted making together an outlay required from the Tithe Owners of say £960.

Of this sum the 2/5ths to be contributed by you amounts to £384 and £200 of this having been already advanced, there remains to be paid by you the sum of £184.

I enclose a copy of Mr Christian's Report on Mr Pearson's estimate for the roof and on hearing from you that you adopt the figures I have stated above, I shall be prepared to make such a communication to Mr Atkinson as will I trust enable him to proceed with the works.

178. To Eccl. Com. from Hall, Wolfreton House, 30 Sept. 1851 (EC)

Sir

Stow Chancel

In stating to Mr Atkinson that I was prepared to contribute 2/5ths of an increased estimate for these repairs, I of course had in my view nothing beyond a "*repairing estimate*". Mr Christian took this as the basis of his calculation of the required expenditure for the roof & desirous as I am, that the works may be proceeded with, I decline to make myself responsible for more than 2/5ths of that which he considers to be sufficient for the purpose.

179. To Eccl. Com. from Hall, Wolfreton House, 8 Oct. 1851 (EC)

Sir,

Stow Chancel

Since my reply to your letter of the 29th Ulto I have been in communication with Mr Atkinson in reference to Mr Pearson's increased Estimate for the roof and after the explanations given by him as to other expences connected with the substantial repairs, but not included therein, my objections to adopting the figures stated by you have been removed.

Accordingly I have signified to Mr Atkinson that on my receiving from him an indemnity against all further claims or liability whatever in respect of the cost of completing these repairs, my proportion shall at once be paid to him.

Trusting that he will now be enabled to proceed with the works

180. To Atkinson from Eccl. Com. (Copy), 11 Oct. 1851 (EC)

Sir

Stow Chancel

I have the honor to acquaint you that I have received a letter from Mr Hall in which he states "that he has signified to you that on receiving an indemnity against all further claims or liability whatever in respect of the cost of completing these repairs, his proportion shall at once be paid to you".

I have submitted to the Commissioners your request as to the payment of the money and also as to an allowance for Architect and Clerk of the Works—to the former the Commissioners cannot accede, and with regard to the latter, you will see that Mr Christian has in both of his Reports allowed an addition of 10 per cent and the Commissioners do not feel called on to go further.

I have therefore only to refer you to my letter of the 29th July and to state that the Commissioners are prepared to carry out the offer therein made, subject to their liability in respect of the cost of the roof being limited to 3/5ths of £377 being the amount of Mr Pearson's estimate.

181. To Eccl. Com. from Atkinson, 14 Jan. 1852 (EC)

Sir

Stow Chancel

I have the honour to inform the Ecclesiastical Commissioners for England that the whole of the substantial repairs, and other works necessary to the complete restoration of this Chancel, are now in a forward state, and with the exception of the tiled floor will be shortly completed.

The Carpentry of the roof will be finished at the end of this week or the early part of next—the Lead is now all at the Church, and will be put on with all proper dispatch—the stone vaulting has been finished about three weeks. Under these circumstances I request that the Ecclesiastical Commissioners will make payment of £100 on account of their proportion of the Cost of the roof.

Mr Hall's proportion of the increased Estimate was paid in October.

182. To Atkinson from Eccl. Com., Accountant (Copy), 17 Jan. 1852 (EC)

Sir,

I have on behalf of the Ecclesiastical Commissioners for England to inform you that the Sum of £100—on account of their Grant for the purpose of reconstructing the Roof of the Chancel of the Church of St Mary's, Stow will be paid on the presentation by a Banker at this Office of a receipt signed by the Treasurer of the "Stow Church Restoration Fund"—

183. To Eccl. Com. from Atkinson, 18 March 1852 (EC)

Sir,

Stow Chancel.

The roof of this Chancel is now in all respects completed according to the plan and specification approved by the Ecclesiastical Commissioners for England, and the Plumber having applied for payment of the sum due to him, I have the honour to request that you will direct the balance of the Commissioners' proportion to the Cost amounting (£100 having been already received) to the sum of £126.13. 8 to be paid to the Treasurer of the "Stow Church Restoration Fund"

The whole of the works will be finished in the course of two or three weeks: when completed I shall have the pleasure of informing you.

184. To Atkinson from Eccl. Com. (Copy), 26 March 1852 (EC)

Sir

Stow Chancel

I am directed by the Ecclesiastical Commissioners for England to acquaint you with reference to your letter of the 18th Instant that upon their being furnished with Mr Pearson's certificate that the roof of the Chancel has been completed and that the sum of £126. 13. 8 is due to the Builder in respect of the Commissioners' proportion of the works, that amount will be forthwith paid as you have requested.

185. To Eccl. Com. from Atkinson, 30 March 1852 (EC)

Sir,

Stow Chancel

I beg to state in reference to your letter of the 26th Instant, that Mr Pearson was here for the purpose of making a final inspection of the Chancel works, at the time it reached me—and he would send a certificate of the completion of the roof on his return to London. This you will, I imagine, have received by this time.

I have this day requested the Treasurer of the Stow Church Restoration Fund to present a receipt through their London House for the Amount—

186. To Eccl. Com. from Pearson, 2 Delahay St, 31 March 1852 (EC)

Stow Chancel

Dear Sir,

Will you be good enough to lay the enclosed before the Board it refers only to the roof as you will see, the other works are however within a few days of being completed.

186A.

St Marys Stow—Lincolnshire
Chancel
No 3.

2 Delahay Street
March 31st 1852

I beg to certify that the new Roof of the Chancel has been put up in accordance with the drawings and specification submitted to and approved of by the Ecclesiastical Commissioners and that the whole is covered in with lead and all Gutters &c completed for carrying off the Water, and that the grant made by the Board towards this Work is now due—

John.L. Pearson.

To the Ecclesiastical Commissioners
of England
James Chalk Esqr Sec:

187. To Atkinson from Eccl. Com., Accountant (Copy), 5 April 1852 (EC)

Sir,

With reference to Messr Smith, Ellison & Co's Receipt for *£126. 13. 8* in respect of the balance of the Commissioners Grant towards re-constructing the roof of Stow Chancel, I beg leave on behalf of the Ecclesiastical Commissioners for England to remind you that Mr Pearson's Estimate of the 8th September last amounted to *£376. 16. 1*, 3/5 of which (less £100 paid 27th January last) is *£126. 1. 7* only, which latter amount will accordingly be paid to Messr Smith Payne & Co—

188. Vestry Book

Stowe, April 12th, 1852

A Vestry Meeting was held in the Church, according to Notice duly given, for the purpose of electing Churchwardens; and a Vestry Clerk for the year ensuing, and for any other business that may be then and there brought forward, "Present the Rev Geo. Atkinson in the chair, the Churchwardens Messrs Harrison and [*blank*]) and the following Parishioners,—Messrs Watson, Ellis, Jos Harrison, Howard, Northing, Taylor, R. Credland, Gor Harrison and others.

Proposed by William Ellis, and seconded by Jos Harrison that Henry Walker be Vestry-Clerk for the year ensuing carried unanimously

Proposed by William Watson, that John Harrison of Stowe, and Henry Walker of Sturton, be the Churchwardens for the year ensuing this was seconded by William Taylor.

The Chairman refusing to put the above proposition to the Meeting Mr Thos Spencer proposed—That whereas the Chairman the Rev Geo. Atkinson refuses to act and put the proposition by William Watson, that another Chairman be chosen, and proposes Mr Wm Ellis be chairman and buisness be proceeded with. this was seconded by Mr Wm Taylor, and carried unanimously

The Chairman hereupon put Mr Watsons proposition, viz,—that Mr John Harrison of Stow and Mr. Henry Walker, of Sturton be Churchwardens for the year ensuing which was seconded by Wm Taylor and carried [unanimously *erased*] by a large Majority.

Signed William Ellis Chairman
John Harrison } Churchwarden

Wm Watson
Wm Taylor
Thomas Spencer
Joseph Harrison
Robert Credland
} parishioners

189. To Eccl. Com. from Atkinson, 4 May 1852 (EC)

Sir,
Stow Chancel

I have the honour to state for the information of the Ecclesiastical Commissioners for England, that the works connected with the Restoration of this Chancel have been finished, and I shall feel obliged by the payment of the balance due on account of these works, so soon as the Commissioners shall have satisfied themselves that the works have been properly executed.

190. Eccl. Com., Estates Ctee, Minutes (Copy), 6 May 1852 (EC)

Stow Church
Chancel Repairs

Mr Christian to Inspect.
No Minute.

191. To Eccl. Com. from Ewan Christian, Lincoln, 12 May 1852 (EC)

Dear Sir,

Stow Chancel

Agreeably to the instructions in your letter of the 8th May, I have this day surveyed the Chancel at Stow, and beg to report that the restoration of that building is now entirely completed, and that the work has been executed in a sound substantial and satisfactory manner

192. To Atkinson from Eccl. Com., Accountant (Copy), 14 May 1852 (EC)

Sir,

Mr Christian having certified the Ecclesiastical Commissioners for England of the complete restoration of Stow Chancel, I am directed to advise you that £149. 16. 0 the balance of their whole Grant, will be paid upon presentation of the Treasurer's Receipt at this office.

193. Vestry Book

Stowe July 1st. 1852

A Vestry Meeting was held at Stowe, according to the following Notice duly given.

Notice is hereby given, that a Meeting will be held on Thursday Next, the first day of July 1852. at the house of Mr Thos. Palmer (the Cross Keys Inn) in Stowe, for the purpose of consulting and determining what Measures to adopt respecting the present unsettled affairs of the Church &c. All those Persons who occupy Church gardens would do well to attend and hear for themselves the Minds of the Parishioners.

Dated June 26th. 1852.

Present Mr John Skill, in the Chair the Churchwardens Messrs Harrison, and Walker, Mr A. Cox, Mr. J. Rose, Mr W. Palmer, Mr. J. Harrison, Mr. Geo Sergeant, Mr. G. Credland, Mr J. Butler, Mr. J. Wilkinson, Mr W. Ellis, &c.

Mr. John Skill proposed the following resolution that all those Persons occupying Church gardens who are in arrears do forthwith pay the respective amounts to Mr John Harrison the Parish Churchwarden, and that all the

Tenants do pay their rents as they become due to the Parish Churchwarden according to the usual custom.

And further that the Tenants be indemnified by the Parish by the delivery of a Receipt on payment, from any loss consequent on proceedings been taken against them by any other parties, this was seconded by Mr William Ellis and Carried unanimously.

The Chairman then enquired if there were any other buisness to come before the Meeting and been answered in the Negative declared the Meeting disolved.

Signed John Skill Chairman
Ashton Cox
Jonathan Rose
Joseph Harrison
George Sergeant John Butler
William Palmer John Wilkinson
George Credland William Ellis

194. To Eccl. Com. from Stow Churchwardens, 4 Oct. 1852 (EC)

To the Ecclesiastical Commissioners
for England.

We the undersigned Churchwardens for the parish of Stowe do hereby certify that whereas there are certain huge heaps of refuse in the Churchyard of Stowe which were accumulated during the repairs of the Chancel, also an unsightly shed which was erected for the accommodation of the workmen, the presence of which is a great inconvenience and annoyance, and altogether unseemly and improper to remain within the sacred precincts of a churchyard.

In obedience to instructions received from the Archdeacon at his Visitation we the said Churchwardens do hereby give you notice to remove the said refuse and shed without delay and clear the Churchyard of all remains pertaining to the repairs.

Signed John Harrison } Churchwardens
Henry Walker }

P.S.—If you have any communication to make, please to direct to us by Name.

Note: This communication and the two following were read at a meeting of the Estates Committee, 23 October 1852.

195. To Mr John Harrison from Eccl. Com. (Copy), 8 Oct. 1852 (EC)

Sir

Stow Church Chancel Repairs

In reply to your letter of the 4th Instant with reference to the state of this Church yard I beg to acquaint you that I have forwarded a copy of your communication to the Revd George Atkinson the Perpetual Curate of Stow under whose direction the recent reparation of the Chancel was executed.

196. To Eccl. Com. from Atkinson, 9 Oct. 1852 (EC)

Sir,

Stow Church

I have the honour to acknowledge the receipt of your letter enclosing a copy of a communication received by you from this Parish. Yesterday I heard from Mr Hall who has received a similar communication, and for the information of the Ecclesiastical Commissioners for England I beg to submit the following statement of the true facts on the subject in question.

1. The persons who have addressed you are not the legal Churchwardens of the Parish, but two persons of no weight or consideration who have been illegally nominated by a small faction of dissenters and other opponents of the Church, in order to obstruct the repairing of the rest of the fabric. Two other Churchwardens were duly elected in Vestry who according to the opinion of two eminent Counsel are the legal Churchwardens. This will explain to you the reason of the request at the foot of their Communication that you would address them by *Name*. I may add that these two persons were severely rebuked by the Bishop at his late Visitation on account of their factious conduct, and for their illegal intrusion into the office.

2. The Archdeacon has had no Visitation since the spring of this year, and I am certain that he gave no such instructions then as they allege, and consequently they must be making an untrue statement in saying that, . . . instructions &c "*at his Visitation*".

3. I need not trouble you with the details relating to the shed rubbish &c on which I am, in fact, in communication with the Archdeacon—but of course neither the Ecclesiastical Commissioners nor Mr Hall can be held responsible for, or be required to remove anything. I myself, as the Contractor in fact for the completion of the reparation of the Chancel, am alone answerable (were there anything to answer for) and this responsibility I am quite prepared to take wholly on myself.

197. Vestry Book

Stowe Nov 8th, 1852.

A public [Parish *del*] Meeting was held, according to Notice to that effect, at the House of Mr Geo. Knowles, (the Red Lion Inn) in Sturton, at the hour of 6 oclock in the evening; for the purpose of consulting and determining what Measures to adopt in the following case.

A demand having been Made, (by order of the Rev Geo. Atkinson,) upon the Parish Churchwardens, of all Books, Monies, Goods, &c, belonging to and connected with the Church, and in consequence of a refusal to deliver up the same, and betray the trust reposed in them by the Parishioners; an Action has been commenced in the "Court of Queens Bench," (at the instance of the Rev. Geo. Atkinson) at the suit of John. H. Locke, and Writs have been issued, and Copies have been served upon the said Churchwardens.

Present Mr. W. Ellis, in the Chair, Messrs W. Watson, Burton, G Sergeant, R Harrison, W Buttry, Webster, J Harrison, W. Hill, G Harrison, J. Middleton, J Howell, J. Wilkinson, J S Gelder, J Buttler, J Lilley, Mr A. Cox, Mr T. Spencer, R Credland, Mr R. Gilbert, Mr J. Jollands, Mr W Hutchinson, Mr G. B. Sikes, the Parish Churchwardens Messrs Harrison, & Walker, Mr E. Watson,

Proposed by Mr Spencer, and seconded by Mr R Harrison, that Mr. W. Ellis, take the Chair, Carried unanimously. Proposed by Mr A Cox, and seconded by Mr John Jollands, that the Churchwardens do enter an appearance against the copies of the Writs, issued from the "Court of Queens Bench", at the suit of John. H. Locke, against them. This Motion was put to the Meeting and declared to be carried unanimously.

Proposed by Mr. T. Spencer, and seconded by Mr. A. Cox, that this Meeting do pledge itself, to indemnify and bear the Churchwardens harmless in any expence they may incur or loss they may sustain in defending this suit. This Motion was put to the Meeting and declared to be carried unanimously.

The Chairman having enquired if there were any other buisness to be brought foward, and been answered in the Negative, he declared the Meeting desolved.

Signed William Ellis Chairman
in behalf of the Meeting.

198. Vestry Book

Stowe in Lindsey } A parish meeting was held according to notice duly given on thursday the twentyfifth day of Novr at 3 oclock in the afternoon in the Church of Stowe for the purpose of submitting to the consideration of the parishioners the Declaration from the "Court of Queens Bench."

Also to take into consideration the recent shame[ful] desecration of the Church yard and the damage done to the graves &c. And for any other buisness which may be then and there brought forward. Proposed by Mr T. Spencer, and seconded by Mr Geo. Sikes that Mr. J. S. Gelder, do take the Chair and preside at this Meeting carried unanimously. Present Mr A. Cox, Mr. T. Spencer, Mr W. Watson Mr J. S. Gelder, Mr R. Harrison, Mr J. Harrison, Mr Geo. Harrison Mr. G. Sergeant, Mr G. B. Sikes, Mr. R. Taylor, Mr. J. Buttler Mr. T. Smith, Mr W. Buttrey, Mr. W. Ellis,

Proposed by Mr A. Cox, that this Meeting do adjourn to the Cross Keys Inn in Stowe, there to transact the buisness of the day. Mr A. Cox proposed That it is desirable (in order to put an end to an action at law brought by the Minister of this parish, the Rev. Geo. Atkinson against Mr John Harrison, & Mr. H. Walker, the Churchwardens elected on Easter monday last by a meeting held for that purpose, that they the said Churchwardens, should vacate their office and give up the books &c held by them to one of those persons, who have been declared by the minister of this parish to have been elected Churchwardens at a meeting held on the same easter monday that is to say Mr W. Hutinchson & Mr John. H. Locke—And also that for the future the parish will concede to the Minister the privilege of choosing one Churchwarden reserving to itself the right of electing the other. And be it understood, that the concession is made solely for the purpose of putting an end to the litigation between the Minister and the parishioners and with the hope that friendship and good feeling will henceforth exist between both parties and that each party will use every means within its power to promote the same. seconded by Mr G. B. Sikes the Motion was lost.

Mr. T. Spencer proposed the following Amendment that the Manuscripts, Books, & Keys, be delivered to Mr J. H. Locke this evening and be it understood, that this concession is made solely for the purpose of putting an end to the litigation between the Minister and the parishioners; and with the hope that friendship and good feeling will henceforth exist between both parties and that each party will use every means within its power to procure the same, seconded by Mr. W. Ellis Carried by a large Majority.

Proposed by Mr. W. Ellis and seconded by Mr. A. Cox, that Mr. John. Harrison, & Mr. Henry Walker, be requested to inform Mr Plaskett the defendants Solicitor of the course persued,—and to ask him to request the plaintiffs solicitor to withdraw the action & get the costs taxed in order that the same may be discharged. Carried unanimously.

Mr T Spencer, moved and Mr G. B. Sikes, seconded the following Motion That a copy of the resolution passed at this Meeting be forwarded immediately to the Rev. Geo. Atkinson, the Minister of the parish and that he be informed at the same time in whose hands the Church books &c. are placed.

And also that he be requested to give instructions to his solicitor to withdraw the action upon the defendants solicitor paying taxed costs, carried unanimously.

Mr. A. Cox Moved and Mr. G. B. Sikes seconded the following Motion,—That as soon as Mr Plaskett obtained an account of the costs, he will be good enough to forward it to the defendants, and that immediately it is received meeting shall be called for the purpose of raising the Money and discharging the account. Carried unaimously.

Mr. G. B. Sikes Moved and Mr. W. Ellis seconded the following Motion.—That the thanks of this parish are due and therefore are recorded by this Meeting to Mr. John Harrison, & Mr Henry Walker, for their fidelity to this parish during the time they have held the office of Churchwardens, and also for their condesention in giving up the Book &c and vacating Office when required to do so by the foregoing resolutions.—Carried unanimously.

Mr. G. B. Sikes, Moved and Mr. A. Cox seconded a vote of thanks to Mr. J. S. Gelder, for the very able and disinterested Manner in which he has fulfilled the duties of his office carried unanimously.

The Chairman having enquired if there were any more buisness to come before the Meeting and been answered in the negative declared the Meeting disolved.

Signed James. S. Gelder Chairman
in behalf of the Meeting

199. Vestry Book

Stowe in Lindsey } A parish meeting was held according to notice given on wednesday the 29th day of Dec 1852. at the Cross Keys Inn in Stowe. For the purpose of opening a subscription to raise money to defray Defendants Costs incurred in the recent suit viz,—Locke,—v—Harrison & Walker.—Also to consider what measures to adopt concerning the Church-Lands under the present circumstances. And for any other business which may be then & there brought forward.

Present the following parishioners Mr. J. Skill, Mr. T. Spencer, Mr. W. Palmer, Mr J. Harrison, Mr W. Ellis, Mr J Watson, Mr R Credland, Mr R Harrison, Mr G Harrison, Mr Jenkinson, Mr J Middleton, Mr G Sergeant, Mr J Buttler, & others.

Mr W. Ellis was unanimously called to the Chair to conduct the business of the Meeting.

Mr John Skill, proposed the following resolution that a voluntary subscription be entered into at this time at the Meeting for the purpose of discharging the said Costs & that a List of the Subscripers be made out which list shall be taken round to all parishioners and what they give be entered & if at the conclusion of the solicitation there be more Money then covers the Debt the surplus to be returned to each subscriber according to the proportion of his subscription. Mr. R. Harrison. seconded this Motion, carried 'Nem.-Con,'.

Mr John Skill proposed & Mr G Harrison seconded the following Motion That Mr John Harrison, & Mr William Ellis, be appointed Collectors of the Church Garden Rents, pay the Parish Clerk, order the repair of the Church leads &c Carried unanimously.

The Chairman having enquired if there where any other business to come before the meeting & been answered in the negative declared the meeting disolved.

Signed in behalf of the Meeting } William Ellis Chairman

200. Vestry Book

A Vestry Meeting was held according to Notice duly given, in the Parish Church of Stowe, on Easter Monday the 28th day of Mar 1853, at a quarter past eleven oclock in the Morning; for the purpose of choosing Churchwardens for the Year ensuing.

Present the Rev. George Atkinson, Incumbent in the Chair.—and the following parishioners; Mr. A. Cox, Mr. T. Spencer, Mr W. Watson, Mr. W. Watson, Mr. W. Ellis, Mr. G. Sergeant, Mr. R Credland, Mr. R. Harrison, Mr. G. Harrison, Mr. J. Harrison, Mr J. Brumby, Mr. J. Jollands, Mr J. Northing, Mr J. Buttler, Mr J Watson, Mr. J. Palmer, and others.

The Rev. G. Atkinson appointed Mr Anthony Gibbs, be one of the Churchwardens for the ensuing year. the Minister refusing to concur with the parishioners in a joint appointment.

Mr A. Cox proposed, and Mr. W. Ellis seconded that Mr John Harrison of Stowe, be one of the Churchwardens for the parish of Stowe for the year ensuing, carried unanimously.

George Atkinson Minister
Chairman—

Mr. T. Spencer proposed the following resolution,—That this Vestry protests against the Assumption of the Incumbent to choose one of the Churchwardens, as a violation of its ancient rights. The records of the Parish plainly showing, that for 140 years Stowe and Normanby have chosen one, and Sturton and Bransby the other. seconded by Mr John Sergeant. The Chairman refused to put to vote the above resolution, it was put by the Mover and carried by a large Majority—

William Ellis	Thos Spencer
George Sergeant	Robert Harrison
John Butler	John Sergeant
George Harrison	

201. *Vestry Book*

Stowe in Lindsey, } A Vestry Meeting was held according to Notice duly given, in the Church of Stowe, on thursday the second day of June, 1853., at the hour of six oclock P.M. for the purpose of calling for the production to the Vestry, of the several Vestry Books, Books of acts, and other documents, pertaining to the office of Churchwardens. This been done will render an opportunity of the acts been passed.

Also to require the delivery up to the Churchwardens of the several Church Goods which any person may posses the Churchwardens been the legal custodiers of all goods belonging to the Church. Also for the purpose of appointing a proper and efficient person to take charge of and to have the custody of all Books, Documents, Papers, Accounts, Vouchers &c belonging to the office of Churchwardens.

Present the following Parishioners viz.—Messrs J Skill, A Cox, T Spencer J S Gelder, W. Ellis, W. Palmer, J. Palmer J Harrison, J Jollands W. Watson J Buttler R. Credland G Knowles G Credland J Spink G Sergeant and numerous other ratepayers. The Rev. G. Atkinson in the Chair.

The Chairman then called for the production of the Books, &c., specified in the Notice, which were immediately produced by Henry Walker, who held them by consent of a Vestry Meeting, held last Easter Monday, the 28th day of March, 1853.

Proclaimation been made for John. H Locke to come forward and produce his accounts has Churchwarden for the year last past but not appearing the Accounts as they stand in the Book for the year commencing Easter 1852 and ending Easter 1853 must stand as they do until Mr John. H. Locke returns. And that for the present there appearing no monies in his hands the Books &c be passed over to the present Churchwardens.

Signed in behalf of the Vestry } George Atkinson Chairman.

202. *Vestry Book*

Stowe in Lindsey } A Vestry Meeting was held according to Notice duly given in the Church on Thursday the eighteenth day of August 1853. at the hour of seven oclock P.M. For the purpose of taking into consideration the condition of the Church and to ascertain the repairs required. Also to consider the best mode of proceeding for the Collection of the outstanding Rents due from the Holders of the Church Lands. And to examine the Accounts of what has been collected. And for any other buisness which may be then and there brought forward.—

Present Messrs A. Cox, T. Spencer, W. Palmer, J. Palmer, W. Ellis, W. Watson, J. Rose, J. Harrison, G. Sergeant, W. Taylor, J. Buttler, R. Hill, and other parishioners & Mr J Harrison Churchwarden. Mr J. Harrison was unanimously called to the Chair to conduct the buisness of the Meeting.

A Letter was handed to the Chairman signed Antony Gibbs, which was read to the Meeting. Mr A. Cox, Moved, & Mr T Spencer, seconded the following Motion.—That Mr Antony Gibbs, not having been considered by the Parishioners one of the Churchwardens in consequence of not been eligible for appointment to the Office, by his non-residence in the Parish previous to the day on which the Churchwardens are chosen; and he has not yet been countenanced in the Office by the Parishioners. That this Meeting declines receiving any dictation from him, has set forth in his Letter addressed to the Chairman of the Meeting.—This Motion been put to the vote, it was carried by a large Majority.

Moved by Mr A Cox, and seconded by Mr W. Ellis, That this Meeting doo adjourn until Thursday, the eighth day of september, 1853., at the hour of three oclock P.M., to allow an opportunity for the Minister to be present.— This Motion been put to the vote, it was carried nem-con,—.

Joseph Harrison Chairman

203. Vestry Book

Stow September 8, 1853

The adjourned Vestry meeting was held this day according to adjournment from the 18th day of August last in the Parish Church of Stow at the hour of three OClock in the afternoon. Present The Reverend George Atkinson the Incumbent in the Chair, Mr Ashton Cox, Mr Jonathan Rose, and Mr John Harrison one of the Churchwardens.

As the attendance of the Parishioners was so small on account of the harvest, it was moved by Mr Cox, and seconded by Mr Rose that this Vestry be further adjourned till Thursday the 6th day of October next at the hour of three o'Clock in the afternoon. This motion was carried and the meeting adjourned accordingly.

George Atkinson M.A Chairman

204. Vestry Book

Stow October 6th 18/53.

The adjourned Vestry meeting of the 18th August last was held in the Parish Church on 6th day of October 1853 at the hour of three o'clock in the afternoon.

Present. The Minister in the chair, The Churchwardens. Mr Cox, Mr Skill, Mr John Sargeant, Mr Ellis, Mr Wilkinson, Messrs J & G Harrison, J. Palmer, W. Hill, J. Watson, J. Rose and others. Moved by Mr A Cox seconded by Mr Skill that no estimate be received from the hands of Mr A. Gibbs no instruction having been given by the parishioners to him to procure any. This resolution was put to the meeting by the Chairman and carried.

A discussion took place amongst the parishioners respecting the amount to be raised for the necessary repairs of the church, which was estimated at about two thousand pounds, a much larger sum than the parishioners were able to provide. The sum of five hundred pounds was considered as large an amount as the parishioners would consent to raise by borrowing, to be paid off in instalments. This would be done provided the further sum required could be raised by subscription.

George Atkinson—Minister— }
Chairman }

205. Vestry Book

Stowe in Lindsey { A parish meeting was held according to Notice given on Thursday 10th November 1853. The Notice is as follows. Notice Stow Novr 5/1853. The parishioners are requested to take notice that in consequence of the parish Churchwarden receiving a monition from the Archdeacon to procure funds to repair the church in a substantial manner. And in case of disobedience to this monition a prosecution to be commenced against the Churchwardens or the Parishioners in the Ecclesiastical Court.

Therefore a Vestry meeting will be held in the Church on Thursday the tenth day of November 1853, at the hour of three O'clock in the afternoon When the Monition will be laid before the Meeting, and to adopt such measures as may appear necessary for making a rate, and carrying such rate into execution.

Also to cause the removal of some earth from the burying ground. And for any other purpose that may come before the meeting. N.B. The Bell to ring at half-past two. The meeting to commence at three

Signed {John Harrison {Churchwardens

Present Mr Joseph Harrison Chairman, Mr W. Palmer, Mr Ellis, Mr Burton, Mr. John Watson junr., Mr John Watson, Mr Hill, Mr Smith, Mr Thos Palmer, Mr T. Dickinson, Mr Joseph Palmer, Mr Spenser, Mr Gelder, Mr Robt Harrison, Mr J. Rose, Mr James Gilbert, Mr George Sargeant, Mr John Wilkinson, Mr Wm Buttery, Mr John Harrison Churchwarden.

John Harrison Churchwarden proposed a rate of sixpence in the pound, in obedience to the Archdeacon's monition, after enquiry being made by the chairman, no one was found to second the motion.

Wheras, Mr Gelder proposed, and seconded by Mr Robert Harrison that no rate be granted until such time as the Incumbent has made recompence to the parish for all the damage that he has done to the interior of the Church, (viz) The singing and ringing galleries, Pews, and stones from the floors, &c this proposition was put to the meeting by the church warden and carried unanimously. Mr Wm Buttery moved that the Clergyman is reprehensible in allowing refuse that he claims as his private property to cumber the graves of his parishioners, and wishes for such refuse to be removed without doing any damage to the graves; this motion was seconded by Mr Robert Harrison, and carried unanimously.

Signed {
Joseph Harrison Chairman
John Harrison Churchwarden
Wm G. Dodsworth,
Vestry Clerk

206. Vestry Book

Stow in Lindsey { A Parish meeting was held according to notice on Thursday 9th day of February 1854. The notice is as follows,

Parish of Stow Febry 4th 1854

Notice that a Vestry meeting will be held in the church on Thursday the ninth day of February at the hour of four o clock in the afternoon, to take into consideration the inadequate salary of the clerk at the present period, as the work he has to perform now is twice as much as what it was at the time he was put into office by the parishioners. viz. First the incumbent taking down the ringing gallery and other causes equally inconsistent. The belfry door being placed in an improper place either for Sunday service or funerals & And for any other purpose that may come before the Meeting.

N.B. That no notes or letters of dictation shall not be received into this vestry unless such notes or letters are accompanied with a Certificate from a Medical Doctor. Feby 4th 1854.

Signed John Harrison, Churchwarden

1st Mr Wm Ellis proposed seconded by Mr Wm Buttery that Mr Joseph Harrison be Chairman for this meeting. Carried unanimously. The meeting was adjourned to the Cross Keys Inn.

Mr William Palmer proposed seconded by Mr William Taylor that the salary of the Parish Clerk, and all other outstanding debts belonging to the nave of the Church be paid by the parish Churchwarden out of any funds, that may come to his hands belonging to the Church. Carried unanimously.

2nd Mr Robert Harrison proposed seconded by Mr William Ellis that the parish Clerk is not to do any more work, than he was engaged to do at the time of his appointment, (viz) to attend the Sunday services, and the Church Clock, and the cleanliness of the seats in the Church. This proposition was also carried unanimously.

3rd Mr Robert Harrison proposed, seconded by Mr Wm Buttery that the key of the original belfry door be demanded for admission to ring the bells at the proper times; and if such key is refused, the bells to remain still. Carried unanimously.

4th Mr William Ellis proposed seconded by Mr Robert Harrison, that the old unbecoming wagon gate leading into the Church-yard near to Mr Middleton's shop, be removed and a small convenient gate be replaced in its stead. Carried unanimously.

The Chairman enquired if there were any other business to come before the meeting, being answered in the negative the meeting was dissolved.

Signed,

Joseph Harrison Chairman
W. G. Dodsworth, Vestry Clerk
John Harrison Churchwarden

Parishioners: William Palmer, William Taylor, William Ellis, William Buttery, William Hill, William Middleton, Robert Harrison

Note: The Notice for the meeting harks back to Atkinson's actions of 1846 (See Nos 8 and 94). The "original belfry door" refers to the external door in the east wall of the north transept just by the old rood screen stairs which in turn gave access to the ringing gallery in the crossing which had been removed in 1846. This door was later blocked up. The "improperly placed" door was the door from outside which gave access to the belfry stairs, then within the nave, but gave no access to the rest of the church as had the "original belfry door". See No. 213 (note).

For the point of Mr Palmer's motion, see pp. xx–xxi.

207. To Eccl. Com. from Atkinson, 23 Feb. 1854 (EC)

Stow Chancel
Sir

I am sorry to have to inform you that within the last two or three weeks malicious damage has been done to the Chancel windows by stones thrown through them

When the first injuries were done I acquainted Mr Cox of Stow Park, who has purchased the lease of the Tithes on his farm from Mr Hall, and he promised to make some enquiry.

This week two fresh windows have been broken, and it is high time that some measures of prevention were taken, as offering a reward for discovery, or there is no saying to what extent further injury may be done.

I am writing to Mr Cox and Mr Hall—if you should think proper to communicate with them on the subject—The address of the former is

Ashton Cox Esq.
Stow Park
Gainsborough

of the latter

The Revd S. W. Hall
Wolfreton House
Hull.

Note: This was not the first instance of malicious damage to the church. In 1852 the Rural Dean, Mr Peel, reported: "The transepts and nave are in a sad state, especially the South transept, in which the windows are very much broken. The Church Wardens complain that the transept was made use of as a workshop by the persons who repaired the chancel. But I am of a very different opinion. The breakage of the windows I perceive is continually going on, and I believe it done by some evil disposed persons. An attempt has been made to break into the church, but it failed." Quoted in *A Stow Visitation* (See No. 27, note) p. 97.

The damage to the church windows continued and resulted in a long correspondence which has had to be omitted for lack of space. Ashton Cox, as resident tithe owner, at first agreed to subscribe his share of a £10 reward for information, but then dragged his feet. He wrote to the Commissioners on 7 May 1855, "I beg leave to recommend that no reward be offered nor other proceedings taken at the present time, but that the past be forgiven, with a hope that the like may not occur again. The old Clerk Middleton has been dismissed by the Archdeacon, and Mr Churchwarden Harrison is not yet allowed to go out alone his brain or mind being injured through illness that he has been suffering since a little time before Easter". The stone throwing nevertheless continued and proceedings were taken against William Middleton. These were discontinued, much to Atkinson's annoyance, on the receipt of an apology from Middleton: "I, William Middleton of Stow beg to express my regret to the Ecclesiastical Commissioners for England for having broken Windows in the Chancel of Stow Church and I firmly believe that at the time I did so my mind was disordered as I am frequently afflicted with fits . . ." This was dated 1 March 1856 and witnessed by the Commissioners' agent, Alfred Search, and by Joseph Palmer. Atkinson's long memorial of complaint, dated 8 April 1856 finished as follows: "It should be mentioned that besides the mischief done to the Chancel windows, a great part of the glazing of the Transepts, including that of one whole window, a large one, has been altogether demolished, and so remains at present, and that since the transaction complained of in this memorial a stone has been thrown through one of the windows of the Nave [in which at this time services were held]—in respect to which also suspicion rests on Middleton".

208. Vestry Book

Stow, April 17/54

A Vestry meeting was held in the Church of Stow this day according to notice duly given for the purpose of choosing the parish churchwardens for the year ensuing. Present The Incumbent in The Chair The Churchwardens Messrs W. Watson Josh Harrison Josh Palmer W Buttery J Butler W Smith Geo Credland J Middleton Burton J Watson W Hill W Ellis J Rose T Palmer W Palmer A Cox Robt Harrison & others.——

It having been proposed that The Minister and parishioners should agree on a joint Choice and it being found that they could not so agree they proceeded to a seperate election.

The Incumbent appointed Mr Antony Gibbs as his Churchwarden for the year ensuing.

Mr Jno Wilkinson proposed and Mr William Burton seconded that Mr Jno Harrison be one of the Churchwardens of the Parish of Stow for the year ensuing. This resolution on being put to the meeting was declared to be carried unanimiously.

George Atkinson, Minister Chairman
Chas G Smith V.C.

Note: The minutes are a bland account if the description of the same meeting in *The Lincolnshire Chronicle* of 21 April 1854 is to be believed. "If anyone wishes to see human nature in one of its lowest and worst states, he should attend a vestry meeting of the Parish of Stow. . . . The vicar . . . chose the same churchwarden whom he had selected in the previous year. This gentleman has made a most magnificent present to the church of an altar cloth and carpet, a complete set of church services, magnificent cloth curtains to cover the two large doors"—the third, the west door was bricked up at this time—"cocoa-nut matting for the floor, hassocks, &c. . . . The vicar in vain hope of obtaining common decency of behaviour towards his churchwarden, directed their attention to his magnificent gift. This was only the signal for fresh insult and contumely. Everything ill-natured and unchristian, which it appeared to be in their power to utter, they poured forth. But, when one of their number, who appeared to have a great deal of right feeling and good sense, stood up to withstand them, and said that, he for one, thought that a vote of thanks ought to be passed to Mr. Gibbs for his kind gift, the yell that was uttered, the ferocious looks that were turned upon him, and the coarse expressions used, might have been supposed to come from so many demons. . . ." It is tempting to guess that it was Ashton Cox who thus exposed himself.

209. Vestry Book

Stowe in Lindsey } A Parish Meeting was held according to Notice on Thursday May 11th. 1854.

Copy of the Notice.

Parish of Stowe 1854

Notice is hereby given that a Vestry Meeting will be held at the House of Mr George Knowles the Red Lion Inn, in Sturton, on Thursday the eleventh day of May instant at the hour of four o'clock in the afternoon for the purpose of taking into consideration the advice which the Churchwarden did receive from the Judge at Lincoln he being defendant in the suit promoted by the Rev. Geo: Atkinson v. Harrison, when such advice will be laid before the meeting, and to adopt such measures as may appear necessary for carrying that advice into execution—and for any other purpose that may come before the meeting.

(Signed) John Harrison Churchwarden
for the Parish of Stowe.

Present—Wm Taylor, Jas Gelder, J. Rose, Geo. Sergeant, Robt Credland, Robt Harrison, Jno Jollands, Wm Hunt, Jas Brumby, Robt Taylor, Wm Howell, Thos Ingham, Jno Middleton, Wm Hill, Robt Smithson, Jno Wilkinson, Jno Watson, Wm Watson Senr, Wm Buttery, Josh Harrison,

Wm Taylor proposed seconded by John Watson that Joseph Harrison be Chairman for this Meeting. Carried Unanimously.

Proposed by George Sergeant seconded by Wm Hill that the Churchwarden employ Wm Plaskitt Solicitor of Gainsbro' to obtain a Prohibition in the Queen's Bench against the Citation Atkinson v. Harrison forthwith. Carried Unanimously.

Signed in and on behalf of this Meeting

Joseph Harrison Chairman
J. W. Hope Vestry Clerk

Note: This meeting presumably planned a move to stop the suit in the Consistory Court described in No. 213N.

210. Vestry Book

Vestery Meeting was held in the parish porch on the 16 of November 1854 at the hour of 3 O Clock in the afternoon and after the Notice being read over Mr Wm Buttery moved that this Meeting adjourn to thee Cross Keys Inn and seconded by John Woodhouse it was Carried.

Parish of Stow Nov 11 1854

Notice is hereby given that a vestery meeting will be held in the Church on Thursday the sixteenth day of November Instant at the hour of three O Clock in the afternoon. After the Meeting has been Open'd by the Notice been read over, that it is intended that such vestery do adjourn to the Cross Keys Inn there to transact the Business of the day (Viz) to appoint a proper person to take the Management of the Parish Clock. Also to order and direct the payment of seven pounds due to Mr Middleton for Clark wages on the eleventh day of October last past. And further for the purpose of removing the gate and posts to their former situation, that is the North side enterance into the Churchyard it been the ancient gate-way and the opening where the said gate now stand be walled up has it was formerly before the Revd Geo Atkinson pulled it down. And for any other busisness that may come before the Vestery.

Dated Nov the 11, 1854

Signed John Harrison Churchwarden

The Revd Objected to Open the Church Door

Present Mr Wm Taylor Messrs Wm Palmer Mr J Skill Mr Watson Mr Jollands Mr J Harrison Mr Spink Mr J Woodhouse Mr Wm Ellis Mr Jonathan Rose Mr Robt Harrison Mr J S Gelder Mr J Middleton Mr J Buttler Mr Buttery Mr T Ingham Churchwarden Mr Robert Credland Mr J Brumby Mr Wm Watson Mr R Thomas Mr Wm Hill Mr G Sergent Mr J Wilkinson

Mr Joseph Harrison proposed that Mr Wm Taylor be Chairman and seconded by Mr Robert Harrison it was carried

Mr Robert Harrison proposed that Mr Wm Middleton look after the Church Clock Seconded by Mr John Wilkinson, Mr W Middleton stated that he would do the work for the sum of five pounds per annum. If he can have peacable access to it if not the Clock to remain silent

this being put to the Meeting by the Chairman, it was carried uniamiously

Proposed by Joseph Harrison that the clerk wages now due be paid as usual out of any funds that coms to the Churchwardens hands. Seconded by Mr G Sergent. Carried unimuosly

Proposed by Mr Wm Ellis that the gate in front of the South porch be removed to the North side of the Churchyard to its ancient place; and the place where it now stands be walled up

Seconded by Mr J Harrison this propistion was carried unimously.

Signed Wm Taylor, Chairman

John Harrison. Churchwarden

Robert Credland Vestery Clark

John Woodhouse	X Thomas Ingham his Mark	parishioners
Robert Harrison	William Hill	
John Butler	William Buttery	
John Middleton	William Ellis	
George Sergeant	Joseph Harrison	

211. Vestry Book

Stow in Lindsey } A parish Meeting was Called in the Church by the Churchwarden according to Notice duly given on Thursday the eighteenth day of January, 1855. The Revd George Atkinson refused to Open the Church door for such meeting Also refused the Key to ring the Bell.

Notice of Vestry Meeting Parish of Stow.

The inhabitants have requested the Churchwarden to Call a vestry meeting in The Church on Thursday the eighteenth day of January Instant at the hour of three O Clock in the afternoon—

For the purpose of taking into Consideration the parish Clock *Which is at present Silent*

Dated this 13th day of Jany 1855

Signed John Harrison.

Church Warden

Present Mr Wm Palmer Mr Wm Ellis Mr Jos Harrison Mr Jno Watson Mr Jas Brumby Mr Jonathan Rose Mr Wm Buttery Mr Jno Middleton Mr Geo Knowles Mr George Sergeant Mr John Buttler

Proposed by Mr J Watson that Mr W Ellis be Chairman and Seconded by Mr Wm Buttery Carried unamisously

Proposed by Mr Buttery that Mr Robert Credland be vestry Clerk for this Meeting, and Seconded by Mr Joseph Harrison Carried.

Proposed by Mr Jos Harrison and Seconded by Mr John Watson That no person what so ever, or whom so ever does any thing to the Church Clock except the person appointed at the former Meeting to wind up the Clock and keep it in order, any person found spoiling or any way doing damage to the Clock will be persecuted, that no person shall have access save him who has been appointed at the former Vestery this being put to the Meeting Carried unanimously

Moved by Mr George Sergeant Seconded by Mr Jo Buttler that if the Revd George Atkinson refused to give up one Key that a New Lock and Key be bought and put on the door to protect the parish Clock and Bells there is nothing there but what is purely Temperal and they belong to the Churchwarden—Carried unanimously

The Chairman enquired if there were any other business to come before the Meeting being answered in the negative the meeting was dissolved

Sined	William Ellis Chairman	George Sergeant
	Robert Credland	Joseph Harrison
	John Harrison Churchwarden	John Butler

William Buttery John Middleton
William Hill John Watson

212. To Bp Jackson from parishioners of Stow, 9 March 1855 (Lincolnshire Times, *17 April 1855*)

The humble petition of the parishioners of Stow (who are churchmen), in the division of Lindsey, in the diocese of Lincoln, to the Right Rev. the Lord Bishop of the Diocese,

Showeth.—That the Rev George Atkinson, M.A., has been incumbent of the parish of Stow for upwards of 17 years.

That nearly the whole of this period the said Rev. George Atkinson and your Lordship's humble petitioners have been on unfriendly terms, if not at open emnity with each other—this state of affairs having been brought about by Mr. Atkinson himself, through his overt and wayward conduct

That the said Rev. George Atkinson has frequently outraged the morals and religious sentiments of your lordship's petitioners by pertinaciously refusing to inter their dead according to the usual form and custom, as prescribed and set forth in the Book of Common Prayer, and to let women return thanks after childbirth, besides many other monstrosities which he has committed, but which your lordship's petitioners do not deem it necessary to now relate.

That in consequence of such indecencies and improper conduct on the part of the said Rev. George Atkinson, he has driven and alienated your lordship's petitioners from their devotional duties in the church in which their forefathers have devoutly and attachedly worshipped for many generations past; and we, their descendants, deeply regret that in consequence of the conduct of our minister, we are unable to follow their pious example.

That the parish of Stow contains about 5,000 acres of land, and 170 ratepayers, and about 1,050 inhabitants, of which inhabitants the following number of adults have attended church on the Sundays specified, viz:—

1853			1854		
May 29	23	adults	March 19	6	adults
June 19.......	21	,,	,, 26	14	,,
July 10.......	20	,,	April 2	12	,,
,, 24.......	21	,,	,, 16	20	,,
Aug 7.........	25	,,			

—All these were morning services.

That if your lordship will be pleased to try and reconcile the said Rev. George Atkinson to your petitioners, whose unreserved amnesty will be readily granted, your lordship will render a great service to the parishioners of Stow.

213. Vestry Book

Stow Saturday March 31st 1855.

A Vestry Meeting was held this day in the Church according to Notice duly given for the purpose of making a formal reply to the Bishop's Letter. Present Mr Wm Ellis. Mr Robert Harrison Mr Wm Buttery. Mr T Spencer. Mr W Watson. Mr Jollands. The Church Warden in the Chair.

The Bishop's Letter was read, and ordered to be inserted in the Vestry Book.

Mr Wm Ellis proposed that a Committee be formed of five parishioners to prepare an answer to the Bishop's Letter to be submitted to a future vestry. Seconded by Robt Harrison.

The following parishioners were proposed to form that Committee and unanimously Chosen. (viz) Messrs John Skill. Wm Ellis. Joseph Harrison. Wm Taylor. J. S. Gelder. With power to add two men more if the Committee sees it needful to do so.

Copy of
The Bishop's Letter.

Riseholme Lincoln
Feby 27th 1855

Sir.

On the 9th inst. a Memorial or petition was presented to me from some of the parishioners of Stow, & as your name is the first Signed to it, I take the liberty of troubling you with the reply.

Of the former part of the document which consists of vague Charges against the Incumbent, expressed in very strong language I must decline to take any notice. When parishioners are compelled to bring complaints against their Clergyman defined by dates & facts & supported by proof, it will always be my duty to attend to them, but general & unsupported accusations which (if I am not misinformed) have already been made at visitations but not proved, it cannot be right for the parishioners to prefer nor for me to receive. With the last request of the Memorial however that I will try to reconcile the Incumbent to the parishioners I shall most gladly comply, and most thankful shall I be, if I could in any way assist in restoring the harmony in your parish which for various reasons has so long been interrupted. I am happy to believe that Mr Atkinson is ready heartly to concur in such an arrangement as I now venture to propose one great source of dissention has been the state of your noble Church.—I would suggest that the parish on the one hand should raise a sum by mortgage of the rates sufficient to complete the substantial repairs—say—£1000, and that Mr Atkinson should make himself responsible for obtaining the additional fund necessary for restoring the Church & making it what it ought to be, a commodious & beautiful place of public worship.

In the case of the Churchwarden Mr Harrison now pending in the Consistorial Court, I shall recommend Mr Atkinson to withdraw the suit, on Mr Harrison paying the costs, & not merely to take no steps with reference to another charge against him, but to consider all the past as forgotten. It will however be more agreeable for all parties that Mr Harrison should not at present accept the office of Churchwarden.

I should be willing to trust to the good sense & good feeling of the parishioners to prevent the recurrence of acts of wanton damage done to the Church doors & which have brought the parish into no very creditable notoriety, & I will venture to promise for the Incumbent that he will earnestly & zealously use his endeavours for the spiritual well being of all his people & for their best interests temporal & eternal.

I have the honr to be,
Sir,
Your Obedient Servant
John Lincoln

John Skill Esqe

Signed John Harrison Chairman
On behalf of this Meeting—

Note: According to the *Lincolnshire Times* (17 April, 1855) "The suit in the Ecclesiastical Court . . . originated in this manner:—About 12 months ago Mr Harrison found that the lock of a door leading into one of the transepts of the church (of which he had one of the keys) had been altered under the direction of the incumbent, so that he was locked out. To "recover possession" (as the lawyers say), he resorted to an ingenious expedient. Watching the sexton enter the belfry to ring the bells, he followed him into the tower and let himself down by a rope from a suitable opening out of the tower into the transept. He then removed the lock from the inside of the door, and had it restored to its former state. For so entering the church and breaking out again, a suit was commenced against him in the Ecclesiastical Court. . . ." As the transept roofs had not yet been raised his route to the floor must have been through a trap door in the ringing chamber floor, and down a rope, well over 30 foot long, to the crossing floor. Harrison was 47 years of age at the time.

The bishop referred also to "another charge against" Harrison, the nature of which has not emerged.

214. Vestry Book

Stow 9th Apl. 1855

A vestry meeting was in the Church of Stow This day according to notice duly given for the purpose of choosing Churchwardens for the year ensuing. Present—

The Rev Geo Atkinson, the minister in the chair; Messrs Spencer, Taylor, Cox J Palmer W Palmer W Watson, J Watson G Harrison Rose, Credland Josh Harrison J Brumby, Gelder W Ellis J Butler, J Wilkinson Hill W Smith and others.

Mr A Cox moved that this meeting for the purpose of choosing Churchwardens in order to give time to reply to the Bishop's letter, be adjourned till this day month, Mr Spencer seconded the motion, which on being put to the meeting by the Chairman was negatived.

The Minister and the Parishioners not being able to agree in the choice of the churchwardens conjointly The Minister chose as his Churchwarden Mr Magnus Hugh Duncan.

Mr John Butler propesd and Mr John Wilkinson seconded that Mr John Harrison be the Churchwarden on the part of the parish. No amendment being moved the chairman declared the above gentlemen elected.

George Atkinson Chairman
Chas G Smith V.C.

Note: This meeting was described in the *Lincolnshire Times*, 17 April, 1855, as follows:—"The meeting on Easter Monday was held in the nave of the church, the only part of the edifice in a fit state. It presents a strangely dilapidated, cheerless, and primitive appearance. The walls have been stripped of their plaster in the nave, the pews have been taken up, and rude benches substituted by the incumbent, and all ornamentation has been removed. The clergyman acted as chairman of the meeting. Mr. W. Palmer and Mr. Gelder were proposed as churchwardens, but these gentlemen objected to serve. Mr Cox then said he would have no objection to stand himself, if Mr. Palmer would serve with him, but he was told to wait till he was asked.—Mr Gelder then proposed the appointment of Mr John Harrison (one of the retiring wardens), and Mr. W. Watson, of Sturton.—Mr. Cox hoped Mr. Harrison's name would be withdrawn. It would be undesirable again to elect that gentleman, seeing that the bishop, whose advice had been asked, had suggested it as the first step towards a reconciliation.—Mr Ellis said they did not ask the bishop to interfere with their rights as ratepayers. They made certain statements to his lordship, and asked his interference to bring their minister to better terms. Without asking them to substantiate those charges, his lordship treated them as unfounded accusations, but offered to decide between the parties on assumptions which could not be submitted to. He believed his lordship to be a very fair man, but he had prejudged their case in this instance, and they could not sacrifice old friends to new. Mr Harrison, their present churchwarden, had been their advisor so far, and having got into the clutches of the law in fighting their battles, they could not throw him overboard now, however much they might desire to please the bishop. ("Hear, hear," and expressions of assent.)—The Rev. G. Atkinson said that as he could not agree to the nomination he should appoint Mr. Wagner Hugh Duncan schoolmaster and parish clerk. The nomination of Mr. Harrison was then put and carried, and the Meeting separated."

215. Vestry Book

Stow 24th March 1856

A Vestry meeting was held in the Church of Stow this Day according to Notice duly given for the purpose of Choosing Churchwardens for the year ensuing

Present. The Revd G Atkinson the minister in the Chair; Messrs Cox J S Gelder Wm Ellis W Palmer J Palmer J Rose Geo Harrison Jno Harrison Jos Smith Jno Northing, W Hill.

The Minister Choose as his Churchwarden Mr Joseph Smith

Mr Rose proposed and Mr W Palmer seconded That Mr A Cox be the Church Warden on the part of the parish

Mr Ellis proposed and Mr Hill Seconded that Mr Jno Harrison be the Churchwarden on the part of the parish as an amendment These motions been put to the vote the amendment was Carried.

The Chairman declared that Joseph Smith, and John Harrison, elected.

Secondary as regards the Churchyard Wall. It was proposed by Mr Geo Harrison and Seconded by Mr J S Gelder that a voluntary subscription be entered into for the repairs thereof

Mr J S Gelder and Mr Jno Sergeant offered their services in the matter

George Atkinson. M.A. Chairman
John Harrison }
Joseph Smith }

216. Vestry Book

July 12th. 1856
Adjourned Vestry of July 10th. 1856
Pursuant to Proposition.

Resolved—That this Vestry respectfully suggest that the Minister, Churchwardens, and Overseers of the Poor for the time being of Stowe, also, the Overseers of the Poor for the time being of the Hamlets of Sturton and Bransby together with the following Freeholders—Ashton Cox, John Skill, John Spink, William Ellis, Thomas Spencer, John Jollands, Joseph Palmer, George Sergeant, Robert Harrison, & James S. Gelder, be a trust for the Charities of the Town of Stowe, and of the Town and Parish of Stowe—namely for "Lady Warwick's Gift", "Burgh's Gifts", and "Tomlinson's Dole", which is a trust as nearly in accordance with the Wills of the Donors as this Vestry can Devise.

Resolved—That this Vestry respectfully suggest that the trust of the Church Lands remains as it stands in the Award.

James. S. Gelder Chairman
Joseph Harrison
John Gilbert
Robert Harrison
By order of John Skill (Joseph Palmer)

James Gilbert
William Markham
George Sergeant
John Jollands

John Clarke	J Rose
John Butler	William Taylor
Robert Credland	Joseph Palmer
Robert Hill	Thomas Spencer
William Lanes	John Harrison
William Hill	William Ellis
Robert Howell	William Buttery
George Harrison	John W. Hope V.C.
John Sergeant	

Note: The minutes of two earlier meetings on this subject have been omitted for lack of space.

217. Vestry Book

Stowe in Lindsey } A Vestry Meeting was called to meet in the Court House but the use of that room having been denied the meeting was adjourned to the Church

Copy of the Notice

Take Notice A Vestry Meeting will be held in the Court House at Stow on Thursday the 29th day of January 1857 at the hour of half past ten O'clock in the morning, to take into consideration the means of defraying the necessary expenses of Divine Service, also the Clerk's Wages, the Clock, and the repair of the Churchyard Wall.

Stow January 24th 1857 Joseph Smith Churchwarden

Present. The following Parishioners viz. Messrs. Spencer, Gelder, R. Harrison, Taylor, Spink, Watson, Jollands and others

The Revd G Atkinson in the Chair.

With respect to the means of defraying the necessary expenses of Divine Service

Proposed by Mr Spink that the Churchwardens provide in the manner that has been done for the last fifty years with such money as they have in their hands and such money as shall come into their hands.

Seconded by Mr Joseph Harrison.

Carried—

2ndly. With respect to the Clerk's Wages

It was discussed but no resolution was come to.

3rdly. With respect to the Church Clock

The Vestry declined paying any thing to the Clerk for keeping the Clock going.

With regard to the Churchyard Wall repair.

The subscriptions received and the expenses of repairs done were examined showing a balance due to Joseph Smith Churchwarden of 4/2.

George Atkinson Chairman
Joseph Smith Churchwarden.

Note: Mr Spink was proposing that the Church Garden rents should be used for all church expenses, and not merely for the fabric.

218. To Sir Charles Anderson from Atkinson, 5 Feb. 1857 (CA)

Dear Sir Charles,

I enclose the suggestions which you requested I would draw up for the Consideration of the Trustees of our Charities.

Will you be so good as to name a week, and as early as convenient, in which you would be able to come to a meeting at Stow—and two or three different days in that week which would suit you, avoiding Tuesday and Friday the Market Days. I would then get George Hutton to see his brother to fix him on one of the days named by you, and when that has been done inform you and the rest of the Trustees of the day, hour, and place of meeting. If we once get a set of proper rules laid down for the management of the Charities, we shall on on easily afterwards—but it is very necessary that the right-minded Trustees should all the present at our *first* meeting in order to secure right and proper regulations for the future—and the three Gentlemen Trustees, with myself and one Churchwarden could turn the scale the right way if anything not right were attempted by the others—

218A.

Stow Charities—4 in number

Trustees 9 viz
The Incumbent
The two Churchwardens } for the time being.
Sir Charles H. J. Anderson Bart.
William Hutton Esquire
The Revd George P. Hutton
Mr John Skill
Mr Ashton Cox
Mr John Spink

No 1. Church Lands

Amount—about £15 per Annum arising from about 6 Acres of Land situated in the Parish, and let out in Garden allotments.

Object—Repairs of the Church according to ancient and modern Terriers—to actual practice till within the last 25 years—and to the Reports of the former Charity Commissions.

N.B. During the last 25 years not less than £250 have been abstracted from this Repair Fund, and applied to the payment of the Clerk's wages and other purposes.

During the last seven years this Fund has been entirely under the management of the Churchwarden chosen by the Parish, Mr John Harrison, who has kept three of the Gardens in his own occupation. . . .

Note: The remainder of the communication described the other charities.

218B.

Suggestions

No 1. Church Lands

First. That the rents should be strictly applied in future to the proper object of this Charity, viz, the Repair of the Church, and—as the Charity must be taken as intended for the benefit of the Fabric, and not for the easement of the Ratepayers from the necessary and usual expenses of mending broken wondows, rapairing leaky leads, and the like—the whole rents, after paying Tithes, Rates and Taxes, should be placed in some Bank in the Names of the Trustees for the purpose of being applied in a proper manner to the Repair of the Fabric.

Secondly—That an investigation should be made into the past management of the Charity with a view to ascertain to what extent the Funds have been applied to other purposes than that of the Repair of the Church—and the result be submitted to the Charity Commissioners for their advice therein.

Thirdly, That the Churchwardens with the advice and consent of the Minister be empowered to let the Garden Allotments which are, or may become, vacant, to give Notices to quit, to collect the rents as they become due, and all arrears now due, and to pay the same, after deducting the outgoings as soon as convenient into such Bank as the Trustees shall direct, and generally to act as Agents of the Trustees in respect to the management of the Land and Gardens. That good Character and conduct and regularity of attendance at Church be considered in the future selection of Tenants from among the labourers residing in the Parish—that the Churchwardens shall not retain any gardens in their own occupation if suitable Tenants can be found—And that they, with the Minister shall give an Account each year to the Trustees of all that they have done in the Management of the Lands of this Charity. . . .

Note: The remainder of this paper described the other parochial charities.

219. Vestry Book

Stowe in Lindsey } A Parish Meeting was held according to Notice on Easter Monday April 13th 1857.

Copy of Notice

Notice is hereby given that a Vestry Meeting will be held in the Parish Church on Easter Monday April 13th 1857 at the hour of half past ten O'clock in the forenoon for the purpose of choosing the Churchwardens for the year ensuing.

George Atkinson Minister

April 4th 1857 Joseph Smith, John Harrison } Churchwardens.

Present Messrs Wm Ellis Wm Buttery Jos Palmer John Spink George Harrison John Watson Wm Hill Ashton Cox Jonathan Rose John Middleton John Northing The Revd George Atkinson and the churchwardens, Jos Smith & Jno Harrison.

The Revd George Atkinson appointed Joseph Smith as his Churchwarden.

Mr Wm Ellis proposed Mr John Harrison as the other churchwarden

Mr Wm Buttery seconded the proposition

Mr Ashton Cox proposed Mr William Watson of Old Hall Farm as the other Churchwarden.

Mr John Northing seconded Mr Ashton Cox's proposition

Upon a shew of hands the majority present voted for Mr John Harrison upon which Mr Cox demanded a poll on behalf of Mr Watson which was accordingly appointed to take place in the Court House on Thursday next the 16th Instant from the hour of 3 O'clock in the afternoon until 7 O'clock. And this Vestry was accordingly adjourned to the place & hour above said for the purpose of taking the poll.

Signed on behalf of the meeting } George Atkinson Chairman

The Poll was taken according to adjournment as above when the number who voted for Mr Harrison was 67 and for Mr Watson 15 upon which Mr Harrison was declared duly elected.

Signed—George Atkinson, Chairman.

Stow April 16—1857 Joseph Smith Vestry Clerk

220. From the Charity Trustees' Minute Book. Minutes of a meeting Monday 15 March 1858. (Misc)

A meeting of the Trustees was held this day in the National School at Stow at 3 o'Clock P.M. instead of 12 (on account of the Eclipse) when the whole of the Trustees were present—viz Sir Charles H. J. Anderson Bt William Hutton Esq. The Revd George T. Hutton, Messrs John Skill, Ashton Cox and John Spink—The Revd George Atkinson, the Incumbent, and Messrs Jonathan Elwis and John Harrison, the Churchwardens of the Parish. . . .

4. Church Lands. The Secretary having gone into the Accounts of Mr Harrison one of the Churchwardens who had for some years previous had the management of this Fund, there was found on Mr Harrison's shewing a balance due from him to the Trustees of £5 – 1 – 9¼. The Collector after repeated applications being unable to obtain payment of this balance laid the Case before the Charity Commissioners, and a correspondence between the Board and Mr Harrison a copy of which was sent by them to the Secretary was read to the meeting, from which it appeared that the Commissioners considered Mr Harrison bound to pay over the Balance remaining in his hands to the Trustees, or to the Treasurer appointed by them. Mr Harrison still refusing to do this, the Commissioners in a letter dated Nov. 3, 1857 which was read by the Secretary, stated that the "Trustees may proceed against him in the County Court under the equitable jurisdiction created by the Charitable Trusts Acts to enforce the payment a certificate from the Board being first obtained, a form of application for which was enclosed—" Mr Harrison was now again requested to pay the Balance remaining in his hands, the Trustees signifying their willingness to return him any deductions out of it which had been paid for him for legal purposes—As however he persisted in his refusal to pay either the £5.1.9¼, or to produce any account of sums which he alleged to have been paid out of such balance, the Collector was directed to proceed to enforce the payment in the manner pointed out by the Charity Commissioners, after having obtained from them the necessary authority to enable him to do so. . . .

Note: John Skill, John Spink, and the Collector, Atkinson, were appointed to be a committee to distribute Burgh's Dole. Minutes in Atkinson's hand.

221. To Eccl. Com. from Atkinson, 17 Sept. 1859 (EC)

Stow Chancel

Sir,

I regret to have to report to the Ecclesiastical Commissioners that the sheets of lead covering the South side of the roof of this Chancel have slipped down, more or less, so as to admit the rain, in several places upon the vaulting, and through it to the floor of the Chancel.

This is owing to sheets not having been fastened to the boarding of the roof, on a proper and sufficient principal in the first instance.

They were merely nailed at the top of the sheet, whereas they ought to have been secured further, by a series of "Keys" worked into the rolls between each two sheets. This, I find, is the plan used at Lincoln Minster where the roofs are much steeper than ours—and it secures the sheets effectually from slipping down.

The sheets on the North side have not moved, from not being exposed to the heat of the sun like those on the South.

I have got Mr John Newton of Gainsborough, the Plumber who did the work, to insert temporarily pieces of lead where the sheets had parted, to prevent further damage from the rain until the sheets can be replaced in their positions and effectually secured, which ought to be done without delay. I send herewith a statement of the plan used at Lincoln which is the best that can be employed.

I exceedingly regret that this failure should have occurred and I shall be ready if the Ecclesiastical Commissioners think fit, to superintend the work, and to see that it is effectually done. The lead "Keys" will require something less than half a Cwt of 7 lb lead, the Cost of which will not exceed 15/– The rest will be all labour, except the nails required, and the entire Cost may be between £5 & £10.

I am happy to say that the works done about the Chancel with the above exception, stand as perfectly as possible.

[*endorsed*]

That the Incumbent be authorized to expend on the repairs referred to in this communication a sum not exceeding *£10*

22 Sep

WD

221A.

Specification of the plan used at Lincoln Cathedral for securing the sheets of lead covering the roofs from slipping down.

---

1. Each sheet is nailed down, along the top, to the boarding.
2. Between each junction of the sheets lengthwise, Keys of lead 5 in. long by 2 in. broad, are nailed down to the boarding, at intervals of from 2 to 3 feet, the other end of the Key is then brought up between the edges of the two adjacent sheets, and is turned over and worked into the roll, which joins the sheets together.

The plan is found effectual as I am assured by Mr Belham the Surveyor of the Fabric, as well as by the working Plumber.

George Atkinson

Note: There are seven further papers on this subject which can be summarised. The secretary asked Atkinson to do as he had suggested, and Atkinson lost no time in seeing Mr John Newton, whom he found "evasive and unsatisfactory in his mode of dealing from a sense of shame . . . that his work should in so short a time want doing over again." Atkinson therefore employed Mr Kent, who was already employed on the other parts of the church. "He has been 7 days at work," Atkinson reported, "with a labourer to assist him, and eleven out of the nineteen rolls on the South side are finished. . . . Kent's charge is 4/– a day for himself, and the labourer's wages are 2/– per day." Atkinson advised that the north side should also be put in order, and this was done at Mr Hall's expense. The Commissioners paid £5–5–5. for the work. These repairs, however, proved to be inadequate—see Nos. 252 and 253.

222. *Vestry Book*

A Vestry meeting was held pursuant to the following Notice

"Notice is hereby given that a Vestry meeting will be held in the National School Room at Stow on Thursday the 9th day of July 1863 at the hour of seven o'clock in the Evening for the purpose of Consulting about the repairing of the Parish Church, and adopting such measures as may be agreed on for promoting and affecting the same

Stow July 4th 1863 — George Atkinson Minister

Signed — James Gelder, Jonathan Elwis } Churchwardens

Present the Minister in the chair, the Churchwardens Messrs Ellis, Spencer, Joseph Harrison, William Taylor, William Spurr, James Gilbert, Jollands, Robert Howell, Robert Gilbert, Hope, Richard Reed, Pycroft, Robert Harrison, James Spencer, Robert Gibson, Llewellyn and Godson

After reading the Notice calling the Vestry the Minister made a Statement with regard to the necessity of repair and the most convenient mode of providing the funds

Mr Godson proposed that this vestry meeting be adjourned to this day fortnight at the same place and hour—this was seconded by Mr Ellis and carried

George Atkinson, Chairman
Jonathan Elwis

223. Vestry Book

A vestry meeting was held pursuant to adjournment present the Minister in the Chair, the Churchwardens, Messrs Ellis, Spencer, Joseph Harrison, Geo. Harrison, John Homer, Willm Taylor, Hope, Woodhouse, Robt. Gibson, Pycroft, Robt. Todd, Burton, Harwood, Middleton, Robt. Hill, Robt. Howell, Geo. Sargeant, Robt. Harrison, Hunt, Jollands, John Needham, Richd. Reed, Godson, Jas. Spencer, Joseph Brumby, Jos. Sharpe, and Lewellyn.

Mr Elwis proposed a Rate of 10d in the pound, for the necessary Repairs of the church and other Legal expenses—This proposition was seconded by Mr Pycroft

Mr Spencer proposed that—"Whereas the Parish of Stow pays £900 a year in the shape of a Tithe Rent Charge it is inexpedient to enlarge this compulsory payment by a Church Rate and therefore that no Church Rate be granted"—this amendment was seconded by Mr Jollands and Carried.

The original proposition was then put and negatived

George Atkinson, Chairman
George Luff
Vestry Clerk for this time

224. To Rev George Ainslie, Secretary, from Atkinson, 8 February 1864 (ICBS)

Dear Sir

We are about to commence the Restoration of the Parish Church of Stow—which was in the Early Saxon times—the Cathedral of the Diocese. The funds are from voluntary subscriptions—and I write to ask for Instructions and Forms to enable me to apply to the Incorporated Society for a Grant towards the work.

All the existing seats in the Church are free—and all the additional sittings which will be a very considerable number will likewise be free.

Waiting for a communication from you I remain.

[P.S.] I have sent with this a copy of the Appeal which has been put out on behalf of the work. It may interest you and enable you to put our Case more fully before the Committee

Note: In his application, Atkinson stated that five sixths of the inhabitants of the parish were of the "labouring class". The restoration of the Chancel had cost £1700, of which £924 had been contributed by the tithe owners, and the remaining £776 by voluntary subscription.

At present, he stated, there were 105 free seats in the church, none of which were exclusively for children. He proposed to add sittings so that there would be an additional 304 free seats for adults and 72 exclusively for children, giving a total of 481 sittings.

He had in hand £2110, of which £126 had come from the Church Lands, and the remaining £1984 from subscriptions. The cost was estimated at £695 for the increased accommodation; £2600 for the work on the roof and walls; £180 for the architect's fees and expenses, and £120 for the Clerk of works. This total of £3595 left a deficiency of £1485.

225. (Misc)

FACULTY

for making certain alterations and improvements in the Parish Church of Stowe in the County and Diocese of Lincoln.

Lincoln 22.7.64 [stamped]

TRAVERS TWISS Doctor of Civil Law Vicar General in Spirituals of the Right Reverend Father in God JOHN by Divine Permission Lord Bishop of Lincoln and Official Principal of the Episcopal and Consistorial Court of Lincoln lawfully constituted TO ALL CHRISTIAN PEOPLE to whom these Presents shall come GREETING—WHEREAS it hath been represented unto us and our Office on the part and behalf of the Reverend George Atkinson Clerk Perpetual Curate of the Perpetual Curacy and Parish Church of Stowe in the County and Diocese of Lincoln and Jonanthan Elwis and James Shankster Gelder Churchwardens of the said parish THAT the Parish Church of Stowe in the County and Diocese of Lincoln is out of repair and requires immediate restoration THAT it has been proposed to remove the present North and South porches and to restore the two doorways covered by the same to take down and rebuild the present Staircase up to the Belfry so as to be outside the Nave to build a new Vestry with small adjoining room the latter to have a vault chamber underneath for warming apparatus to repair the Buttresses of the Nave to repair the Walls of the Nave and Transepts and to reconstruct and repair the present roofs over the same to pave the floors of the Transepts Tower Vestries &c with 6in Common Staffordshire Tiles to take up the floor of the Nave and relay and repair the same to lay the floor of the Chancel with Tiles preserving the old gravestones and to make a platform properly elevated for the Communion Table to be placed on to repair the old open seats in the Nave and to provide new Seats of Oak for the Nave and Transepts where required to provide a new pair of folding doors of Oak for the North doorway and also new doors of the same character for the South and West doorways if the present ones be found incapable of being repaired and to glaze with Cathedral glass the whole of the Windows of the Nave Transepts and Vestries according to certain plans (copies of which are now filed in our Registry) THAT the cost of carrying out the said works has been estimated by Mr J. L. Pearson an experienced Architect at Two thousand seven hundred pounds which sum has been raised by voluntary subscription THAT it has also been proposed to raise the existing Steeple or Tower which is disproportionately low by a single stage of about Eighteen feet so as to give space for the ringing of the Bells from the uppermost floor of the Tower as it now exists to replace the Screen at the entrance of the Chancel by a new Screen and to provide an Organ to be placed in such part of the Church as may be found most suitable according to the aforesaid plans THAT the cost of carrying out the said last mentioned works has been estimated by the said J. L. Pearson at the further sum of Five hundred pounds and the said George Atkinson has undertaken not to commence the aforesaid works until such further sum of Five hundred pounds has been raised WHEREFORE they the said George Atkinson and Jonanthan Elwis and James Shankster Gelder have prayed our License and Faculty to be granted to them and the Incumbent and Churchwardens of the said parish for the time being for carrying into immediate effect all and singular the works firstly mentioned and for carrying into effect the remainder of the said works so soon as a sufficient sum of money shall be collected for paying for the same according to the said plans and specifications and for selling such of the old materials as shall not be used in carrying out the said intended works AND we being inclined to grant the same unless sufficient cause was shewn to the contrary caused all and singular the Parishioners and Inhabitants of the same Parish of Stowe in special and all others in general having or pretending to have any right title or interest in the premises to be cited to appear at a certain time and place to them prefixed and now elapsed then and there to shew cause if they had or knew any why our Licence or Faculty should not be granted to the said Perpetual Curate and Churchwardens and the Perpetual Curate and Churchwardens of the said parish for the time being for the purposes by them desired with Intimation that if they some or one of them did not appear at the time and place aforesaid or appearing did not shew good or sufficient cause to the contrary We our Surrogate or some other competent Judge in this behalf did intend and would proceed to grant our Licence or Faculty to the said Perpetual Curate and Churchwardens and the Perpetual Curate and Churchwardens of the said Parish for the time being for the purposes aforesaid their absence or contumacy in anywise notwithstanding AND WHEREAS upon the due execution and return of the said Citation with Intimation all persons cited as well in special as in general being called and none of them appearing they were pronounced to be in contempt and in pain of such their contumacy or contempt a Licence or Faculty was decreed to be granted to the said Perpetual Curate and Churchwardens and the Perpetual Curate and Churchwardens of the said Parish for the time being for the purposes aforesaid Justice so requiring WE THEREFORE the Vicar General and Official Principal aforesaid in pursuance of the said decree do as far as by the Ecclesiastical laws of this Realm and the Temporal laws of the same we may or can give and grant our Licence or Faculty to the said Perpetual Curate and Churchwardens and the Perpetual Curate and Churchwardens of the said parish for the time being to carry into immediate effect all and singular the works firstly mentioned and also to carry into effect the remainder of the said works so soon as a sufficient sum of money has been raised for that purpose according to the said plans and specifications to use in the said proposed works so much of the old materials as may be used with advantage to sell the residue and to expend the money arising from such sale towards defraying the expences of the said works they the said Perpetual Curate and Churchwardens and the Perpetual Curate and Churchwardens of the said Parish for the time being rendering and passing a just account of their doings and transactions herein when lawfully required IN TESTIMONY whereof we have caused the seal of our Office to be hereunto affixed the seventeenth day of February in the year of our Lord one thousand and eight hundred and sixty five

John Swan
Deputy Registrar & Notary Public

Note: The Cash Book, No. 254, shows that the work had already been started in March 1864. See above No. 224.

226. The Lincoln Gazette, *Saturday, 27 May 1865*

STOW.—*Death of the Rev George Atkinson.* We deeply regret to announce the death of the Rev George Atkinson, somewhat suddenly, on the 23rd inst. Presented to the Perpetual Curacy of Stow in 1836, he then became the first resident Incumbent in the memory of man, and through his unflinching struggles in behalf of justice, and his uncompromising fidelity to the church of England, he quickly incurred the hostility of some of the inhabitants of Stow, but he lived to see those who withstood him dispersed, and the undoubtedly great work he took in hand, viz., the restoration of the ancient church committed to his charge, almost completed. . . . Although unassisted by the parishioners, through great self denial and munificent subscriptions from his relations and friends, he at length procured the means to accomplish what his heart so earnestly desired. It was intended, we believe, to have opened this venerable old church again with solemn service in the course of this year, but whether this event will take place, we cannot say. Perhaps no one in the diocese of Lincoln has prepared for himself so fine a monument, and this unconsciously, as Mr Atkinson has done; for as long as the now restored church of Stow stands, it will gratefully speak of his name, and his name will then require no other monument, and his good work no inscription. . . .—*Correspondent.*

227. To Sir Charles Anderson from Frederick Atkinson, Stow, 5 June 1865 (CA)

My dear Sir,

Your letter by Mr Pearson expresses pretty accurately my own views of what should now be done in the matter of the restoration of the Church.

My brother's death was, we may say, so sudden & unexpected, that there was no opportunity of receiving his instructions on the subject & it is therefore most necessary that some definite understanding should be come to.

I think your suggestion of writing to the Archdeacon of Stow (Mr Giles) to acquaint him with the state of the funds, & that they can be used in no other way than in carrying out the restoration according to the views which my brother had decided upon, a very proper one, & I shall be glad if you will carry it into effect. For your information I may say that the state of the funds at the present time is this:—

Invested in Railway shares . . . (say)	—	760. 0. 0
Cash now in Bank . . .	,,	50. 0. 0
Subscriptions promised but not yet paid	,,	150. 0. 0
Grant from Ch. Building Society		150. 0. 0
		£1110. 0. 0

The grant from the Ch. Building Society is to be spent in seating the Church according to the plan submitted to & approved by them—the subscriptions it is hoped will all be paid, but you will see there is no money to be going on with but the small sum now in the Bank. The money invested in Shares it is desirable to retain until this half year's dividends have been secured & which I expect to produce nearly £20. Nor indeed should I be willing to pay over any part of the sum I now hold, until I see what are the future arrangements with respect to the restoration.

Would not the best plan be to endeavour to get in the subscriptions now out—the parties might I think be written to without any offence being given, as the death of my brother would quite justify such a step. I think also your plan of inserting a short notice in the county papers, announcing that the works are going on & that it was hoped they might be completed according to my brother's wishes, most desirable. At the same time, the public might be urged to further contributions, as the funds now in hand would not complete the restoration. If £500 or £600 more could be raised I think the work might be brought to a happy conclusion—this is not a large sum for the county to raise, when it is recollected that the bulk of the money already subscribed has been procured from other sources.

I ought to have mentioned after the statement of the funds in hand &c. that at the present time very little is owing on account of the work at the

Church. As far as I know there is only owing a *small* sum for stone, a little to the blacksmith, & a balance to the plumber (who has had £100 on account). These accounts have not yet been sent in, but they cannot be of much amount.

Some money will be wanted for wages this week & perhaps you will be good enough to draw a Cheque for £40 for that purpose; as this sum will last for three or four weeks, it will be unnecessary to trouble you for some time to come.

The Cheque book is here & shall be sent you if you wish it. I am going to Manchester this afternoon but propose returning tomorrow night, when I expect to remain until the Monday following.

My sisters are upon the whole pretty well & are much obliged for your enquiries.

228. To Sir Charles Anderson from Frederick Atkinson, Stow, 9 June 1865 (CA)

My dear Sir,

I think the notice for the papers will do very well. I am of the opinion however that it would be better to omit the last paragraph which says "If the Tower is raised, which by many is wished, a separate fund should be raised for that special purpose."

If the Stow people see this, it may be reasonably inferred from their well known character & from the experience we have had of them, that they will immediately conclude that their best plan will be to do nothing, and it is probable if they only stand out, other people will do it for them.

I have made three copies of your letter, to be sent to the Mercury, Chronicle & Lincoln Gazette, but as I have taken the liberty of making an omission, I do not think it right to send them for insertion until I had your approval.

I enclose you the copies & if you approve perhaps you will be kind enough to forward them.

I think you are quite right in not taking any active part with the Stow people respecting the Tower. It will be much better to wait until the new Incumbent arrives. If the parishioners really wish to do anything, there is a very fair & easy mode of raising the money by borrowing it on security of the Church rates, from the Board of Works in London, who will lend on such security:—the amount with interest to be paid back in 20 years. By this means the annual payment for the outlay would be very easy & it appears to me also the fairest plan.

You appear to have forgot about the cheque for wages which I named. If it had not been that £10 of subscriptions had come most unexpectedly into our own hands, we could not have paid wages this week. Perhaps you will be kind enough to say if we must send you the Cheque book?—money will be required for next week.

As your letter to the county papers reached me too late for insertion this week, I did not consider there need be any hurry about sending it, particularly as I have been & am so much occupied.

Note: The letter, as published in the *Stamford Mercury* on 16 June 1865, was dated "Lea, June 10 1865" and read as follows:

Sir,—As the subscriptions for Stow Church were placed in the joint names of the Rev. G. Atkinson and myself, I think it is my duty, now that excellent man is gone, to let the public know how affairs stand at present. The roof of nave and transepts are completed, and all bills paid. Remaining to be done are vestry, warming apparatus, plastering the walls and pointing, paving with tiles, glazing, and seating. The funds at present available are, cash in bank 50*l.*, and grant from Church Building Society 150*l.* Also 700*l.* invested in railway shares belonging to the Atkinson family, which will be available, provided the works are carried on according to the original plan and the late Incumbent's intentions. More will be required to complete the work satisfactorily.

229. To Sir Charles Anderson from Adn Giles, Willoughby Rectory, 17 June 1865 (CA)

Dear Sir C Anderson,

I was much obliged by your letter of the 14th.

I certainly should not have supposed the work remaining to be done at Stow, exclusive of the Tower, would have cost £1000. I think this estimate must include some decoration in colour or carving.

I do not consider raising the Tower essential to the success of the work. I think that the external appearance is quite *satisfactory*—Within, a lantern would be very fine; but I dare say a very good effect would be produced by only raising the ringing floor.

I think that an energetic and conciliatory man, going into the Parish at once, might get £200 or even more from the Parishioners, by loan on rate, as a testimonial to Mr Atkinson. But the iron should be struck while still hot.

I am very much pleased with the idea of putting a plate on the pier—I always thought it wise to leave the pier in statu.

I trust the church will have the benefit of your counsel & inspection—A new Vicar may have the best intentions, but spoil all by thinking himself a competent judge of architecture.

230. To Sir Charles Anderson from Miss Mary Atkinson, Stow Parsonage, 4 July 1865 (CA)

Dear Sir Charles

Your letter which came by post to day we have duly forwarded to our brother in Manchester. I am sure he will be very glad of your suggestions and will no doubt confer with you on the subject.

With regard to a Cheque being required I am glad to say that we shall not want any this week and possible not next either as Fred got yesterday a Dividend of £9 on some of the shares, and a subscription card of one of our friends has been sent in with a £5 note and 18d worth of stamps. Also Fred got a subscription of £5 from a friend in Lancashire to whom he had written to ask for something for the Church. So we shall have enough for the next fortnight for wages.

With regard to our not knowing about what subscriptions are not yet paid. I think if I forward the book to the Bank at Lincoln and ask them to enter any subscriptions since paid, I could then give you a list of those we know of. Mrs Kaye's I do not know about. Mr Haskins the new Incumbent has got £11 for Stow Church which he told my brother he would bring to pay wages &c. £10 he has got from Vice Chancellor Page Wood who knew some of his family.

Thanking you for all your kindness. With kind regards to Lady Anderson and yourself

P.S. The work is going on well.

231. To Sir Charles Anderson from Frederick Atkinson, Stow, 26 July 1865 (CA)

My dear Sir,

Will you please to draw Cheques in payment of the inclosed bills, viz:

John Wilson 1. 12. 0
Lockwood, Blagden & Crawshaw 3.3.5

Please also to draw a separate cheque of £20 for the work at the church—we have only in hand what will pay this week's wages.

There will then remain only about £10 in the Bank, but if no more subscriptions come in, I shall be able to find in a week or two, money enough to go on with for some time.—We shall in all probability finally leave Stow on

Monday August 7th. I will have the books balanced & ready for Mr Haskins—though as he hates writing, I fear he is not likely to be in love with the keeping of accounts.

If you will return the Cheques & bills to me, I will forward them to the respective parties.

232. To Sir Charles Anderson from Pearson, 22 Harley Street, 3 August 1865 (CA)

Dear Sir Charles

I intended only to put in plain glazing into the quarter foils but if have some old painted glass that will do for them I will not order any glazing for them. With regard to the large circles I fully intend to have the iron work so arranged that painted glass of old design may be introduced into them without any necessity to alter [them.]

I am very sorry that [I have] made arrangements for [this week] and go into Yorkshire early on Monday otherwise I should have been so glad to have paid Stow a visit just now. I wrote to Mr Atkinson the other day upon the same subject. I am much grieved to hear of the appointment the Bishop has made I am afraid it will be very uphill work with the new man.

I will endeavour to get the apparatus used at Westminster Abbey for applying the shellac & bring it with me when next I come down.

Young Codd has left London this Morning for Lea for his Holiday he intends to be at Stow tomorrow (Friday) to see the carpenter & to attend to several matters that require consideration—I believe I have now put nearly everything into working order the heating apparatus is on its way the seats are in hand for the Transepts, the windows are also being prepared so are the doors too The tiles for the floors & the steps alone remain to be ordered.

I wish something could be done to raise some more money so that the whole of the works might now be finished short of raising the Tower.

233. To Sir Charles Anderson from Frederick Atkinson, Stow, 12 Aug. 1865 (CA)

Dear Sir Charles,

We take our final leave of Stow today & I send you the accounts of the Restoration balanced up to Saturday last.

The book which accompanies this note, is an exact copy of the original

Cash book in my brother's handwriting & which for reasons you will readily understand, we all feel a wish to retain.

I have supplied Bates the foreman at the Church with a Cash book which I will show him how to keep.

He will send me every week an account of the wages &c. and all bills after examination are to be forwarded to me. I shall send Bates each week a Cheque upon Smith Ellison & Co Gainsborough, with whom I have opened an account. You will thus be saved the trouble of keeping the accounts as will also Mr Haskins.

It seems at first sight as if Mr Haskins was the proper person to undertake this duty, but from his entire unacquaintance with the affairs of the Church & the lack of interest he appears to take in the work, conjoined with two extremely unpleasant interviews I have lately had with him, I think it best to keep the matter in my own hands.

As I have now supplied you with an exact transcript of my brother's accounts you will be in a position to answer any enquiries which may be made.

I also enclose a list of unpaid subscriptions which you can deal with as you think fit. Perhaps you will drive over to the Church occasionally & keep an eye upon what is going on?

With thanks for your many & continued acts of kindness, believe me

P.S. The books & documents, Bank book &c. connected with the Stow Charities, we have placed in the hands of the Revd Mr Haskins: We have paid into the Bank this week £14. 12. 6 on account of the Church Land Charity. Would it not be desirable to have this amount transferred to the Restoration Fund?

Unpaid Subscriptions

The Bishop of Lincoln	– – –	£20
Archdeacon of Stow	– – – –	10
Sir C. Anderson Bart.	– – –	10
Mr Godson, Normanby	– – –	10
Mr J. Lewis Ffytche	– – –	5
Captain Boucheret	– – – –	1
Revd T. Lowe	} promised to	5
Revd Dr Parkinson	} Mrs Kaye	
		£71

Note: The Cash Book referred to is No. 254.

234. To Sir Charles Anderson from Frederick Atkinson, Higher Broughton, 21 Aug. 1865 (CA)

Dear Sir Charles,

I enclose you the Bank book of the "Stow Church Restoration Fund".

There appears to be a balance of £35. 9. 8 in favour of the fund, but there have been two or three cheques drawn which are not entered on the Dr side, which will reduce the balance to about £10.

In the Stow Charities Bank book, there is about £15 on the credit side, arising from the Church land money which we paid in before leaving Stow. I much wish that you & any other Trustee (should it require one) would please to order the amount to be transferred to the Stow Church Restoration Fund.

There would then be about £25 to the credit of the Fund: and if you could send me a cheque for £20 the balance might remain for the present, until augmented by fresh accessions.

I am anxious that the Church land money should be transferred to the Restoration Fund, because from some words which Mr Haskins dropped, I believe he has an intention of using the funds of this charity, for the lighting of the church for evening service, which he has decided permanently to establish.

Without giving any opinion as to the propriety of appropriating the money for this purpose, I think there can be no doubt, that as the fund has been left for the repair of the "fabric" of the church, it ought to be strictly applied to that purpose, so long as the fabric needs repair & the funds in hand for such reparation are insufficient. This is exactly the case at Stow at present & I hope if you take my view, you will see that the transfer is made.

I had occasion last week to write to Mr Pycroft my late brother's churchwarden & I asked him to take the trouble of going to the Church as often as possible to see how the work goes on. This may be some little check on both the foreman & workmen—I am having the new brass plate which is to be affixed to the pier, engraved here, & I will take care that it is thoroughly well done.

235. To Sir Charles Anderson from Frederick Atkinson, Higher Broughton, 30 Aug. 1865 (CA)

Dear Sir Charles,

I have received your Cheque for £25 on the Stow Church Restoration Fund & for which I am very much obliged.

As I am just about starting into Shropshire for a couple of days, I must defer noticing the contents of your letter until my return home.

236. To Sir Charles Anderson from Frederick Atkinson, Higher Broughton, 5 Sept. 1865 (CA)

Dear Sir Charles,

I do not see that we are likely to get into any unpleasantness with Mr Haskins about the seating, because that is a matter already settled.

The plan for the seating was submitted to the Church Building Society:— it met with their approval & they made a grant of £150 towards the cost.

This plan (which I have now in my possession) has their seal stamped upon it, dated April 18th 1864 & to it is affixed the following notice "If in the execution of the work, any alteration is made in regard to the construction or arrangement either of the building or of the seats, as shown by these drawings & described in the accompanying Specification without the previous sanction of the Board, the grant made by the Society will therefore be forfeited."

Mr Pearson has already put the seats in hand & they are being executed by two separate contractors & I should think by this time a good deal has been done. If all this is not sufficient to prevent Mr Haskins' interference, I could as a last resort stop the supplies, which in such a case I should certainly do.

He appears determined to have an evening service both winter & summer, but I think he will find some difficulty in accomplishing it. As to his plan of lighting the Church with gas, there are two great rocks ahead.

First, how or where will he get the money for the first outlay for the necessary apparatus & Second, how will be obtain the funds for meeting the regular after expenditure.

As far as our experience of Stow goes, he is not likely to meet with much success there & as to the offertory (in my brother's time) it rarely exceeded six or seven shillings above what was contributed from the Parsonage.

I myself disapprove of an evening service during winter—the nights are dark, the roads & weather frequently bad & evil effects will probably arise from the dispersion of the congregation at such seasons, while all the old & infirm are cut off from such services.

I do not think anything of his large congregations—they are no more than were accustomed to assemble when my brother had evening service. On such occasions I have repeatedly seen the Chancel so full, that the people had to stand about the door & what was better the congregation were almost entirely his own parishioners & not drawn from other neighbourhoods.

He appears to have quite changed his views about the school. When he came to stay with us to be ready for the Sunday duty, he was all for having an efficient *master* at Stow & a mistress at Sturton.

We advised caution, as it would be a serious expense, but nothing less would satisfy him. He seemed determined to root out Hope (the schoolmaster at Sturton) & get the whole education of the children of the parish into his own hands.

He has now probably begun to count the cost & finds with the other irons which he has in the fire, that it will be too great a drain on his resources.

I quite agree with you that a Schoolmistress however clever, is not adequate to deal with growing lads.

If Mr Haskins persists in his present plans, the inevitable effect will be, that he will have the mortification of seeing all his big boys drafted off into Hope's school at Sturton.

I am obliged by your letter—its kindness & firmness of tone has much encouraged me.

I am sorry to say that my oldest sister is now very seriously ill. She was not well before my brother's death, but since we left Stow she has become rapidly worse. Her disease seems to be a kind of atrophy, deep seated & of long standing. She was always thin, but now she is almost reduced to a skeleton. She has I am thankful to say no pain, but her weakness is excessive. I hope she may be spared to me some time longer, but her condition is I fear precarious.

My other sisters are quite well & all join me in kind regards.

237. Vestry Book

Vestry Meeting September 21st. 1865—

Copy of the Notice.—

A Vestry meeting will be held in the School room Stow on Thursday Sept: 21 to consider what the Parishioners are willing to contribute towards the Church Restoration Fund and the raising of the Tower and whether by Rate or Voluntary Subscription.

Proposed by Mr Churchwarden Pycroft that a one shilling rate be raised in this parish to be paid in two equal instalments the first moiety to be paid on the 1st. of October 1865 the second moiety on the 1st. of March

Seconded by Mr Joseph Harrison

For the Rate 7

Against the Rate 23

A poll demanded for Thursday next the 28th. of Sept. to begin at 10 A.M. to close at 4 P.M.

The following Resolution was proposed by Mr Thos Spencer.

Resolved. It is the sense of this meeting that a Church Rate of a shilling in the pound would be inexpedient inasmuch as it would fill the parish with heartburnings and distress the people generally. The Parish of Stowe pays upwards of nine hundred pounds a year Tithe Rent Charge and that is sufficient for all Church purposes.

This meeting was held after due notice in the Parish School room. Present the minister and Churchwardens and others.

E H Haskins
Incumbent
Joseph Pycroft

238. To Sir Charles Anderson from Frederick Atkinson, Higher Broughton, 22 Sept. 1865 (CA)

Dear Sir Charles,

My late brother I know was anxious to have had painted windows in the chancel at Stow & had he lived a few years longer, I have no doubt his wish would have been accomplished.

He was moreover particularly anxious that the round window at the west end should be filled with the best stained glass & had he lived & if the funds at his disposal had permitted, this would have been done.

The subject he had fixed upon for this window as the most appropriate was the baptizing of Blecca the heathen governor of Lincoln in the river Trent at Torksey, by Archbishop Paulinus. From its being so solemn & interesting event in the history of christianity in the diocese of Lincoln—from its having taken place near to Stow: & considering that the window was near to & overlooked the font in the Church, he thought a more appropriate subject could not be selected.

Mr Haskins' notion of what the window should be, is no doubt for the purpose of defeating any plan for having figures. I have heard him say, that as long as he was incumbent of the Church, no windows with figures should ever be put in. Perhaps he may live long enough to have a different view & learn that it is one of those rash vows, which is more honoured in the breach, than the observance.

I should not be surprised if his views will be somewhat modified by the expression of different opinions from those of his own, by the gentlemen present at the meeting.

I think he will scarcely like to be in direct opposition to gentlemen of standing & influence.

I hear from Bates every week, so that I am kept well informed about the progress of the work at the Church. I feel much obliged to you that you go over occasionally & see how things are going on, as it no doubt operates as some check on the men.

I think for various reasons it will be better for me not to attend the meeting on the 27th—at the same time accept my thanks for your kind invitation.

239. A pencilled note on the back of letter No. 236 (CA)

The Archdeacon Rural Dean Incumbent Sir C A[nderson] Mr Trollope Mr Godson Mr Webster Mr Garfit [*erased*]	That a sum be now raised for the restoration of the Church & in memory of the late Mr Atkinson

240. To Sir Charles Anderson from Frederick Atkinson, Higher Broughton, 4 Oct. 1865 (CA)

Dear Sir Charles,

Many thanks for your very interesting account of the meeting at Stow on the 27th September last.

It seems to have passed off quite as well as could have been expected, particularly when we consider how hurriedly it was got up. Mr Cayley did not know of the meeting until my sister Mary who was writing to Mrs Cayley apprized him of it.

We feel deeply the kind feeling shewn to our dear brother's memory & value highly the estimation in which he was held—still none but his own family can have any adequate knowledge of his life of devotion & self denial.

I hope the meeting may be the means of completing the restoration of the Church—an event which he so patiently waited & so ardently longed for.

The painting in the north transept is very interesting—I was afraid from what I saw, that it was so mutilated that it could not be made out.

I have heard from Mr Pearson several times lately—he is anxious not to exceed the means at his disposal, a determination of which I highly approve.

I have written him today to say that the expenditure up to the present time is £1860 & that a bill of £80 is still owing to the plumber, which could raise the amount to £1940.

The money in hand is about £660—& in addition to this there are the outstanding subscriptions which I estimate at about £50 & the Church building grant of £150.

This would make a total of £860 still to expend, but as I have named to Mr Pearson, he can only safely depend upon the £660 as the outstanding subscriptions may remain unpaid for some time & the Church building grant will not (I suppose) be available until the seating is finished according to the plans submitted to the Society.

As I fear Mr Pearson cannot with the funds at command, complete the seating, the £150 grant is practically of no benefit to us at present.

I do not know whether my estimate of the unpaid subscriptions is correct—perhaps you may be able to inform me. I am not aware how the account stands at the Bank—if there is anything in hand, perhaps you will be good enough to draw me a Cheque for pretty nearly the amount?

I am most thankful to say that my sick sister is now much better & there is every prospect of her restoration to health, an event which appears to us all who saw her, little less than miraculous.

All my sisters join me in kind regards.

Note: There was a thanksgiving service at Stow on Wednesday, 27 September, and a meeting was held afterwards at the west end of the church. The High Sheriff proposed that funds be raised to complete the restoration and "to do honour to the memory of the Rev. G. Atkinson, to whose almost sole exertion the building has been rescued from utter ruin". A committee was formed of the archdeacon of Stow, the rural dean (the Rev. E. Garfit), the Revs E. Trollope, E. Haskins, and T.K. Webster, Sir Charles Anderson, and Mr Godson. At the same occasion a collection of £12.0.4d was taken towards the cost of heating and lighting the church, and Trollope showed the newly discovered Becket mural in the north transept (*Stamford Mercury*, 29 September 1865).

241. To Sir Charles Anderson from Frederick Atkinson, Higher Broughton, 10 Oct. 1865 (CA)

Dear Sir Charles,

I am coming to Stow on Friday next to see how the work at the Church is going on, & I shall remain until the Monday following. I shall be staying with Mr Hawke, who has kindly offered me a bed. On Saturday morning I purpose to go over to Saxilby, but hope to be back again at Stow by about 2 o'clock. As you wished me to inform you of my next visit to Stow, I thought it better to send you a line, so that you may know my movements.

242. To Sir Charles Anderson from Frederick Atkinson, Higher Broughton, 5 Nov. 1865 (CA)

Dear Sir Charles,

I lose not a moment's time in replying to your letter received this morning. I fear you are labouring under some misconception which I will do my best to remove.

1st then I gather from your letter that you & the other gentlemen are under the impression that the parish is seriously disturbed about what we are doing at the west end of the Church & that we are likely to be involved in legal proceedings with them in consequence.

This is entirely erroneous:—a parish meeting was called on the 26th Octr last to consider this very business & the result was that our proceedings are sanctioned by it. We had the express permission of the meeting to go on with the north part of the new wall according to a sketch laid before it:—it is true that with respect to the south west corner some persons in the meeting *thought* it came out too far into the road, but as the meeting did not decide that it must be altered, I have let it remain as it was.

Mr Ingham the Surveyor informed me of the decision of the meeting—I replied on the 31st ulto stating that we should go on with the new wall as indicated & that as the south west corner was built up I thought it perhaps better not to disturb it, as I hoped no inconvenience would be found to arise from it. I have heard nothing from Mr Ingham since & I therefore conclude there is no further objection.

2nd. In what we are now doing at the west end, the object is not to save the parishioners pockets but to secure a most important improvement, which if not now effected, will probably either never be done or done most inefficiently.

This is to bring out the church yard wall at the west end, so as to be able to walk round the west end of the church without being compelled to go into the road, as is the case at present.

This effected by our plan while at the same time we leave the road sufficiently wide & good for every purpose. If the parish is satisfied on the subject, I do not think there is any occasion to trouble ourselves any more about it. I can assure you that I have no idea of being involved in legal proceedings in regard to this matter—if the meeting had ordered the south west corner to be taken in, I should at once have given Bates orders to that effect, but if the parish is content with our proceedings, I trust no indiscretion on our part may disturb the harmony which exists.

I think you will see how great is the improvement from the following sketch.

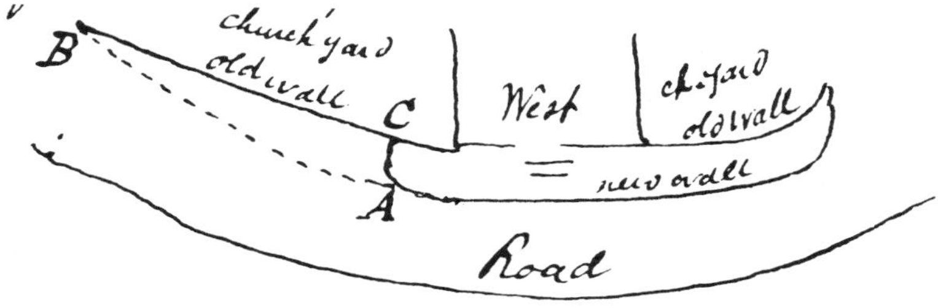

The new wall terminates abruptly at AC, but we have the permission of the parish to carry it on from A to B in a straight line, enclosing a small strip of land shown by the dotted line, which is of no use to anyone.

I will write to the Archdeacon tomorrow & give him a statement similar to the above.

243. To Sir Charles Anderson from Rev. E. Garfit, Parkfield House, Derby, 22 Nov. 1865 (CA)

Dear Sir Charles.

On my way here yesterday I called at the Lincoln Bank to make enquiries as to the payments to the "Stow restoration" & the "Atkinson Memorial Funds." One of the Clerks informed me that he believed you were in possession of the Bank Book containing payments to the *Stow Restoration Fund*. If so, you will perhaps be kind enough to forward it to me here that I may be enabled clearly to understand & to distinguish between those friends to the undertakings who have *already paid* their subscriptions, and those who have given in their names as Subscribers but have *not yet paid*.

You will—I am sure—agree with me that as Secretary to the Committee—I should be able thus to distinguish between paid & unpaid.

I have not been altogether idle in Stow matters since my appointment. Mr Trollope sent me a list of 20 or 24 names to whom I might write with a probability of success. I have written to 20 or so of the number.

On the accompanying list of Subscribers those with a mark x against their name are those who have given in answer to my appeal—Some have written to say they have already subscribed & cannot do more—others have not yet replied to my notes.

I have the Lincoln Bank Book for the Atkinson Memorial Fund with me here.

We hope to remain with our Friends here until the middle or towards the close of next week. Free from *Parochial* work it gives me leisure to attend to Stow matters—and the Diocesan Educational work.

244. To Eccl. Com. from Adn Giles, Willoughby Rectory, 19 March 1866 (EC)

Stow Church,
Archdeaconry of Stow,
Diocese of Lincoln.

Sir,

I have been for sometime past anxious to bring under the consideration of H:M: Ecclesiastical Commissioners the case of the Church of Stow, from which my Archdeaconry takes its name. But I have been prevented from making any application by serious illness, from which I am only now beginning to recover—In the mean time, I greatly fear that the funds in hand have been exhausted, and that the work must be suspended, now that it has very nearly been completed—

I am unequal to lay before the Commissioners such a statement as I could wish—I must throw myself on their indulgence, rather than delay my application—

I trust that they may feel themselves justified in completing the Chancel, which only requires paving and fitting with suitable stalls &c.

I hope also that they may be able, as having, I believe, land in the Parish, to make some small grant towards the general Work—

Since the Circular, of which I have the honour to enclose copies, was printed, about £200 has been subscribed; and less than £1000 would complete all that could be desired, within and without—

The church exhibits extensive remains of an Anglo-Saxon Cathedral of the earliest times, distinct in character from the later Norman work, and, I think, superior to it—

244A. Printed Circular.

STOW CHURCH,
THE ANGLO-SAXON CATHEDRAL

of LINDSEY, was built A.D. 672, in memory of the resting of ST. ETHELDREDA on the spot, by her husband, Egfrid, king of Northumbria, who, six years later, founded a Bishop's See at Stow.

It was burnt by the Danes A.D. 870.

The Transepts were restored, and the present Nave built, during the Episcopate of Eadnoth 2nd, A.D. 1034—50. The great Earl of Mercia, LEOFRIC, and his wife, THE LADY GODIVA, aided liberally in the building and endowment.

The present Chancel was built about A.D. 1090 by Remigius, 1st Bishop of Lincoln.

The great work of restoring this venerable Church was begun about 12 years ago, when £1700. were expended on the Chancel. More recently, £2800. was raised, of which no less than £1100. was contributed by the late self-denying and liberal Incumbent of Stowe, the Rev. G. Atkinson, and his family. The Nave and Transepts are now, as well as the Chancel, substantially repaired, roofed at the original pitch, and covered with lead. But near £1200. is still required to complete so extensive a work, including paving, seating and other fittings, warming and lighting.

Two Subscription Lists have been opened—one for a special MEMORIAL, connected with the work, to the late REV. G. ATKINSON—the other, for the work generally.

I cannot but hope that many, throughout the land, will be interested in the preservation of our only Anglo-Saxon Cathedral, still shewing on its solemn walls the traces of the Danish fires.

J. D. GILES,
Archdeacon of Stowe.

Willoughby Rectory,
1st Jan., 1866.

245. To Sir Charles Anderson from Frederick Atkinson, Higher Broughton, 16 April 1866 (CA)

Dear Sir Charles Anderson

I much regret that you are dissatisfied with the arrangement of the new seats in the transepts & also with the seats themselves.

I have not seen any of the new seats nor any drawings of them. Bates in answer to my enquiries gives a good account of them both as to their "comfortableness" & execution—to use his own phrase, they are a "very good job".

However, whatever they are Mr Pearson is responsible for them and not I.

As to the present arrangement of the seats being both impracticable & unmanageable, I really cannot understand it, seeing it is the ancient arrangement & which had existed for hundreds of years before my brother was presented to the Church 30 years ago.

For some years he preached from the pulpit affixed to the north eastern pier, looking westward & found no difficulty in making himself heard to the west end of the church as well as the transepts.

It is true that since then the roofs have been raised to a much higher pitch & which circumstances may render it more difficult for the preacher to be heard in the same position. If so, it is certainly to be regretted, but I hope the difficulty is not so great but that it may be overcome by contrivance & patient experience.

My brother never intended the pulpit to be a fixed one after the Church was restored, but to be movable, so that it might always be placed in the best position both for seeing & hearing.

The fact is he never intended to have a distinct pulpit, but a movable lectern, which was to serve also as a pulpit & in the plans laid before the Church building Society it is so arranged.

I know that I am speaking the mind of my late brother when I say, that nothing could ever have induced him to consent to the plan you recommend, viz: fitting up the choir for the congregation & leaving the transepts and nave unoccupied.

The piers are as you observe enormous, but it must be recollected that they are no bigger now than in ancient days when the present arrangement of the seats existed.

I hope you will have Mr Pearson over this week, when he can confer with you on the subject—he had intended to be at Stow last week, but Bates tells me that a severe illness had prevented him.

246. To Eccl. Com. from Ewan Christian, 8 Whitehall Place, 30 April 1866 (EC)

Dear Sir,

File No 6498.
Corringham cum Stow and Stow-in-Lindsey Prebends Estates.
Stow Parish.
Chancel Repairs.

Agreeably to your Instructions I have surveyed the Chancel of this Church, and met at the building Archdeacon Giles and the Rural Dean Mr Garfit. So far as the Chancel is concerned but little has been done since my former survey in 1852, the steps have been fixed, and the ground levelled for the paving, and hot water pipes laid down, but neither tile floor nor fittings are yet put in. Mr Pearson the Architect employed, wishes to lay down a very simple plain tile floor, but to put benches of oak in accordance with those in the Church.

The cost of the floor would be about £96. 0. 0
Of the fittings and rail about £78. 0. 0

The work done in the Chancel has stood very well, but a sheet or two of lead had been lifted by the gales of last winter to which I directed the Foreman's attention, and he promised to have it repaired.

A great deal of work has been done in the Church. The Nave and Transepts re-roofed, the Walls repaired, and floors laid, and the Transepts fitted with permanent oak seats; More work remains to be done but the Funds are I believe now exhausted. The Church in its restored state is a very grand, and interesting building.

247. Vestry Book

May 1866

A Vestry Meeting is called for Wednesday next May the 9th at Eleven o clock in the forenoon in the Vestry of Stow Church when a Rate will be proposed to provide for the payment of a Sexton and to defray other necessary and legal Parish Expenses

Signed E H Haskins
Incumbent of Stow
Joseph Pycroft
James S Gelder } Churchwardens

Agreeably to the above Notice Meeting was held in the Vestry when the Notice was read whereupon Mr Joseph Harrison proposed and Mr E Howard seconded a rate of 1s in the pound and Mr Robt Gilbert proposed as an amendment a voluntary subscription & Mr Howell seconded it—

For the amendment The proposer and seconder Mr Jolland & Mr Sergeant = 4

For the rate The proposer & seconder and Mr J Pycroft = 3

Present in addition Mr Gelder Parish Churchwarden

Signed E H Haskins
James Gelder
Joseph Pycroft
Joseph Harrison

Note: The churchwardens collected £5.11.1½ in Sturton and Bransby, and Joseph Harrison collected £6.3.9 in Stow and Normanby. A donation of £2 was also received from Mr Godson (Church Book, p. 165).

248. To Adn Giles from Eccl. Com. (draft), 16 May 1866 (EC)

The Ecclesiastical Commissioners for England have had under the consideration a report from Mr Christian in reference to the chancel of Stow Church, and I am now directed to acquaint you that they will be prepared to make a contribution of one hundred and seventy four pounds towards the provision of a plain tile floor & new fittings for the chancel, but that they are unable to entertain your application for assistance towards the restoration of the other parts of the church.

Note: An Estates Committee minute dated 10 May 1866 refers.

249. To Rev G. Ainslie, Secretary of ICBS from Rev Edward Garfitt, Saxilby, 13 June 1866 (ICBS)

Dear Sir

You may probably have heard that shortly after the death of the Rev. George Atkinson, late Incumbent of Stow a committee was formed for carrying on the restoration of the Parish Church at Stow. Of that Committee I was requested to act as Secretary. In this position I write to you as Secretary of the Church Building Society to enquire whether—on a formal application being made the Society will be willing to pay the Grant of £150 towards the Church, as promised to the late Incumbent.

From a want of sufficient funds, it is not at present practicable to provide the whole of the seats intended to be placed in the Church, but a portion of the new work is already completed, and old seats and chairs lately purchased are elsewhere so arranged as to afford the amount of accommodation at present required—It is the wish of the committee to proceed with the restoration as soon as further funds are raised: but before doing so, it is thought advisable to pay off present liabilities. If towards enabling the committee to do this the Church Building Society will pay its promised Grant the committee will be greatly obliged.

I shall be happy to furnish you with any particulars you may require, & to attend to any suggestions or instructions you may be kind enough to offer—

I think it probable that before the receipt of this, you may have seen Mr Pearson the architect, also the Archdeacon of Stow. If so, these Gentlemen will have given you full information

250. To Rev. G. Ainslie from Frederick Atkinson, Higher Broughton, 9 July 1866. (ICBS)

Dear Sir,

About a week ago I had a letter from Mr Pearson Architect of 22 Harley St London, desiring me to forward you the plan for re-arranging the seating of Stow Church Lincolnshire, towards which the Incorporated Church Building Society made a grant of £150.

This plan to which the seal of the Society is affixed, came into my possession through the death of my brother the Reverend George Atkinson the Incumbent of Stow, in May 1865.

I now forward you the plan by book-post & also the sealed specifications, the receipt of which perhaps you will be good enough to acknowledge.

There is a circular letter dated 19th April 1864 from you to my brother informing him that in answer to his application the Society had been pleased to grant One Hundred & Fifty Pounds.

This document is also in my possession & if you require it, I will forward it without delay.

251. To Rev. G. Ainslie, ICBS from Rev E. Garfitt, Saxilby, 15 July 1866. (ICBS)

My dear Sir,

I thank you most sincerely for your kind note received by this morning's post, & beg to offer similar thanks to the Church Building Society for having consented to pay one hundred pounds on account of the grant made to Stow Church. I can safely say that the remaining portion of the work required by the Society will DV be proceeded with as soon as we have money in hand to meet the expenditure.

I am the more indebted to you for your note from a knowledge of your own willingness to further the wishes of the committee to obtain a portion of the Grant. Both the Archdeacon of Stow & Mr Pearson have informed me of the kind & curteous attention you paid to them when they called upon you on this subject.

The payment of the £100 (if agreeable to yourself & the Church Building Society) can be made in the Bank of Messrs Smith Ellison & Co Lincoln, to the account of the Stow Church restoration fund.

I shall gladly attend to any document that may require signing &c for I shall be glad, on hearing from you, to forward agreeably to the directions you may give—

I will endeavour to obtain the particulars you require as given on the printed Form "For insertion in the Church Builder".

252. To Eccl. Com. from Rev. E. H. Haskins, Stow, 2 August 1866 (EC)

Sir

The enclosed estimate, having been sent by me to Mr Search he has sent it back thinking that the expenditure contemplated requires the sanction of the Commissioners. The Chancel roof has long required putting in a thorough state of repair but probably you will employ some person on whom you can depend to take the estimate before incurring so large an outlay as the one proposed

253. To A. Search from Wm Wilson, Plumber, Marton, 27 July 1866 (EC)

Sir,

The lead of the chancel to repair which I received orders is in such a bad state that I thought it better to let you know about it. The sheets are all slipping as they have done before time. I find the seams so much broken from previous repairs that it will be necessary to cut them all out and work the lead over again, and put the sheets on in widths to correspond with the other part of the roof as they are much too wide and to do that I find it will take 2½ tons of new lead and the old relaying and properly keying on. There will be about 1 Ton 8 cwt of old seams to take to, to take them and complete the work will cost the sum of £76.

An answer as early as convenient will oblige

P.S. I had begun of the work and got one sheet off but found I could make nothing of them

254. Cash Book (Copy) (CA)
Transepts and Nave Accounts

254.1

1863			Contra	Cr		
Sept^{r}	8	By	Packing and carriage of Photographs		2	7
	,,	,,	Note paper		2	9
	,,	,,	Carriage of circulars from London		2	
	11	,,	Engraving of Church for appeal	7	17	6
	,,	,,	Carriage of Photographs to Louth		1	
	17	,,	Blocks from Clays London			10
	30	,,	Printing of Appeals & stamped Envelopes	7	3	4
Oct^{r}	2	,,	Postage Stamps		10	
Dec^{r}	15	,,	Ja^{s} Mudd for Photographs of Stow Church	6		
1864						
Jan^{y}	30	,,	Cousans for collecting Cards & Index Book		14	6
March	31	,,	G.N.R. Carr^{e} Tons 5 cwt 14 Ancaster Stone	1	9	
April	11	,,	d^{o} 4 Casks Cement		8	
	16	,,	Ja^{s} Barton Wages—4 days	1	4	
	18	,,	Taylor Bro^{s} Stone saw 14/– Files 4/6		18	6
	,,	,,	Ja^{s} Foottit—Dust Sieve		3	
	23	,,	Wages as per Book	4	11	6
	,,	,,	Carriage of Saw 1/– Plaster of Paris 6^{d}		1	6
	,,	,,	Sheet of Zinc 7/– P.O. order 3^{d} Brush 2/–		9	3
	30	,,	Wages as per Book	4	12	
	,,	,,	Twigg for a Brush		1	
			Carried forward	£36	12	3

			£	s	d
		Contra C^r^ by Cash paid			
1864		By Amount brought forward	36	12	3
May	7	,, Wages as per Book	4	17	6
	,,	,, G.N.R^y^ carr^e^ T 19 C 2 Ancaster Stone	4	17	2
	,,	,, Beer allowed to men for overwork		1	
	,,	,, 2 Pails 3/8 Brush 2/4 as per Gibson's bill		6	
	14	,, 6 Loads of Road Dirt & leading to Thos Richardson		7	6
	,,	,, Wages as per book	7	0	4
	21	,, Wages as per book	2	12	1
	25	,, Carriage of Timber from Hull. G.N.R.	2	9	
	26	,, Scaffold Timber &c. R. Wade Sons & Co	21	8	6
	,,	,, Stamped Cheque Book		3	
	28	,, Wages as per Book	4	16	2
	30	,, Carriage of Tons 5 Cwt 12 Lime. G.N.R.		15	10
June	4	,, Wages as per Book	7	3	2
	,,	,, Blacksmith's bill—Wm Hill		11	3
	,,	,, Carpenter's D^o^—Wm Smith		10	3
	,,	,, Beer allowed to Carters		2	8
	,,	,, Barton's paper, postage stamps &c.		3	4
	11	,, Wages as per book	5	13	3
	18	,, Wages as per book	7	9	3
	,,	,, Wm Smith, Carpenter, as per bill		18	9
		Carried forward	£108	18	3

			£	s	d
		Contra Cr By Cash paid			
1864		By Amount brought forward	108	18	3
June	23	,, G.N.R. Carre Tons 14 Cwts 9 Ancaster Stone	3	13	5
	28	,, Mr Jno Wilson 518 feet Ancaster Stone as p Invoice	21		10
	25	,, Wages as per Book	7		8
	,,	,, A File		1	3
July	2	,, Wages as per Book	9	6	4
	,,	,, Wm Smith, Carpenter as per bill		18	3
	7	,, Henry H. Earl for 6 cwt. Hoop Iron as per bill	3	7	3
	9	,, Wages as per book	8	12	2
	,,	,, Wm Hill, Blacksmith as per bill		16	6
	,,	,, Do for allowance of beer to Carters		9	3
	18	,, Carre Tons 19 cwt 5 Ancaster Stone G.N.R.	4	17	10
	16	,, Wages as per book	8	17	9
	,,	,, Carre Hoop Iron from Sheffield 6 cwt.		2	6
	,,	,, Beer to Carters		3	
	,,	,, Do to Quarrymen at Ingham		1	6
	,,	,, A Scuttle		1	10
	26	,, Invoice of Oak Timber from Roe & Son— less Disct	75	6	8
	,,	,, Invoice of Lime 11¼ Tons from Lockwood & Co less Disct	4	18	7
	23	,, Wages as per book	9	13	1½
	,,	,, Nails as per Barton's Acct.		4	10
		Carried forward £	268	11	9½

			£	s	d
		Contra C^r By Cash paid			
1864		By Amount brought forward	268	11	9½
July	23	,, G.N.R. Carr^e 5¾ Tons Lime		16	5
	,,	,, D^o ,, Roofing Boards		19	8
	,,	,, Twigg for Carriage of Crab		1	
	,,	,, Woodhall for 100 Drain Tiles		4	
	,,	,, Beer to Carters		6	3
	,,	,, Chalk &c.		1	3
	30	,, Wages as per book	8	9	4
	,,	,, Barton's expenses to Lincoln		4	
	,,	,, Gibson 2 Buckets } as per Barton's acc^t		4	
	,,	,, Stool repairing }		1	
	,,	,, 25 Ladder staves }		2	9
	,,	,, Barton's paper & postage May 21 to July 29 }		6	3
	,,	,, Beer to Carters		3	3
Aug^t	4	,, G.N.R. Carr^e 10 Tons Oak Timber from Derby	5	19	2
	6	,, Wages as per book	11	12	10½
	,,	,, Soap & Tallow for New Rope 2/9½ Tin Tacks 2^d		2	11½
	,,	,, Beer to Carters leading Stones from Ingham		6	3
	13	,, Wages as per book	13	15	10
	,,	,, Carriage of Ropes & block from Minster		1	
	,,	,, Beer to Carters 4/6 D^o to Labourers 6^d		5	
		Carried forward	£ 312	14	0½

Contra C^r By Cash paid

				£	s	d
1864			By Amount brought forward	312	14	0½
Aug^t	13	,,	Barton's expenses to Gainsbro'		3	
	,,	,,	Clarke for sawing & barrows repairing as per Bill	1	10	
	,,	,,	150 Nails		1	
	24	,,	C.D. Bourn for Ropes as per Invoice	6	19	10
	,,	,,	Wade & Co for battens & sawing as per Invoice	18	7	8
	,,	,,	Roe & Son for E. Oak Timber as per Invoice	19	14	6
		,,	Wages as per book for week ending 20th	20	11	
	27	,,	Wages as per book	19	16	1½
	,,	,,	Beer to Carters 1/– Nails 4^d Brush 8^d Carr^e of Ropes 3^d		2	3
	,,	,,	G.N.R. Carriage of 6½ Tons Lime		18	5
Sept^r	2	,,	Simpson & Co 28 lbs floor nails as per bill		4	
	3	,,	Wages as per book	20	3	6
	,,	,,	Wm Hill, Blacksmith as per bill	1	7	8
	10	,,	Wages as per book	23	9	7½
	,,	,,	G.N.R. Carriage of Tons Ancaster Stone	1	8	3
	,,	,,	Sweet Oil 10^d Beer to Carters 7½^d		1	5½
	17	,,	Wages as per book	22	15	4½
	24	,,	Wages as per book	17	12	8½
	,,	,,	G.N.R. Carriage of 4½ Tons Oak Timber from Derby	2	16	7
	,,	,,	D^o D^o Tons 18 cwt 2 Ancaster Stone	4	12	
			Carried forward	£ 495	9	

			£	s	d
		Contra C^r By Cash paid			
1864		By Amount brought forward	495	9	
Sept^r	24	,, 500 Nails		1	3
	,,	,, Barton's paper & postage stamps		2	4½
Oct^r	1	,, Wages as per book	19	1	5½
	,,	,, Carriage of Nails 6^d. Beer for Carters 3^d			9
	8	,, Wages as per book	20	4	5
	13	,, Roe & Son for Oak Timber as per Invoice	47	5	7
	15	,, Wages as per book	16	8	8
	17	,, Carriage of 6 Tons Timber from Derby G.N.R.	3	11	6
	21	,, Newsam for boards for spouting of S. Transept	1		6
	,,	,, G.N.R. Carriage 6½ Tons Lime		18	5
	,,	,, Twigg Carr^e blocks, sheets & boards from Lincoln		2	6
	,,	,, Wm Hill's Blacksmith's Bill	4	8	4
	,,	,, Repairing Cuts 2/10½ Paint 6^d Sulphur 5^d Axe Shaft 8^d		4	5½
	22	,, Wages as per book }	19	9	8½
	,,	,, Omitted—Geo. Morris }	1	3	10
	,,	,, Sulphur 2/8 Screws 1/8 Shell Lac 3^d		4	7
	,,	,, Beer to Carters for Lime & Timber leading		3	6
	,,	,, Paid to Minster men for getting their crab out		2	
	29	,, Wages as per book	19	3	9
Nov^r	5	,, Jno Wilson for Ancaster Stone—on acc^t	20		
		Carried forward	£ 669	6	7

254.7

Contra C^{r} By Cash paid

1864		By Amount brought forward	669	6	7
Nov^{r}	5	,, Carr^{e} of Crab 2/– Nails 1/– from Lincoln Beer to Carters 1/– as per Barton's a/c Octr 29		4	
		,, Screws, Nails, Paint &c. from Wm Smith as per acc^{t}		4	4½
	,,	,, Wages as per book	23	5	2½
	,,	,, G.N.R. Carr^{e} 4 Tons Oak £2.9.2 Spirits of Salts 4^{d}	2	9	6
	9	,, Roe & Son for E. Oak Timber as per Invoice	58	15	9
	12	,, Wages as per book	22	19	6
	,,	,, Lockwood & Co for 13 Tons Lime	5	17	
	18	,, Horner & Fell for 65 cwt. 2 Qrs. Lead as per Invoice	69	11	10
		,, G.N.R. Carr^{e} 13 Tons 5 cwt. Stone (15th)	3	7	4
		,, D^{o} D^{o} Timber from Hull (3 Tons 9 cwt.	1	3	1
		,, Oil 4^{d} carr^{e} of Nails 3^{d} as per Barton's acc^{t}			7
	19	,, Wages as per Book	22	12	6
	23	,, Roe & Son for E. Oak as per Invoice less 2½ disc^{t}	40	10	3
	(19)	,, G.N.R. for Carr^{e} T6 C8 Ancaster Stone	1	12	6
	,,	,, Barton's paper & stamps		2	11
	19	,, Wm Smith for Nails &c. as per bill		4	11
	26	,, Wages as per Book	20	18	10
	,,	,, G.N.R. Carr^{e} T7. C13 Ancaster Stone	1	18	11
	,,	,, D^{o} ,, 7. 5 Warmsworth Lime	1		7
	,,	,, D^{o} ,, 3. 8 E. Oak from Derby	2		6
		Carried forward	£ 948	6	8

		Contra Cr By Cash paid			
1864		By Amount brought forward	948	6	8
Novr	26	,, G.N.R. Carr^e T13. C10 Warmsworth Lime	1	18	2
Decr	3	,, Wages as per book	20	13	2½
	,,	,, Jos^h Harrison Ash Poles as per bill 3/– Carr^e 6^d Oil 4^d		3	10
	,,	,, Beer to men on getting up last Truss on Nave		5	3
	10	,, Mr George Thrush, Plumber on acc^t	50		
	,,	,, Wages as per book	23	8	5
	,,	,, Expense of fetching Truck from Minster		1	
	17	,, Wages as per book	27		3½
	,,	,, Wm Smith for repairs, paint &c. as per bill		10	10
	20	,, Roe & Son for English Oak	31	10	4
	24	,, Wages as per book	14		11
	31	,, Horner & Fell for 80 Pigs of Lead Cwt86. qu2. lb5 @ 21/3	91	19	2
	,,	,, G.N.R. Carr^e 3 Casks Cement as per bill		13	4
	,,	,, F.G. Smith for Nails & Screws as per bill, with carriage		3	4
	,,	,, Soft Soap for Minster Ropes 7lb		3	8
	,,	,, Gee & Twigg for Carr^e as per Barton's acc^t		2	3
	,,	,, Wages as per book	12	8	5
	,,	,, Barton's Stationery from Novr 19		2	5½
1865					
Jan^y	7	,, Wages as per book	8	13	8½
	,,	,, Pail 2/– Soot 1/– Carr^e 5^d as per Barton's acc^t		3	5
		Carried forward	£ 1232	8	8

254.9

Contra C^{r} By Cash paid

				£	s	d
1865			By Amount brought forward	1232	8	8
Jan^{y}	14	,,	Wages as per book	10	15	4
	18	,,	Wade & Co for Roofing Boards for Nave, less Disc^{t}	18	8	
	,,	,,	G. & T. Eadle for 4 Casks of Cement	1	18	
	,,	,,	White & Brothers for 3 Casks Portland Cement	1	13	
	21	,,	Lockwood & Co Tons 20. Cwt18 Lime @ 9/3 less 3^{d} disc^{t}	9	8	
	,,	,,	Wages as per book	11	12	7
	28	,,	Wages as per book	5	17	4½
Feb^{y}	4	,,	Wages as per book	7	7	11
	11	,,	Wm Hill for Ironwork on acc^{t}	14		
	,,	,,	Wages as per book	9	16	6½
	18	,,	Wages as per book	8	9	3
	23	,,	Wilson on acc^{t} for Ancaster Stone	10		
	25	,,	Wages as per book	8	6	11
	28	,,	Horner & Fell for 20 Pigs of Lead	21	15	5
March	3	,,	Newsum for spouting boards		14	
	4	,,	Wages as per book	9	12	8
	11	,,	Wages as per book	10	14	11½
	13	,,	Mr Geo. Thrush, Plumber on acc^{t}	50		
	19	,,	Wages as per book	11	3	4½
	26	,,	Wages as per book	11	6	5
			Carried forward	£ 1465	8	5

			£	s	d
		Contra Cr By Cash paid			
1865		By Amount brought forward	1465	8	5
April	1	,, Wages as per book	7	14	1
	,,	,, New Skip 2/– Carr. & 1/4 lb Umber 3d		2	3
	8	,, Wages as per book	8	11	5
	,,	,, Wm Smith for Paint & Jobbing work as per bills		13	2½
	13	,, Wages as per book	5	5	2
	18	,, Carre of Cask cement London to Saxilby 3/5 thence 7d		4	
	20	,, Wilson for Ancaster Stone, Balance	8	1	3
	22	,, Wages as per book	6	18	4
	25	,, Gee for carriage of Minster Tackle		4	6
	29	,, Wages as per book	6	8	11½
May	6	,, Wages as per book	7	13	11
	,,	,, Widow woman for leading Smithy Ashes		1	6
	8	,, Mr C. F. Mawer for Ingham Stone 300 yds @ 1/–	15		
	13	,, Wages as per book	6	7	8½
	,,	,, Beer to Carters for 17 Loads Ingham Stone		4	3
	,,	,, Thos Simpson & Co for files & Wire as per bill		3	
	,,	,, Advertisement in Nottm Guardian for plasterers		2	
	20	,, G.N.Ry Carre T6. C8 Ancaster Stone	1	13	1
	,,	,, Wages as per book	7	4	7
	,,	,, Beer to Carters 6d, Oil 1d			7
		Carried forward	£ 1548	2	2½

				£	s	d
			Contra C^r By Cash paid			
1865			By Amount brought forward	1548	2	2½
May	27	,,	Wages as per book, includes beer 1/– Carr^e of tub 2^d & a lb of Umber	9	0	3½
	,,	,,	D^o Jos^h Wilson's back money 9 weeks @ 1/6		13	6
	29	,,	G.N.R^y Carr^e T6.C14 Ancaster Stone @ 5/2	1	14	7
June	3	,,	Wages as per book	10	6	7½
		,,	Blacksmith putting Tire on Wheel of Cutts		1	6
		,,	2 lb of Umber			6
		,,	½ ,, Ochre 1½^d Beer to Carters 1/6		1	7½
	10	,,	Wages as per book	9	15	2
	,,	,,	Beer to Carters for 4 loads Ingham Stone & 4 of sand		2	
	,,	,,	Oil 1^d & one sheet of drawing paper 7^d			8
	16	,,	Wm Smith Jobbing as per bill		1	4
	17	,,	Wages as per book	10	17	2½
	,,	,,	Fred. G. Smith sheet of zinc as per bill		5	10
	,,	,,	Beer to Carters for 6 Loads of Sand from Torksey		1	6
	,,	,,	Envelopes & Paper 7½^d Postage Stamps 6^d (for Jno Bates)		1	1½
	,,	,,	Carr^e of Zinc from Gainsbro'			3
	24	,,	Wages as per book	12	6	6½
	,,	,,	Beer to Carters for 3 loads of sand			9
	,,	,,	2 Sheets of Pasteboard & Carriage		1	
			Carried forward	£ 1603	14	2½

254.12

			£	s	d
		Contra C^{r} By Cash paid			
1865		By Amount brought forward	1603	14	2½
July	1	,, Wages as per book	12	7	3
,,	,,	,, Beer to Carters 4 loads of stone from Ingham		1	
,,	,,	,, D^{o} 5 loads of lime from Torksey		1	3
,,	,,	,, D^{o} 2 loads sand (Jos^{h} Palmer) from Torksey			6
,,	,,	,, D^{o} 2 loads sand (T. Richardson) D^{o}			6
	8	,, Wages as per book	11	14	6½
,,	,,	,, Beer to Carters 2–2 horse loads sand from Torksey			6
,,	,,	,, D^{o} 6–2 horse loads sand D^{o}		1	6
,,	,,	,, Sheet of drawing paper			2
	10	,, M. S & Lin^{c} Railway Carr^{e} Truck of Lime T7.C3 @ 4/–	1	8	8
	8	,, Jno Wilson, Ancaster Stone (on a/c)	5		
	15	,, Wages as per book	11	17	
,,	,,	,, Tracing paper		1	
,,	,,	,, Pipe Clay for taking Casts & Carriage		1	8
,,	,,	,, Oil			2
,,	,,	,, Four inch glazed Drain pipe 8^{d}, Carriage 2^{d}			10
,,	,,	,, Robt Gibson, Galvanized buckets as per bill		4	
	20	,, Thos Simpson & Co Nails &c. as per bill	6	5	
,,	,,	,, Jos^{h} Fambrini, Cement & Plaster as per bill		19	
		Carried forward	£ 1653	18	9

254.13

Contra Cr By Cash paid

			£	s	d
1865		By Amount brought forward	1653	18	9
July	22	,, Wages as per book	10	14	1
	,,	,, 2 Sheets of Paper			1
	,,	,, Beer for Carters leading Walling Stone from Ingham		2	6
	,,	,, Carriage of 150 Slates from Lincoln		1	3
	,,	,, Carriage of box of Plaster Casts to Gainsbro'			8
	26	,, J.B. White & Bros Portland Cement as per bill		11	
	28	,, J & R Swan for obtaining Faculty as per bill	7	10	
	29	,, Wages as per book	10	13	9
	,,	,, Carre of Plaster 6d do bundle of laths 6d		1	
Augt	1	,, Lockwood Blagden & Co T7. C1 Lime less disct	3	3	5
	,,	,, Jno Wilson, Ancaster Stone, Balance	1	12	2
	,,	,, Wm Hill, Blacksmith as per bill	3	6	
	5	,, Wages as per book	9	1	2½
	,,	,, Beer for Carters 10–2 Horse loads of Stone from Ingham (Mr Godson)		2	6
	,,	,, Do 10–2 Horse loads do do (Mr Motley)		2	6
	,,	,, Do 6–2 Horse loads do do (Mr Howard)		1	6
	,,	,, Quire Brown Paper for taking window patterns		1	6
	,,	,, Carriage of do			2
	,,	,, Beer for Stone getters at Ingham		2	
	,,	,, J. Hannam for tracing paper as per bill		2	8½
		Carried forward	£ 1700	18	9

254.14

Contra Cr By Cash paid

			£	s	d
1865		By Amount brought forward	1700	18	9
Augt	5	,, Balance in hand	12	8	1
			1713	6	10

INDEX OF PERSONS AND PLACES

Note. **V** indicates a person recorded as having attended the Vestry, and names in **heavy type** are those of the leaders. Most of the information, unless otherwise stated, is true for the year 1851. "Ch. gdn" means that the person rented a Church (or charity) Garden, "ag. lab.", an agricultural labourer, "donor" to the Restoration Fund or the Atkinson Memorial Fund. "Stow", in most cases, refers to the township rather than to the parish. A query indicates an uncertain identification. Arabic figures refer to Document numbers.

Abraham, John, **V**, Knaith, Lincs. 38
Ainslie, Rev. George, sec. of ICBS see Subject Index
Ancaster see Wilson, Jn.
Anderson, Sir Charles, Bart, Lea Hall, Lincs., donor x, xi, xxiii, xxviii, 10, 12, 25, 111, 218, 218A, 220, 227–36, 238–43, see Codd
Anderson, Lady, wife of Sir Chas. 230
Ashton, Mr, master mason 111, 141, 144A
Ariosto 66N
Atkinson, Francis, Rochdale, cotton spinner, father of Rev. Geo., donor xi
Atkinson, Frederick, Claremont, Higher Broughton, Manchester, cotton merchant, brother of Rev. Geo. x, xi, xxv, xxviii, xxix, 227, 230–6, 238, 240–2, 245, 250, copied 254
Atkinson, Rev. George, perpetual curate of Stow 1836–65 *passim*
  character described xi, 8, 26, 66, 81, 226, 240
  publications xxxii
  death 226
Atkinson, the Misses Eliza, Francis, Mary, and Sarah, sisters of Rev. Geo. xi, 227, 230, 236, 240

Baines, Joseph, Stow, ag. lab., ch. gdn., b. c.1812 149
Barker, James, Esq., Severn Stoke, Worcs., donor 65
Barton, James, clerk of works for nave 254.1–.8
Basset, Rev. John, curate of Stow 1789–1805 78
Bates, John, foreman of nave restoration 233, 238, 242, 245, 246, 254.11
Baxter, William, **V**, Stow, ag. lab., b. c.1796 42
Bayley, Ven. Henry Vincent, adn of Stow 1823–44 xxxi, 8, 56, 67, 74, 80
Beckett, Rev. George, preb. of Corringham cum Stow 1822–43 xxxi
Beckett, Sir John, Somerby Park, Lincs, lessee of Corringham prebendal tithe, owned in 1839 105a let to Thos Spink 2A
Belham, Mr, surveyor of fabric at Lincoln Minster 221A
Blecca, 7th C Christian convert 238
Blow, Samuel, **V**, Sturton, in 1839 rented 59a of Wm Watson, parish CW 1847 1, 42

Bonney, Ven. Henry Kaye, adn of Lincoln 1845–62 xxxi, 66, 105, 106, 111
Boucheret, Capt., N. Willingham, Lincs, donor 233
Bourn, Charles Day, Lord St, Gainsborough, ropemaker 254.5
Bransby see Stow
Brocklesby, Charles, **V**, Sturton, farmed 28a, b. c.1807 42, 44
Bromehead, Edmund Arthur, James St, Lincoln, attorney and proctor 74
Brooke, William & Benjamin, High St, Lincoln, booksellers & printers 65, 83
Broughton, Higher see Atkinson, Frederick
Broughton, Rev. Robert, curate of Stow 1752–89 78–80
Brown, John, brother in law of Robt Broughton, CW 1757–89 79, 80
Brownlow, Lord, Belton House, Lord Lieutenant, donor xxix, 41, 60, 65, 83, 142, 154
Brumby, James, **V**, Sturton, proprietor of houses, father in law to Jn Middleton, b. c.1784 ?200, 209, ?210, 211, ?214
Brumby, Joseph, **V**, Sturton, ag. lab., b. c.1814 ?200, ?210, ?214, 223
Burnham, Robert, **V**, Stow Park, in 1839 rented 488a of S. W. Hall 10, 12, 38, 90
Burton, George, **V**, Bransby, farmed 94a rented of Thos Spencer, prim. meth., CW 1850, b. c.1792 1, 38, 40, 42, 64, 84, 88, 90, 93, 100, 103, 110, 111, 128, 129A, 146, 149, 205, 208, ?223
Burton, George, ?**V**, Sturton, in 1861 farmed 112a, son Geo. Burton, b. c.1832 ?223
Butler (Buttler), John, **V**, Stow Pasture, farmed 14a, child baptized "schismatically" in 1856, b. c.1812 44, 90, 193, 197–202, 208, 210, 211, 214, 216
Butterworth, Thomas, Rochdale, brother in law to Rev. Geo. Atkinson, donor xxix
Buttery, William, **V**, Stow, carpenter & wheelwright, b. c.1797 42, 44, 53, 72, 88, 197, 198, 205, 206, 208–11, 213, 216, 219

Carr, Rev. John, rector of Brattleby, rural dean of Lawress 27
Cayley, Mr and Mrs 240
Chalk, James J., assistant secretary then secretary to Eccl. Com. x, 118, 120, and *passim*
Chaplin, Charles, Blankney Hall, Lincs., donor xix, 115
Christian, Ewan, consultant architect to Eccl. Com. xxiii, 136–41, 143–5, 147, 152–4, 156–62, 171–8, 180, 190–2, 246, 248
Clarke, John, **V**, Bransby, wheelwright, b. c.1826 216, 254.5
Clay, London, supplied blocks 254.1
Clayton, Henry, **V**, Stow, ag. lab., shopkeeper in 1855, ch. gdn, donor, b. c.1801, 42
Coates by Stow 87, see Motley
Codd, John, Pearson's head clerk, architect, son of Wm Codd who was Sir C. Anderson's farm bailiff xxv, 232
Codd, Rev. Mr 9
Cottam, Robert, **V**, Stow, baker & grocer, b. c.1800 44
Coultas, **V** 146
Cousans, Edward R., printer & publisher of *Lincolnshire Chronicle* 254.1
Cox, Ashton, Esq., V, Stow Park, bought 488a of S.W. Hall in 1849 with the lease of the tithe, left in 1857 162, 172, 173, 176, 193, 197, 198, 200–4, 207, 208, 214–16, 218A, 219, 220
Credland, George, **V**, Stow, farmer's son (125a), brother to Robt, b. c.1821 38, 40, 42, 44, 53, 72, ?90, 193, 201, 208, ?214
Credland, John, ?**V**, Stow, ag. lab., ch. gdn., b. c.1821 ?44
Credland, John, ?**V**, Stow, cattle dealer, b. c.1807 ?44
Credland, Robert, **V**, Stow, farmer's son (125a), brother to Geo., b. c.1824 42, 53, 72, ?90, 103, 110, 149, 188, 197, 199–201, 209–11, ?214, 216

Dickinson, Tobias, **V**, Stow, shoemaker in 1855 205
Dodsworth, William G., **V**, vestry clerk 205, 206
Duc, Violet le xxiii
Duncan, Magnus Hugh, **V**, Stow, National School master, parish clerk 1854–55, CW 1855 1, 214
Durham xxiii

Eadle, G. & T., cement suppliers 254.9
Eadnoth II, bishop of Dorchester 244A
Earl, Henry H., Sheffield, supplied hoop iron 254.3
Egfrid, king of Northumbria 244A
Ellis, Jesse, Stow, CW 1824, father of Wm xvi
Ellis, William, V, Stow, farmed 16a inherited from Jesse, grazier in 1855, "staunch churchman", b. c.1799 xxx, 38, 40, 42–4, 48–53, 64, 72, 88, 90, 103, 110, 146, 149, 188, 193, 197–202, 204–6, 208, 210, 211, 213–16, 219, 222, 223
Elwis, Jonathan, **V**, Sturton, cottager in 1861, parish clerk 1857, CW 1858–64, b. c.1818 in W. Indies 1, 220, 222, 223, 225
Emery, Joseph, clerk of works to chancel restoration 144, 144A, 154, 158A, 165, 176, 180
Etheldreda, abbess of Ely xxi, 244A

Fambrini, Joseph, Waterside N., Lincoln, plaster figure maker 254.12
Ferrey, Benjamin, consultant architect to Eccl. Com. 120
Ferriby, N., Yorks. E. Riding 11, 13
Ffytche, Mr J. Lewis, Thorpe Hall, Louth, Lincs., donor 233
Foottit, James, Stow, bricklayer, son of Sam., supplied dust sieve 254.1
Foottit, Samuel, **V**, Stow, bricklayer, father of Jas, b. c.1793 42, 44
Foster, Robert, **V**, Sturton, farmed 23a, CW 1848, b. c.1786 1, 37–53, 55, 61, 63, 72, 84, 88
Fox, Joseph, **V**, Stow, farmed 6a, b. c.1807 40, 44, 64
Fraser, Rev. Peter, preb. of Stow in Lindsey 1831–53 xxxi, 4, ?83

Garfit, Rev. Edward, vicar of Saxilby, donor 239, 240N, 243, 249, 251
Gee, William, ?**V**, Sturton, farmed 33a, b. c.1795 ?44
Gee, William, ?**V**, Sturton, cattle doctor, b. c.1824 ?44
Gee, see Twigg
Gelder, James, Sturton, bricklayer, charged with drunkenness xii
Gelder, James Shankster, V, Sturton, farmed 26a, CW 1859–70, rarely at service, b. c.1795 1, 37N, 38, 40, 42–4, 48–54, 63, 64, 72, 84, 88, 103, 197, 198, 201, 205, 209, 210, 213–17, 222, 223, 225, 247
Gibbs, Anthony, **V**, CW 1853–54 xxix, 1, 200, 202, 204, 208, 209
Gibson, John, **V**, Sturton, ag. lab., b. c.1794 44
Gibson, Robert, **V**, Sturton, joiner, in 1861 grocer joiner & wheelwright, signed 1851 Census for Sturton Wesleyans as Local Preacher, b. c.1819 222, 223, 254.2, .4, .12
Gilbert, James, **V**, Bransby, farmer's son (Robt), in 1861 farmed 68a in Bransby, b. c.1828 205, 216, 222
Gilbert, Robert, **V**, Bransby, farmed 126a rented of Wm Mason, father of Jas and Robt, ? Prim. Meth. local preacher, CW 1851, d. 1856, b. c.1789 1, 44, 146, 149, 197
Gilbert, Robert, **V**, Bransby, farmer's son (Robt), in 1861 farmed 52a in Sturton, ? Prim. Meth. local preacher, chaired Prim. Meth. meeting in 1861, b. c.1823 222, 247

Sidnacester xxi, xxii, 116
Sikes, George Booth, **V**, Sturton, farmed 286a, married daughter of Thos Spink, convicted of manslaughter in 1853 having killed Sam. Makins, b. c.1817 42–4, 90, 197, 198, see Makins
Simpson, Thomas & Co., High St, Lincoln, nail makers 254.5, .10, .12
Skill, John, V, Stow, in 1839 owned and farmed 79a White House Farm, and rented 77a in Sturton, and the 520a of Normanby, his daughter married Wm Godson to whom the Normanby tenancy was transferred, chief constable in 1856, brother of Thos, churchman 12, 38, 42, 84, 88, 193, 199, 201, 204, 210, 213, 216, 218A, 220
Skill, Thomas, Stow, formerly maltster, unmarried, was left in 1833 malt kiln, seed yard and public house called "Jackhalls Den" by father, died 1852, b. c.1789 xvi, xvii
Smith, Charles, Sturton, journeyman shoemaker 110
Smith, Charles Gowen, **V**, Stow, schoolmaster in Sturton, son of Wm Smith the grocer, correspondent to *Stamford Mercury*, vestry clerk, translator of *Domesday Book* for Lincolnshire in 1870, b. c.1829 xix, 42, 72, 88, 90, 103, 116, 117, 124, 146, ?205, 208, 214
Smith, Ellison & Co., High St, Lincoln, and Lord St, Gainsborough, bankers (Miss Ellison a donor) 82, 111, 112, 115, 125, 131, 134, 187, 227, 231, 233, 240, 243, 251
Smith, Frederick George, Market Pl., Gainsborough, ironmonger 254.8, .11
Smith, Joseph, **V**, Stow, National School master, parish clerk 1855–7, CW 1856–7 1, 215, 217, 219
Smith, Payne & Smith, London, bankers 112, 131, 187
Smith, Thomas, **V**, Stow, butcher, lived with Wm Pearce, b. c.1825 44, 149, 198, ?205
Smith, William, **?V**, Stow, grocer, father of Chas G. and Wm, at Thatched Cottage where it was said the first Methodist Class Meetings in Stow were held, b. c.1789 ?205, ?208, ?214
Smith, William, **?V**, Stow, wheelwright, b. c.1815 ?205, ?208, ?214, ?254.2, .3, .7, .8, .10, .11
Smith, William, **?V**, Stow, carpenter, son of Wm Smith, grocer, b. c.1827 ?205, ?208, ?214, ?254.2, .3, .7, .8, .10, .11
Smithson, Robert, **V** 209
Spencer, James, **V**, Bransby, farmed 156a belonging to brother **Thomas**, Quaker, in 1861 farmed 125a in Sturton, b. c.1825 in USA xviii, 88, 146, ?217, 222, 223
Spencer, Robinson, **V** 44
Spencer, Thomas, V, Bransby, farmed 40a, owned in 1839 435a some let to Wm Taylor, children born in USA, in 1861 farmed 160a in Sturton, Quaker, b. c.1793 xviii, xix, xx, 38, 40, 42, 44, 48, 53–5, 64, 65, 72, 74, 84, 88, 89, 130, 146, 188, 197–202, 205, 213, 214, 216, ?217, 222, 223, 237
Spink, John, **V**, Stow, farmed 90a, in 1856 married widow Purvis, in 1859 built "The Mere", in 1861 was farming 600a, CW 1848, b. c.1814 1, 37–53, 55, 61, 63, 68, 72, 146, 201, 210, 216, 217, 218A, 219, 220
Springthorpe, Lincs. xi
Spurr, George, **V**, Sturton, in 1861 proprietor of houses, b. c.1817 44
Spurr, William, **V**, Bransby, farmed 36a, in 1861 20a, b. c.1820 44, 222
Spurr, William, parish clerk 1838 xvi, xvii
Stonehouse, Ven. William Brocklehurst, adn of Stow 1844–62 xi, xiii, 1–127 *passim*
Stothard, James **V**, 44
Stothard, John, **V**, Sturton, brickmaker, b. c.1808 44

Wilkinson, John, **V**, Stow, farmed 108a, son of **William**, b. c.1828 193, 197, ?204, 205, 208–10, 214
Wilkinson, Samuel, manager of Lord St, Gainsborough, branch of Smith, Ellison, & Co.'s bank 125
Wilkinson, William, V, in 1839 owned 22a in Sturton let, in 1848 described as of Stow, of Hackthorn in 1852 poll book, father of John 42–4, 48–52, 63, 64, 84, 88, 90, 103, 149, ?204
Willson, E. J., antiquary xvi, xxi
Wilson, John, owner of Wilsford Quarries, supplied Ancaster stone 231, 254.3, .6, .9, .10, .12, .13
Wilson, Joseph, wage earner on nave restoration 254.11
Wilson, William, Marton, plumber 253
Wood, Vice Chancellor Sir William Page, donor 230
Woodhall, William, Danesgate, Lincoln, brick dealer 254.4
Woodhouse, John, **V**, Sturton, machine feeder, son of Rich., b. c.1826 210, ?223
Woodhouse, Richard, **?V**, Sturton, machine maker, in 1855 a blacksmith, father of John, b. c.1801 ?223
Wordsworth, Rt Rev. Christopher, bishop of Lincoln xxxi
Wrawby, Lincs. 98N

Yarborough, Earl of, Brocklesby, Lincs., donor 111, 115

INDEX OF SUBJECTS

Arabic figures refer to Document numbers.